Keslhofer '96

The Archaeology of Wealth

Consumer Behavior in English America

INTERDISCIPLINARY CONTRIBUTIONS TO ARCHAEOLOGY

Series Editor: Michael Jochim, *University of California, Santa Barbara*
Founding Editor: Roy S. Dickens, Jr., *Late of University of North Carolina, Chapel Hill*

Current Volumes in This Series:

THE ARCHAEOLOGY OF WEALTH
Consumer Behavior in English America
James G. Gibb

CASE STUDIES IN ENVIRONMENTAL ARCHAEOLOGY
Edited by Elizabeth J. Reitz, Lee A. Newsom, and Sylvia J. Scudder

CHESAPEAKE PREHISTORY
Old Traditions, New Directions
Richard J. Dent, Jr.

DARWINIAN ARCHAEOLOGIES
Edited by Herbert Donald Graham Maschner

DIVERSITY AND COMPLEXITY IN PREHISTORIC MARITIME SOCIETIES
A Gulf of Maine Perspective
Bruce J. Bourque

HUMANS AT THE END OF THE ICE AGE
The Archaeology of the Pleistocene–Holocene Transition
Edited by Lawrence Guy Straus, Berit Valentin Eriksen, Jon M. Erlandson,
and David R. Yesner

PREHISTORIC CULTURAL ECOLOGY AND EVOLUTION
Insights from Southern Jordan
Donald O. Henry

REGIONAL APPROACHES TO MORTUARY ANALYSIS
Edited by Lane Anderson Beck

STATISTICS FOR ARCHAEOLOGISTS
A Commonsense Approach
Robert D. Drennan

STONE TOOLS
Theoretical Insights into Human Prehistory
Edited by George H. Odell

STYLE, SOCIETY, AND PERSON
Archaeological and Ethnological Perspectives
Edited by Christopher Carr and Jill E. Neitzel

A Chronological Listing of Volumes in this series appears at the back of this volume.

A Continuation Order Plan is available for this series. A continuation order will bring delivery of each new volume immediately upon publication. Volumes are billed only upon actual shipment. For further information please contact the publisher.

The Archaeology of Wealth

Consumer Behavior in English America

JAMES G. GIBB

London Town Foundation
Annapolis, Maryland

PLENUM PRESS • NEW YORK AND LONDON

Library of Congress Cataloging-in-Publication Data

Gibb, James G.
    The archaeology of wealth : consumer behavior in English America /
James G. Gibb.
        p.   cm. -- (Interdisciplinary contributions to archaeology)
    Includes bibliographical references and index.
    ISBN 0-306-45233-2
    1. Consumer behavior--United States--History--17th century.
2. Consumption (Economics)--Social aspects--United States-
-History--17th century. 3. Wealth--United States--History--17th
century.   I. Title. II. Series.
HF5415.33.U6G53 1996
306.3--dc20   96-7999
                                                             CIP

ISBN 0-306-45233-2

© 1996 Plenum Press, New York
A Division of Plenum Publishing Corporation
233 Spring Street, New York, N. Y. 10013

10 9 8 7 6 5 4 3 2 1

Printed in the United States of America

Foreword

The purpose of theory is to connect facts with conclusions. In historical archaeology, facts are of two kinds—archival records and the archaeological record, composed of architectural remains, artifacts, features, and their contextual associations. Conclusions from these data explain how and, sometimes, why people lived the way they did in the past. It follows that theory in historical archaeology uses evidence from both excavated sites and archival collections to create and test hypotheses about former lifeways.

The Archaeology of Wealth: Consumer Behavior in English America addresses the lifeways of the English settlers in the upper Chesapeake Bay region during the mid- and late seventeenth century. James Gibb takes his archaeological evidence from various sites, mostly in Maryland. Two particular digs, at Compton and Patuxent Point, receive detailed attention. In combination with contemporary historical material, Gibb uses the data from these sites to frame hypotheses about early English settlement in the area based on consumer behavior.

As Gibb defines it, consumer behavior is how households spend the wealth that comes within their control. It is not limited to items such as food and clothing. Rather, it encompasses the entire budget of a seventeenth-century English settler household, including investment in tools, equipment, and farm animals. In fact, Gibb notes, consumer behavior extends to the way people bury their dead.

The Archaeology of Wealth proposes that individual decisions about the allocation of wealth reflect culturally defined goals and the strategies employed to reach those goals. Three broad classifications of decisions are considered: buildings and their positionings; ceramic and glass remains; and family cemeteries. The artifactual and archival records indicate that the mid- and late-seventeenth-century English settlers sought land along Chesapeake Bay that was suitable for

v

growing the area's main cash crop, tobacco; was near navigable water; and was far enough from centers of governmental authority to avoid the more serious effects of regulation and taxation. They initially constructed simple structures that they maintained only to a limited extent. On the other hand, the settler families brought with them and/or acquired while in America some fairly elaborate household items—such as window glass—and expensive, as well as less expensive, ceramics. At the end of their lives, they were interred in household cemeteries segregated between the members of the planter family and the servants and slaves.

Gibb's goal is to identify "larger social patterns through analyses of individual and household behaviors." He appeals, as did Walter Taylor in 1948, for the reconstruction of cultural contexts and states that "indeed, the reconstruction of cultural contexts—the identification and modeling of systems of meaning—is the interpretive process." He credits this intellectual inspiration from reading the works of Ian Hodder (1991), Daniel Miller (1987), and Grant McCracken (1988).

Gibb's conclusions indicate that the Chesapeake Bay was not colonized by people intending to create a utopia or seeking the freedom to persecute others for their religious beliefs without interference from the British government. Rather, most of the settlers seem to have been intent on making money in commercial agriculture. They sought to establish their families in comfort, honor, and prosperity by participating in the world economy of the day. In the process, they engaged in a very extensive form of agriculture and, at least initially, were willing to live in houses that failed to meet the standards of the Stuart middle class, even though they were often embellished with the small luxuries of that era. All of this took place in a physical environment very different from that of England and in a peculiar political and legal environment shaped by the Calverts' proprietary agreement with the British crown and the institutions of indentured servitude and slavery.

Consumer behavior theory enables Gibb to integrate the facts generated by historical archaeological research with conclusions about seventeenth-century Chesapeake Bay settlers on the basis of economic actions take by individual household units. Since those units are what occupied the homelots or farmsteads that archaeologists investigate, and since those units are often the subject of contemporary historical documents, *The Archaeology of Wealth* stands on a firm theoretical foundation. The theory used to explain the facts is commensurate with those facts; hence, the explanations offered about the settlers' lifeways are tied down in a nonspeculative, empirical fashion. Moreover, the facts and the explanations are linked by a theory based on economic behavior. We are here concerned with what households actually did with their money and other wealth, not what they said they did or wished they did. As a result, Gibb's conclusions are strongly supported by his evidence.

His emphasis is on examining social behavior in the context of household decision making "for developing meaningful cultural contexts," and he points out that this goal is "far from being realized by archaeologists." This statement echoes those of Walter Taylor (though Gibb does not draw on Taylor 1948:89), who urged "the construction of cultural contexts for the purpose of picturing the mode of life of by gone peoples" and who, like Gibb almost a half-century later, pointed out the need for—and the scarcity of use of—such an approach by archaeologists.

Taylor, and Gibb, see a pertinent question as "What may be inferred today from present evidence as to those things that were relevant, significant, meaningful *to the bygone individuals and societies under investigation?*" (Taylor 1948:122). From Gibb's presentation we believe he would also agree with Taylor that the primary obligation of the archaeologist is to interpret a site "in terms of the human group or groups which used it. This is nothing more or less than the construction of a cultural context for the site or its separable components" (Taylor 1948:147).

In this book Gibb has emphasized, as did Taylor, the need for the construction of meaningful cultural contexts through a "conjunctive approach" using the historical record and archaeological data in the form of artifacts, architecture, burials, and their contextual associations to make a contribution toward understanding the lifeway of the English settlers in the upper Chesapeake Bay region during the mid- and late seventeenth century. That need is still with us today.

The materialistic, empirical approach taken by Gibb is particularly important given his subject matter. Too often the origins of European settlement in what is now the eastern United States are obscured by contemporary ideological positions. Some scholars justify such settlement on the grounds of democracy and religious freedom concepts that in their late twentieth-century forms would seem peculiar to seventeenth-century English people. Others examine such settlement on environmental and human rights grounds that would have been equally unfamiliar to the people who actually established British North America. Gibb, on the other hand, offers a set of explanations that is tied to actions taken by the settlers themselves, not the ideological beliefs of their contemporary supporters and critics.

REFERENCES

Hodder, Ian
  1991 *Reading the Past: Current Approaches to Interpretation in Archaeology.* Cambridge University Press, Cambridge [UK].
McCracken, Grant
  1988 *Culture and Consumption: New Approaches to the Symbolic Character of Consumer Goods and Activities.* Indiana University Press, Bloomington.

Miller, Daniel
 1987 *Material Culture and Mass Consumption.* Basil Blackwell, New York.
Taylor, Walter W.
 1948 A Study of Archaeology. *American Arthropologist.* Memoir 69. Vol. 50, No.3(2).
       American Anthropological Association.

HALCOTT P. GREEN and STANLEY SOUTH
University of South Carolina
Columbia, South Carolina

Preface

"Live plentifully, and be rich." Twentieth-century scholars could misinterpret this expression. Wealth, and particularly great wealth, is something that twenti-eth-century Westerners associate with the individual. Accumulated through the cunning of a securities broker, or the skills of a major league baseball player, individuals earn and enjoy wealth. Regardless of form, wealth represents the individual: the achievements of the individual, and his or her self-image. The premise of this work is that pamphleteer George Alsop (author of the above quote) and his seventeenth-century contemporaries conceived of wealth in ways fundamentally different from widely held twentieth-century conceptions. Never-theless, wealth in its material forms provides for many of the same household needs of both periods. The ways in which people use—or do not use—their accumulated wealth tells us a good deal about how they conceive of themselves, as families and as households.

In pursuing this line of thought, I attempt to move beyond the simple equa-tions of consumer choice = social status, or ethnic identity, or place within the rural–urban continuum, or ideological expression of the structure of society and the place of one's class within it. I am concerned with the fundamental unit of production and consumption during the seventeenth and early eighteenth centu-ries: the household. The interpretive framework, drawn primarily from the theo-retical works of Grant McCracken (1988) and Daniel Miller (1987), places the immediate needs of the household—material, psychological, symbolical, juridi-cal, and organizational—above the relationship of the household to the larger society of which it is a part. In other words, I am concerned with how the house-hold views itself and organizes itself through its choices.

Used in its widest possible sense, "consumer choice" includes decisions about every facet of resource allocation, from pottery purchases to cemetery organization on the plantation. One might criticize this approach as yet another foray, and a belated one at that, into the realm of decision-making theory. To such a charge, I plead *nolo contendere*. Consumer behavior theory is a species of decision-making theory, identifying larger social patterns through analyses of individual and household behaviors.

Households make choices within the realms of culturally derived, and socially sanctioned, goals and means. To the extent that those choices vary is an indication of the range of morally acceptable means and goals defined within a particular cultural context, and an indication of the extent to which unanimity has not been achieved. Chapter 4, in particular, illustrates the point that the meanings of certain concepts falling within what we might term the economic sphere of culture were not agreed upon by all English-speakers in England and its American colonies. Attitudes of the many non-Anglo colonists and Native Americans are not addressed, but we must consider that they too differed from those held by England's ruling elite.

The last three chapters of this book interpret the material expressions of households: statements made by the household to itself through the acquisition, use, and discard of material culture. Here I deviate somewhat from the general trend in consumer behavior studies. Most students of consumer behavior view household choices as statements made by the household to the larger community about the household's place—actual or anticipated—within that community. For reasons enumerated in Chapters 2 and 6, I see the focus of these material expressions on the houselot, as each household speaks to itself about itself. Competition for status at the community level is an extension of the basic dialogue occurring on the houselot.

Inspiration for this particular approach grows out of my reading of the works of Ian Hodder (1991), Daniel Miller (1987), and, most especially, Grant McCracken (1988). To these individuals I owe both a scholarly debt and a personal apology for any violence that I may have committed to their arguments. To the large number of historical archaeologists who have dealt with consumer behavior theory, many of whom are cited in the text, I also extend both my thanks and apologies.

The data in this work derive from two sources, the one archival and the other archaeological. I am particularly indebted to the staffs of the Library of Congress, St. Mary's College Library, the Maryland State Archives, the Maryland Historical Society Library, and the respective staffs of the Maryland Historical Trust and Jefferson Patterson Park and Museum for access and assistance in using their collections. My colleagues Susan C. Buonocore and Esther Doyle Read were particularly helpful in "mining" the site files at the Maryland Historical Trust for the analysis presented in Chapter 6. Permission to excavate the Patuxent Point site and funding for the excavation of the Compton site were furnished by CRJ Associates of Camp Springs, Maryland.

Many individuals assisted in the collection, cataloging, analysis, and interpretation of the archaeological data. All of them deserve mention and a public statement of my indebtedness for their collegiality and comradeship. Stuart A. Reeve figures most prominently among them for his (nearly) unflagging good humor, perseverance in the field, and willingness to bat around ideas. To the core of the archaeological team, to whose efforts can be attributed any success we may have had in salvaging the Patuxent Point site, I offer my sincere appreciation and respect. Alexander Lavish, Paula F. Mask, Denise E. Stephenson, and Gretchen Seielstad gave freely of their time and skills for no remuneration other than comradeship and a sense of accomplishment. Dennis J. Pogue is to be lauded, not only for his assisting on several occasions with the excavation of Patuxent Point, but also for his fine job in training the above four individuals to a level of skill that meets—and in many cases surpasses—that of my professional colleagues. Esther White, Kevin Fitzpatrick, and various members of the Mount Vernon archaeological field schools provided timely assistance, as did Henry M. Miller, Silas D. Hurry, Monique Renuart, and Patricia J. McGuire.

Volunteers who have assisted in the excavation and processing of materials from Patuxent Point, most of whom came from the ranks of the Archeological Society of Maryland, are many, and I list as many of your names as I can remember. I hope you will forgive any omissions. Your commitment and good cheer came as an important reminder that archaeology need not be a solitary search, nor a pastime of small bands of social misfits, as portrayed by such writers as Paul Bahn. While I may forget the names of individuals, I will never forget what you brought to us in that sun-baked field on the Patuxent: Kent Slavin, Leona Slavin, Tom Hohenthaner, Diane Hohenthaner, Abigail Turowski, Susan Buonocore, Ethel Eaton, Tom Davidson, Alice James, Alexandra Fotos, Sally Hughes, Kay Spruell, Dale Carlson, Stephen Israel, Michele Bucci, Atwood Barwick, Elaine Huey, Beth Cole, Claude Bowen, Dick Johnson, Marjorie Johnson, Scott Sassier, Ned Ward, Pat Ward, Gary Grant, Karen Davis, Becker LeChien, Wayne Clark, and at least two dozen others whose names no doubt will reveal themselves to me in time.

My good friend Wesley J. Balla prompted my interest in seventeenth-century Dutch-made coarse earthenwares and opened doors that might otherwise have been difficult to unlock. Julia A. King, Southern Maryland Regional Archaeologist and my coprincipal investigator, provided logistical support and access to research facilities. I also thank Wayne E. Clark and Ronald Orr of the Maryland Historical Trust for their kindnesses and encouragements. Karen White, among my newest of friends, advised me on the production of artwork, and Bonnie L. Persinger and Tara D. Pettit assisted in the preparation of some of the graphics.

Any faults the reader may find in the drawings stem not from their advice but from my failure to follow instructions.

There are a number of colleagues who played little direct role in my work with seventeenth-century materials, but who deserve of my thanks, respect, and admiration. These are the people who extended a hand of welcome during my tenure in Maryland and who accepted me into the community of practicing archaeologists. In no particular order, they are Silas Hurry, Kate Dinnel, Laurie Steponaitis, Al Luckenbach, Ester Doyle Read, Carol Ebright, Mike Smolek, Tim Riordan, Stephen Israel, Beth Cole, Richard Hughes, Don Creveling, Marian Creveling, Louise Akerson, Martha Williams, Dan Mouer, Dennis Pogue, and Chuck Fithian. My staff worked diligently and responsibly, allowing me to divert my attention from the daily work routine during the final revision of this work. Tara D. Pettit, in particular, picked up the slack and pitched in to complete some of the graphics. Nina M. Versaggi and Karen L. Davis encouraged me to publish my findings, and conspired with Randall H. McGuire, Albert A. Dekin, Jr., and Vincas P. Steponaitis to convince me that it was time to finish my research.

Stanley South and Halcott Green have been very gracious and generous with their time and comments. I realize that this is not the book that either of them would have written, but I hope that it will justify your efforts and good opinion. Eliot Werner, Executive Editor for the Medical and Social Sciences at Plenum Press, has been particularly patient: thank you for overlooking the difference between July 30 and August 10. My old school chum, Christopher T. Hays, commented extensively on an earlier draft of this work and I benefited greatly over the years from our often animated discussions on anthropological theory.

For my wife, Bonnie L. Persinger, I offer this book as a wedding present—poor compensation for my self-imposed confinement and dereliction of household duties, but one that will always remind me of our choice and our particular definitions of household and family.

Contents

Chapter **1**

Introduction

OVERVIEW

Consumer behavior theory joins a growing body of analytical approaches in historical archaeology. Regarded as a "middle-range" approach and as a "paradigm," archaeologists have used consumer behavior models to link artifacts recovered from domestic sites to such large-scale historical processes as status display and class conflict. In this respect, consumer behavior modeling is useful in a field where the link between data analysis and theory often is tenuous, if not discordant.[1]

The leap from the features and artifacts of a single site to status display and ideological conflict, however, may be too great, obscuring the rich variability among assemblages and among the individuals and groups by whom they were created. The consumer behavior concept can be used to focus on variability and to reassert the priority of decision making and strategic thinking at the household level of social organization.

Many published studies and limited distribution technical reports use consumer behavior theory to organize, analyze, and interpret archaeological data for very late eighteenth- through early twentieth-century assemblages, those dealing with ninteenth-century materials being most common. These are domestic site assemblages, the material remains of households that operated within the social and economic bounds defined by wage labor, factory production of goods, and growing consumerism. Indeed, many of the case studies undertaken to date deal with highly urbanized, and often industrialized, contexts (e.g., Henry, 1991; LeeDecker, 1993; but see Lees and Majewski, 1993, and McBride and McBride, 1987, for rural examples).

1

NEW DIRECTIONS

In this book I demonstrate the applicability of consumer behavior modeling to a society that was neither industrial nor entirely capitalist in its social and economic structure. In terms of colonial studies, I propose a model detailing what Anglo-American colonists were trying to do, and how they used various classes of natural resources and manufactured goods to achieve those ends.

Of broader interest to anthropology is the relationship between social forms and consumer behavior. Patterns of consumption may relate to societywide behavioral patterns, but most consumer behavior is directed inward on the household: articulating values, promoting strategies, and reconciling conflict within the basic residential group of a colonial society. Plantation siting, the creation, maintenance, and modification of architectural spaces, interment of deceased household members in specific parts of the plantation cemetery, and choices in crockery all are direct attempts by households to maintain their identities and to achieve the identities and forms to which they aspire. Such a perspective, of course, does not reject status display and ideological conflict within communities: consumer behavior theory places them within a wider range of behaviors— expressed through material consumption—that is centered on the dynamic social relations that exist within the lot lines and dwelling walls of homelots.

ORGANIZATION OF THE WORK

Chapter 2 presents the basic concepts, intellectual history, and applications of consumer behavior theory in archaeology. It focuses on the archaeology of historic period sites since, to date, scholars have applied consumer behavior theory and analyses primarily to sites and assemblages of the historic past, and particularly to those from North America. The survey of conventional applications of consumer modeling to historical assemblages reveals very narrow limitations. We can overcome those limitations by viewing consumer behavior within a larger, contextual theory of material culture, wherein consumption and production are a single process of group definition, and the defining group is the household.

Chapter 3 presents a model of acquisition and use, derived principally from the theoretical works of Grant McCracken (1988) and Daniel Miller (1987). The model accepts all nondiscarded material culture as wealth. Wealth is situated in the household where household members use it to create household relations on a daily basis. Re-creation of household relations can be studied through several categories of material culture: houselot site locations, architecture and refuse disposal, kitchen utensils, and grave placement within a family or community cemetery. The categories derive from my reading of Anglo-American literature of the early Modern period (elaborated in Chapters 4 through 7), the kinds of data recovered from seventeenth-century sites in the Chesapeake Tidewater region (see Chapters 8 and 9), and the corpus of commonly used analytical techniques in historical archaeology.

Chapter 4 examines and defines a number of key English concepts of the late sixteenth through early eighteenth centuries, the initial period of rapid colonial expansion. Among these are wealth, property, land, labor, and commodity. Historical archaeologists and historians rarely define these terms (e.g., Carr and Walsh, 1977; Gibb and King, 1991). More important, late twentieth-century capitalist definitions of wealth, land, labor, and commodity may be incompatible with those used during the early Colonial period. Uncritical use of these terms also implies a degree of consensus among the people to whom they are applied—a consensus that may not have existed at the time, and that may not exist today. Analysis of these seventeenth-century terms reveals a great deal of ambiguity, and even conflict, over their meanings. Conflicts over the concept of land ownership and the degree to which labor was free were particularly prominent in the social and political lives of English-speaking peoples. The colonists reveal those conflicts through the varied ways in which they viewed their relationships and responsibilities to the land and to one another.

Definitions from Chapter 4 serve as background for the overview of the history of European colonization of the Chesapeake Bay region, presented in Chapters 5 and 6. Social historians and historical archaeologists have been studying the region intensively since the 1970s (e.g., Miller and King, 1988; Rheinhart and Pogue, 1993; Tate and Ammerman, 1979), resulting in a large body of data and techniques and methods appropriate to the analysis of colonial American society. Archival and archaeological data from the northern and southern colonies are included where appropriate.

Most scholars of early colonial Chesapeake history have adopted functionalist/evolutionist or historical materialist perspectives, with a great deal of reliance on demography (e.g., Carson et al., 1981; Earle, 1979; Horn, 1979; Keeler, 1978; Kulikoff, 1986; Neiman, 1990; Rutman and Rutman, 1979; Walsh, 1979a,b). I reappraise some of their conclusions, partly on the basis of the definitions from Chapter 4. Specific patterns in population (insofar as they pertain to labor) and land acquisition are examined through a series of quantitative analyses in Chapters 5 and 6. Patterns in land acquisition and abandonment are identified and related to ambiguities inherent in philosophical and legal concepts of the period. Relating cultural ideals to social practices leads to insights into the systems of meaning of the colonists, while avoiding some of the presentist biases that exist in many archaeological and historical studies of seventeenth-century Chesapeake society, and of Anglo-American colonial society in general.[2] The systems of meaning provide contexts within which to examine consumption.

Rather than isolate households from the larger social and cultural systems of which they are a part, I explore the dialectic of household actions and cultural values. Changing land-use patterns in the Chesapeake Bay region during the early Colonial period had little to do with the evolution of world capitalism: rather, they were part of a process wherein some tenants rejected the claims of a socially and geographically distant hereditary lord. Individual households directed historical developments through their actions as much as they were directed by those developments. The 'Georgian' horizon as manifested in Palladian–inspired mansions was not part of some intangible metaphysic, but the product of innumerable conscious choices made by households, objectifying not only their concepts of a rational and moral social order but their places within that order. Decisions as to what kinds of ceramic and glass vessels to acquire and use had less to do with expressing social status and ethnic identity to the community and more to do with a household's dialogue with itself about membership, identity, power relations, and mutual reliance and affection. That dialogue—the discussions and compromises among household members—extended into household cemeteries in terms of grave placement. To examine each of these object domains and still focus on competition for status in the community is to tell the story of a society's elite, and not of the society as a whole.

THE ARCHAEOLOGICAL DATA AND TESTS

Two domestic sites or homelots situated on the shores of the Patuxent River in Calvert County, Maryland, serve as test cases for the model. Compton (18CV279) is the earlier of the two (ca. 1650s–1660s), preceding and possibly overlapping with the occupation of Patuxent Point (18CV271), a site that dates to the 1660s and 1670s.[3] Only 800 ft. apart, these two homelots appear to have been situated on the same 100-acre (40 ha) tract and may have been occupied by elements of the same household. Chapter 7 describes the environmental and historical background of the William Stephens Land plantation, with period sources providing the details of the Chesapeake Tidewater environment and its rapid colonization. Chapters 8 and 9 present details of the archaeological fieldwork and laboratory analyses for Compton and Patuxent Point, respectively.

The feature and artifact assemblages described in Chapters 8 and 9 provide data for exploring the questions posed in Chapter 3. Chapter 10 interprets feature and artifact patterning at the two sites in terms of consumption patterns and the households' attempts at defining themselves. These patterns are compared to patterns reported from several other sites of similar age in the region, and from published sites in New England.

The concluding chapter addresses the question proposed at the outset: Can consumer behavior models be applied productively to the analysis and interpretation of seventeenth-century colonial assemblages? The answer is yes. A contextual approach to consumption provides insight into the ideals, practices, and strategies of European colonists. The social status-oriented approaches characteristic of consumer behavior studies are rejected. In their stead, I propose a theoretical approach to consumption and production, a theory that substitutes meaningful cultural context for universal, positivist abstractions, and that addresses the relationship between household organization and the acquisition and use of material culture.

European colonists can be characterized as acquisitive. Some sought to recreate feudal social forms already obsolete in England. Others attempted to build communities on utopian models. The majority of the Chesapeake colonists probably attempted to create static social forms based on an ill-defined model of the household as a self-sufficient commonwealth, and the focus for the generational accumulation of wealth and perpetuation of family honor.

The Chesapeake colonists tried, often successfully, to achieve these goals through the acquisition, use, and maintenance of objects that ranged in size and complexity from simple clay pots to the overall settlement system. Success, however, did not come easily or cheaply in the seventeenth century: high mortality, social instability, and intolerance characterize the time and the place. Monocropping, high rates of tenancy, and dispersed settlement led to severe environmental degradation, poverty, and widespread illiteracy.

Consumption provides a point of departure for analyzing and interpreting European colonization in the Chesapeake Bay region and throughout English America. It does so by examining consumption within its cultural–historical contexts, rejecting simplistic, positivist concepts of consumption as a direct expression of status, and recognizing the indivisibility of production and consumption, and the instrumental quality of material culture.

NOTES

1. Leone and Crosby (1987) regard consumer behavior as middle-range theory, while Spencer-Wood (1987a) calls it a paradigm. See Spencer-Wood (1987b) and Klein and LeeDecker (1991) for a number of consumer behavior studies differing both in method and approach. C. Carr (1987) uses the term "discordance" to describe the lack of fit between archaeological theory and data.
2. Carson et al. (1981), for example, attribute ephemeral housing to high mortality rates and the rapid exhaustion of agricultural soils. They do not consider the laws and customs underlying land tenure, and they use a value-laden twentieth-century con-

cept—impermanence—to divine the motivations of the colonists (Cranmer, 1990:109).

3. Archaeologists in Maryland and Virginia use the Smithsonian trinomial cataloging system, the first number representing the state (assigned consecutively to the states in alphabetical order), the letters representing the county or municipality, and the last number assigned to each site in order of its registration for the county or municipality.

Chapter 2

Consumer Behavior Theory in Historical Archaeology

INTRODUCTION

Like its older sibling, prehistory, historical archaeology is a theory "consumer," borrowing concepts from biology and paleontology, sociology, political science, and anthropology. Each borrowed concept lends insight into the historic past, and each has its limitations in historical interpretation (Leone and Potter, 1988). A brief review of some of the principal theoretical approaches current in historical archaeology highlights some of the strengths and attractions of consumer behavior theory. Not intended as a definitive critique of the principal theories and approaches in historical archaeology, this review characterizes the "climate of opinion" (*sensu* C. Becker, 1932) in which consumer behavior theory developed.[1] The remainder of the chapter examines some of the applications of consumer behavior to the analysis of material culture from historic period sites.

THEORETICAL APPROACHES

Perhaps the most widely used approaches in historical archaeology are variants of evolutionary theory and cultural ecology (e.g., H. Miller, 1984; Spencer-Wood, 1980; Stewart-Abernathy, 1986; and see Neiman's [1990] doctoral dissertation for an extreme example of evolutionary theory that is explicitly neo-Darwinian in its approach). South's (1977) "science of cultural evolution," which draws heavily on the works of Binford (e.g., 1962, 1964, 1965, 1967), Flannery (e.g., 1972a,b, 1973), Steward (1955), and L. White (e.g., 1945, 1947), is among the most detailed and best-articulated theoretical approaches in historical archaeology.[2] South developed this approach, along with appropriate methods, as a means of identifying and explaining material culture patterning. The patterns were to be used in the derivation of laws of culture change. The "Brunswick Pattern of Trash Disposal," and the "Carolina" and "Frontier" artifact patterns, defined by South (1977) and developed by others (e.g., Zierden and Calhoun, 1986), are products of pattern-oriented research aimed at a science of cultural behavior.[3]

The abstract, ahistorical character of this approach, and its limited potential for incorporating documentary data analysis,[4] has won South few adherents in recent years; this despite the widespread use of several of his analytical techniques (e.g., mean ceramic dating, definition of characteristic artifact disposal patterns).[5] Many researchers use South's Artifact Pattern Analysis to analyze intrasite artifact distributions and to compare artifact assemblages (e.g., Seifert, 1991; but see Farnsworth [1992] for a critique). This approach is particularly evident in the functional analyses of artifact distributions on seventeenth century colonial sites (e.g., Cranmer, 1990; Faulkner and Faulkner, 1987; Gibb and King, 1991); King and Miller, 1987; Pogue, 1988), although only King (1988:17) acknowledges this influence. Most studies of early colonial sites stop well short of addressing the processes of cultural evolution as defined by South. Only Miller (1984) fully explores the adaptationist/evolutionary approach to the historical development of the Chesapeake colonies, and he does not use South's approach to the problem.

In a more recent statement of his position, South (1988) recommends development of energy flow models based on artifact data that relate artifact patterning to the exploitation of resources through class distinctions and the consequent evolution of world cultural systems. This approach converges with that of the world systems theorists.

World systems theory, inspired by Frank (e.g., 1966, 1967) and developed by Wallerstein (e.g., 1974), also influences the field. World systems theory provides a framework for studying cultural change in terms of large-scale processes that function through a spatial division of labor, spatial inequality in terms of access to the means of production, and extraction and expropriation of surplus value from producers. It describes the processes by which these changes occur and the effects of those processes on specific parts of the developing world system.

Paynter's (1982) experiments with spatial models, developed by geographers, can be credited to a large extent with bringing this approach to the attention of archaeologists. His models, however, deal almost exclusively with settlement patterning rather than with the bricks, nails, and potsherds that are recovered during the course of most archaeological field research. Paynter's (1982) work in the Connecticut River valley demonstrates how a developing world system created settlement and exchange systems (promoting spatial inequality and the expropriation of surpluses by core areas) during the seventeenth through nineteenth centuries. His analysis explains the emergence of a peripheral area and its growth into an industrial, commercial, and political core area.

World systems theory integrates ecological, economic, and political variables into a single model. It reminds historical archaeologists that individual sites are parts of larger wholes, and archaeological remains are products of economic and political forces, shaped by the environment. Paynter (1982), for example, interprets developments in the Connecticut River valley of south-central Massachusetts in terms of large-scale historical processes occurring within certain environmental constraints. The conquest and settlement of Massachusetts, and the transformation of its landscape, was a political-economic process centered in the core area of northwestern Europe, but spanning the globe.

One of the principal weaknesses of the world systems approach is that it depends on developments in the core, while tending to ignore acts of resistance and fraternization in the periphery (cf. Paynter and McGuire, 1991). Peripheral areas, such as colonial North America, are portrayed as stages upon which core "scripts" are performed, the playwrights little affected by the actors' interpretations. Large-scale processes overshadow individual action, and the nature and direction of those processes are predictable and ahistorical.[6] Leone and Potter (1988) criticize world systems theory, characterizing it as essentially functionalist and systemic in perspective.

Moving from the large-scale spatial models derived from world systems theory to the features and artifacts recovered from archaeological sites has proven difficult.[7] Nonetheless, the explanatory power of world systems theory is not easily dismissed, and its influence can be seen in Mrozowski's (1988) call for a cross-cultural approach to the study of world urbanism, South's (1988) recommendation that international energy transfers be studied through artifact patterning, Deagan's (1988) suggestion that historical archaeology focus on the expanding European world system, and a series of papers emphasizing a global perspective (e.g., Falk, 1991; Posnansky, 1992).[8] None of these papers offers an example of how one can relate the archaeological remains of a site that is smaller than a fort or a city block to the larger-scale processes of peripheralization and core formation.[9]

A variety of historical materialist approaches that are Marxian in inspiration, but that lack the emphasis on systems analysis, also emerged in the 1980s. Kohl (1981), focusing on developments in prehistoric archaeology, describes historical materialism as an approach that "accepts a conflictual, as opposed to consensual, theory of society in which conscious political actions of social groups or classes remain central and paramount, however firmly or loosely related they may be to their economic base" (1981:109); that is, institutions and interest groups do not necessarily interact like the inner workings of a machine.

Leone (1984) has been at the forefront of Marxian approaches in historical archaeology, emphasizing the priority of material production over the synchronous spheres of politics and ideology, and the importance of conflict and dialectical processes in creating, maintaining, and altering social formations. Dialecticism and history replace systems and abstract laws of cultural evolution, and archaeologists recognize themselves as participants in the creation of culture rather than as detached observers (McGuire, 1992:248). Marxian approaches have sustained the greatest development and continuity of all of the theoretical approaches current in historical archaeology (e.g., Leone and Potter, 1988; McGuire, 1992; Paynter and McGuire, 1991), with the possible exception of cultural evolution/functionalist theories (e.g., South, 1977).

Marxian theory often is criticized for its focus on class conflict and its explicit political, as opposed to positivist-science, agenda.[10] Moreover, the distinction between the actions of an individual, as an individual, and those of a person representing the needs and goals of a particular socioeconomic class (*sensu* Marx) is often unclear.[11] For example, William Paca designed and had built a formal garden at his home in Annapolis, Maryland, in the second half of the eighteenth century. According to Leone (1984, 1988), Paca utilized the rules of perspective to reify certain aspects of the social order. One wonders, however, for whose benefit Paca made this ideological statement. If he was representing the interests of his class, then the statement probably was lost upon its intended audience, the general population of Annapolis: they could neither see the spatial illusions that were fully visible only from the rear of Paca's house, nor—as most undoubtedly were unfamiliar with the rules of perspective employed in the garden's layout— were they likely to understand, much less accept, the social allusions.[12]

Daniel Defoe, a writer with a keen sense for details of social behavior and the cultural landscape, described the influence of King William on the built environment of southeastern England:

> But I find none has spoken of what I call the distant glory of these buildings. There is a beauty of these things at a distance, taken *en passant*, and in perspective, which few people value, and fewer understand; and yet here they are more truly great, than in all the private beauties whatsoever.... Take them in a remote view, the fine seats among the trees as jewells shine in a rich coronet; in a near sight they are mere pictures and paintings; at a distance they are all nature; near hand all art; but both in the extremest beauty. (Defoe, 1971 [1724–1726]:176).[13]

The only group of people in Annapolis likely both to view and understand the statements created by William Paca through his formal landscape were the elite, a group with whom Paca may have been attempting to negotiate his own status; clearly, Paca's landscaping endeavors were the actions of an individual in pursuit of his own interests, or those of his family at most. Marxian scholars, with their concern for class conflict and emphasis on shared consciousness and access to the means of production, often overlook the all-important conflict within classes, and the role of individuals in fostering or quelling class conflicts.[14]

Marxian analysts tend to downplay elite conflict, but they do not reject it out of hand:

> [N]on-elites often do not share the dominant ideology of the elites, and in fact have ideologies of resistance. This suggests that the dominant ideologies, in which royal burials, pyramids, megaliths, and so on, participate, were better suited to securing the coherence of the dominant class than the submission of the subordinates. (Paynter and McGuire, 1991:10)

Such an interpretation may be appropriate for the William Paca garden, although—as Hodder (1991:70) points out—we still need to demonstrate that gardens functioned in the ideological realm of eighteenth-century Annapolis society.

In contrast to the materialist perspectives of the world systems theorists and others (e.g., Orser, 1987), there is a mentalist perspective that has flourished in historical archaeology since Deetz (1977), inspired by the work of Glassie (1975), introduced structuralism to the field. Deetz's concern for mental templates and structural binary oppositions flavors many interpretations of material culture patterns, particularly in regard to the postulated shift from the "medieval" mind-set of seventeenth-century New England society to the modernist-rationalist "Georgian" mind-set of the late eighteenth-century English-speaking world.[15] Organic models of society and culture, deduced primarily from architectural patterns, were replaced by patterns of bilateral symmetry and rational segmentation and separation (Deetz, 1977). This model has been particularly popular with those researchers concerned with changes in architecture, foodways, tablewares, and funerary monuments: indeed, the popularity of Deetz's approach largely stems from his treatment of artifacts as uniform categories. Every class of material culture in a society is the product of a single mental template structured in terms of analogous binary oppositions (Leone, 1982:743–744); hence, a society's mental template is accessible through the entire range of its material products.

Researchers representing a wide range of theoretical perspectives (e.g., Dent, 1990; Leone, 1984; King and Miller, 1987; Yentsch, 1990a) use the term "Georgian mindset," giving it the stature of a technical term rather than the hypothesized culture manifestation that it was intended to represent.[16] Deetz's characterizations of seventeenth-century New England as "medieval" in outlook and the eighteenth-century Anglo-American world as Georgian also are simplistic and stereotypical. For example, the architectural patterns taken to be reflections or products of the Georgian mindset are clearly visible in Restoration period England (e.g., Hutchinson's [1976] study of the life and work of Christopher Wren). Macfarlane (1978) also questions the characterization of rural English folk as communally oriented peasants within a feudal order (see also H. Miller, 1988).[17]

Perhaps the weakest aspect of a structuralist approach, apart from its ahistorical perspective,[18] and one with which structuralists have been contending since Claude Levi-Strauss introduced it to anthropology in the 1960s, is its inability to deal with culture change: structuralism lacks a theory of practice (Hodder, 1982). Whereas change can be described as an alteration of a society's mental template or worldview, the locus of this change is unclear, as is the manner in which it occurs.[19] The role of the individual in effecting change is uncertain, possibly irrelevant, and, perhaps, theoretically impossible. More important, variations within society are unrecognized in favor of ideals. Such differences as occur are attributed to Chomsky's concept of incompetence, as understood by Glassie (1975), or as products of external constraints operating on an individual's competence, a process likened to genetic drift. Primacy is accorded to competence (Glassie, 1975:17):

> The folk artist is no gambler; his work is continuous in planes of space and time. His innovation is inevitably a truce with time, a compromise in social assertion. A close analysis of the folk maker's product leads to a clear view of him modestly tinkering with given ideas that he can predict will be acceptable to those who must use them. A search for the sources of the genius of a [Frank Lloyd] Wright depends upon an intricate analysis, but even an impressionistic depiction of the folk architect's building reveals it to be a mediation between rejection and submission. It is the perfectionist's compromise: young enough to be arrogant, old enough to be loved. (Glassie, 1975:112)

Tinkering is an interesting concept, one that may not be in accord with structuralist theory. Why would a folk artist "tinker"? Can any individual have a "competence" beyond that embodied within his or her culture? In other words, can an individual anticipate changes in grammar through the creation of novel forms? How is variability in meaning and use addressed?

> Different forms can be identical, but the meanings and uses different people associate with these forms can only be similar. Thus, though the analyst's account may be complete and efficient, it must always be hypothetical. This is a reason for separating problems of meaning and use from the statement of the competence and holding them aside for separate analysis, even though the thoughts of usefulness informed the actual competence at every step. (Glassie, 1975:21)

We are left with a hypothesis that is not entirely testable, and that resists the incorporation of conscious individual action and redefinition. Leadership is denied. Barth's (1963, 1966) entrepreneur (and economic behavior, in general) does not figure into this paradigm, nor do the ideology-mongers of Leone's (1984, 1988a,b) eighteenth-century Annapolis. Clearly, such individuals exist in every society, and a culture is as readily defined by its variability as it is by its ideals. Consumer behavior provides a framework for examining variability, and to a limited extent individual action, through artifact patterning.

CONSUMER BEHAVIOR THEORY

Elements of consumer behavior research appeared sporadically in historical archaeology throughout the 1970s and 1980s (e.g., Hudgins, 1980; Toulouse, 1970), but explicit discussions of consumer behavior theory were virtually absent until the late 1980s.[20] Spencer-Wood broke new ground with the publication of her edited volume *Consumer Choice in Historical Archaeology* (Spencer-Wood, 1987b).

The explanation of "household variations in historic consumer behavior through combined analyses of archaeological and documentary data" is the stated goal of the volume (Spencer-Wood, 1987a:xi). The primary hypothesis: "socio-economic stratification significantly affects certain consumer behaviors, involving choices to acquire, and later archaeologically deposit [read *discard*], relatively expensive versus inexpensive goods" (Spencer-Wood, 1987a:xi; see also Baart, 1987:2). The contributors use quantitative and comparative site analyses to identify variations, explaining those variations through analyses of documentary data on the social status and other social characteristics of the households under study.

> [The] principal application [of the consumer behavior framework] lies in explaining why goods of differing quality or price were selected for acquisition and archaeological deposition by different cultural subgroups in a market economy; . . . The market-oriented consumer choice framework provides a theoretical basis for hypothesizing connections between site-specific archaeological data and levels of cultural behavior from the household level to cultural subgroups and the national market. It forms a conceptual bridge between archaeological data recovery and cultural behavior. (Spencer-Wood, 1987a:9)

The motivation for this volume appears to have been the growing frustration with the chasm between data from archaeological sites and the fascinating, but somewhat ethereal, theories proposed over the previous 10 years.[21] Clearly, this frustration was, in part, behind Binford's (1983) conception and development of middle-range theory. Following Leone and Crosby (1987), Spencer-Wood introduces consumer behavior as a systemic framework or model functioning as middle-range theory: systemic because it addresses various aspects of social differentiation (e.g., market access, ethnicity, household size, and life cycle, as well as social class) and biases in the archaeological and documentary records, and a framework, model, or paradigm because it structures the kinds of questions to be asked and the kinds of data to be collected and analyzed.[22]

Although Spencer-Wood emphasizes socioeconomic status as the principal determinant behind household consumption patterns, several of the other contributors regard this variable as only one among many variables that influence household decisions regarding tableware and food purchases, or that contribute to their representation in the archaeological record (e.g., Baugher and Venables, 1987; Reitz, 1987). Shepard (1987) and LeeDecker, et al. (1987) also suggest patterns that are far more complex. Orser (1987), employing a historical materialist approach, states that it is the relations of production—patterns in the creation, extraction, and distribution of surplus value—that should concern those involved with plantation archaeology. Caste-class models, such as those used by Otto (1984), obscure the fundamental occupational and class aspects of plantation life. Orser (1987:125) also reminds us of our basic undergraduate anthropology when he points out the dynamic nature of status and its contextual aspects.[23] McBride and McBride (1987:158) also note the "almost casual use of the term 'socioeconomic status,'" but suggest that it may be appropriate in the study of Western societies from the fifteenth century onward since social and economic statuses became increasingly intertwined with the development of world capitalism.

Concern for the other social phenomena underlying consumer behavior is made even clearer in a special theme issue of *Historical Archaeology*, entitled "Models for the Study of Consumer Behavior" (Klein and LeeDecker, 1991). The editors compiled this special issue because they felt that existing models of consumer behavior were implicit and narrow in scope. They attributed difficulties in synthesizing data from a variety of urban contexts not so much to incompatible typologies and analytical methods but to the lack of a clearly defined historical context or model for interpreting purchase, use, and discard (Klein and LeeDecker, 1991:1). Henry (1991) models the variables with the aid of a flow diagram that relates household income, internal influences (a "black box" of psychological and individual physiological needs), and external influences on consumer choices. Many of the variables and their relationships are drawn from the works of economists and marketing researchers (e.g., Abraham Maslow's [1943] hierarchy of needs).

Huelsbeck (1991), implicitly criticizing Reitz's (1987) analysis of a large number of faunal assemblages from sites along the east coast of the United States, stresses the importance of using culturally meaningful units in analyzing consumer patterns. Unless minimum numbers of individuals or butchering units (e.g., a side of beef) correspond to the units in which meat was purchased, they should not be used in an analysis of consumer behavior. Although Huelsbeck's comments are concerned specifically with faunal analysis and the need to identify the "unit of acquisition," they are equally valid for other classes of material culture, particularly ceramics and glass vessels (e.g., Gibb, 1993a; Yentsch, 1990b).

Friedlander (1991), in her study of the estates of a midnineteenth-century farmer—Thomas Hamlin—and several storekeepers in northwestern New Jersey, discovered that consumer socioeconomic status could be expressed in terms of consumer behavior patterns, but some classes of property were more revealing than others. Thomas Hamlin achieved a "threshold of comfort" with the purchase of some amenities, but then used his resources to buy additional land and livestock, expand his dwelling, construct new outbuildings of specialized function, and purchase other "durable" goods. Analysis of local store inventories clearly demonstrated that market access and availability of goods did not preclude purchases of fancy tablewares, mirrors, and heating stoves.

> The discrepancy between the relative value of Thomas [Hamlin's] household and his relative position as defined by land, livestock, and farm equipment, suggests that durable household goods, including those picked up [inventoried?] by the executors of his estate, may not be the most important ways that farmers displayed their status. Having achieved a certain threshold, marked by coarse earthenwares and bed/table linen, farmers seem to have chosen to invest in land and livestock and perhaps the dwelling, with expenditures on non-durable goods that were either consumed [e.g., coffee, sugar] or, like clothing, became devalued by the time the estate was entered into probate. . . . Economic scaling based on ceramics, may have limited utility in studies of consumer behavior while analyses of shelters and foodways, including diet, food preparation and service, beckons. (Friedlander, 1991:27)[24]

LeeDecker (1991) echoes Friedlander's suggestion that levels of analysis should be taxonomically higher in archaeological studies than they have been (e.g., the more inclusive, generic category of furnishings rather than the narrow, more specific category of tablewares).[25] Noting that a number of political economists, historians, economists, and sociologists since the seventeenth century have used the more inclusive categories of food, clothing, rent, fuel, and sundries, LeeDecker suggests that we retain the analytic categories now widely used in historical archaeology, but undertake analyses at these more inclusive levels. For example, food has been the largest household expense for most families up until very recently, with the percentage of household budgets devoted to food purchases negatively correlated with household income. LeeDecker recommends that we examine consumer behavior in terms of food, and to a lesser extent clothing.

From a practical perspective, food is highly visible in the archaeological record, represented by discarded containers, preparation and serving vessels, bone, and plant remains. But is food a consumer good? Urban households purchased most of their foodstuffs through markets. But was this true of rural households as well, the type of household in which the vast majority of Americans lived until the early years of the twentieth century? Robert Beverley (1947 [1705]:291) provides some insight into this issue for the late seventeenth and early eighteenth centuries in Virginia:

> The Families being altogether on Country-Seats, they have their Graziers, Seedsmen, Gardiners, Brewers, Bakers, Butchers, and Cooks within themselves: they have a great Plenty and Variety of Provisions for their Table; and as for Spicery, and other things that the Country don't produce, they have constant supplies of 'em from England.

In early eighteenth century Virginia, much of what was consumed at home was grown at home, at least among the wealthier people with whom Beverley would have been most familiar. The case may be somewhat overstated for the less affluent, who purchased more of what they could not produce for lack of sufficient household labor or equipment. Regardless of relative wealth, however, most colonists produced most of their own foodstuffs. Anderson (1971) reached the same conclusion for the farmers of seventeenth-century England, with the poorer husbandmen and wealthier gentry relying to a greater extent than the yeoman farmers on purchased foods. Menard et al. (1988) also suggest that subsistence goods composed a very high percentage of the gross product of seventeenth-century tobacco plantations in the Chesapeake region, with clothing and other manufactured goods making up the bulk of market purchases.

PATTERNS IN THE STUDY OF CONSUMER BEHAVIOR

Archaeological studies of consumer behavior exhibit a number of common features. Principal among these is the focus on the household as the locus of decision making. Household members make decisions, guided by their prescribed roles (*sensu* Goodenough, 1965) within larger social, cultural, and economic contexts. Implicit in all consumer behavior studies in historical archaeology is the notion that all artifacts represent consumer goods that can be purchased in a market economy. The purchasing behavior of a household is quantifiable and comparable to the consumer behavior of other, although not necessarily all, households (see Klein, 1991:88; also Gasco, 1992). Most important, patterns of consumption, in very complex ways, reflect cultural behavior at the household level and at larger, poorly defined levels of social integration.[26]

Household as the Unit of Analysis

The greatest strength of consumer behavior modeling is its emphasis on households. Individual behaviors, in all but the most unusual circumstances, are obscured archaeologically by the material effects of the behaviors of others in the household. The household, then, is an aggregate of individuals: the homelot is the collection of buildings, fences, and yards that is both the product and medium of the household's aggregate behavior.[27] The unit of analysis corresponds to the unit of data recovery—the archaeological site. In practice, of course, this is seldom strictly true, particularly when the site in question is in an urban area where more than one household may have occupied the same or overlapping spaces.[28] A homelot occupied by successive generations also can be said to have been occupied by more than one household, despite genetic continuity in the succession of households.

Implied in many archaeological studies of households, and particularly those that employ consumer models, is that it is a *household* that is under study: the nature of the cultural unit usually is not defined, and the demographics of the specific household under study are either unknown or only partially known (e.g., Gibb and King, 1991). In a special issue of *Man in the Northeast* (1984), several archaeologists identified the household as an important unit of analysis. Beaudry (1984), borrowing from Laslett (1972), defines household as a coresident group sharing the same physical space (the homelot) for basic life processes. Citing Wilk and Rathje (1982), she lists production, distribution, transmission, and reproduction among those basic life functions. Starbuck's (1984) study of the Shaker concept of household, however, calls into question the importance of the reproductive function; the Shakers relied on recruitment as a means of perpetuating their social formation.[29]

More recently, Purser (1991) demonstrated that households can be more fluid, at least on a seasonal basis, in terms of membership and the spaces in which the basic life functions occur. Herlihy (1985), in his analyses of the lives of saints and fifteenth-century Tuscan *castatos* (a species of census return), suggests:

> Not all medieval households were centers of production or even reproduction, if we include in the latter category the rearing of children without interruption to adulthood. . . . This means that the study of households everywhere cannot be limited to individual domestic units, taken in isolation. Rather, the system joining them must be reconstructed and examined. The system, together with separate households, helped [in fifteenth-century Tuscany] to assure that reproduction and production could be carried on somewhere in society, and that this civilization would survive. (Herlihy, 1985:158–159)

Wilk (1991), in his study of Kekchi Maya household ecology, portrays the household as the locus of adaptation to the social and biotic environments. His choice of the household as a unit of analysis is guided by several limitations inherent in the concept:

1. Households are not corporate entities with well-defined boundaries and motivations.
2. Households are not isolated and autonomous, but are embedded within wider social and economic networks.
3. Individuals have different degrees of household membership.
4. The household economy is always abridged by law, custom, or community.
5. There are no functions that are universal to all households, making static definitions very difficult.

Wilk identifies three dimensions of households: morphology, activity, and culture. In terms of morphology, the household is the most common social unit in society, useful as a census unit but of dubious value in an analysis of culture change. As an activity or process, the household is an open group, with more or less fluid membership, in which the basic life processes of production, transmission and trusteeship of property, distribution and consumption, biological and social reproduction, and coresidence occur. Cultural resources and systems of meaning constrain and define strategies and meaning.

This dynamic, and rather complex, model of households is very different from those employed by archaeologists (see LeeDecker et al. [1987] for an interesting exception). Nass (1989), for example, identifies single structures and associated features and activity areas as households in the study of the Fort Ancient aspect (late twelfth/thirteenth century) Incinerator site near Dayton, Ohio. The several structures could represent a single household composed of several "household clusters" (*sensu* Wilk, 1991:205ff.).[30] The household cluster concept may be particularly appropriate for the study of Shaker villages and other utopian communities, as well as for those households that Purser (1991) examines in the American West and that Herlihy (1985) documents for fifteenth-century Tuscany, although the spatial connotation of cluster would be inappropriate for the latter two as the individual units were widely dispersed.

The attribution of single or multiple dwellings to a single household must be demonstrated, not assumed. The assumption that a single dwelling or homelot represents a single household has been made in many archaeological studies, often in situations where household demographics and activities cannot be determined through archival sources.[31] In most cases, archaeologists deal with homelots or, more accurately, with the material remains of homelots. The homelot consists of the principal dwelling, other dwellings, outbuildings, and workyards of a homestead. It represents a culturally meaningful category to its occupants and to those from neighboring homelots, but to what extent a specific homelot can be associated with a specific household is uncertain, particularly given the fluid nature of households. This point is particularly relevant in this study since two homelots appearing to occupy the same plantation tract, and possibly representing a single household or parts of a larger household, provide the archaeological data with which consumer behavior on the seventeenth-century Chesapeake Bay frontier is examined.

Consumer Goods and Status

The focus on socioeconomic status appears in several of the earliest papers dealing explicitly with consumer behavior, and—in practice—archaeologists often infer status from the artifacts recovered from a particular site. For example, a decorative prunt from a German-made roemer (an ornate, and presumably expensive, drinking glass) may be submitted as evidence of the high status of a seventeenth-century site's occupants.[32] Does possession of such a piece indicate high status, and if so, how much higher would the status of the occupants have been had the remains of a second roemer been found? Does the roemer reflect the status of the household, the household head, or the head of household's nuclear family? More important, what is high status? As noted above, scholars (e.g., Orser, 1988, 1992) are beginning to address this naive notion of status, as well as the various transformational processes that could account for the appearance of a roemer, or any other artifact, on an archaeological site (e.g., Henry, 1991).

The complexity and dynamic nature of social status is recognized by many working with consumer behavior models, and its analytical value is limited. Klein, for example, falls back on a typological approach:

Future research should examine each household "site" to the fullest extent possible using standard types of archaeological analyses (e.g., Miller's ceramic scaling, vessel counts, pattern analysis, form/function analysis, etc.), and place the archaeological materials associated with the household in the appropriate social and economic "context" of that particular household. . . .[The] household-specific context should include site location (i.e., along the rural/urban continuum) and the role of women within the household. Juxtaposed to this context should be the configuration of the ceramic market for the time period under study.

This is a very descriptive approach, but it provides historical archaeologists with an attainable goal. Based on the results of these archaeological and historical analyses, *individual households are aggregated into groups of households with shared characteristics*. Each household study then becomes a building block, enabling historical archaeologists to move to a higher level of abstraction [emphasis added]. (Klein, 1991:88)

Classification is the sine qua non of anthropology, as it is for all scientific endeavors, but a classification must have a purpose; otherwise it is of little or no value. Klein's quandary represents a stumbling block that confronts all students of consumer behavior modeling, and particularly those concerned with status: where do we go from here? Using a "snowball strategy" for sampling (Bertaux, 1981), without specific questions in mind, will not explain variability in historic period consumption patterns. In the same volume, Henry provides a sophisticated, generalized model of consumer behavior (1991:5). She ends her article with the following apologia: "Regrettably, there are no neat, clean hypotheses or easy answers here that can be put to work immediately" (Henry, 1991:12). Do we have a method without a theory? A construct paradigm (*sensu* Clark, 1987)? Is there a point in quantifying and comparing patterns without first identifying meaningful questions?

The difficulty stems, in part, from the way in which the various researchers view material culture and its role in human behavior. There is the implicit assumption that humans have an innate desire of Malthusian proportions to consume, guided in their choices by various ascribed and achieved social characteristics, and lacking only the means and opportunity to satisfy their desires.[33] For the logic of this approach, we can look to Schumpeter's (1961:4–5) explanation of the scientific process in economics: "When we succeed in finding a definite causal relation between two phenomena, our problem is solved if the one which plays the 'causal' role is noneconomic." By grounding consumerism in human biology or psychology, we have provided ourselves with an a priori explanation that requires only such historical details as are necessary to explain the availability of specific products and the means of acquiring those products. Our goal is no longer the explanation of consumption, which is attributed to inclination, but the description of the various forms that consumption takes and the social and ecological constraints on its form and rate.

Artifacts are portrayed as passive, static objects that are sought and purchased because they somehow reflect the needs and values of their would-be purchasers. There is a measurable relationship between objects and social needs. Given our full knowledge of its various social characteristics, would any of the above-cited researchers agree that the purchasing patterns of a particular household are predictable? Perhaps. Market researchers, some of whom are cited by Henry (1991), certainly would, at least within definable confidence intervals. The issue, however, is that prediction of household consumption patterns, given independent archival evidence of the household's social status, is the logical conclusion to many consumer behavior studies; particularly, but not exclusively, those that deal with socioeconomic and ethnic statuses. Noncorrespondence between the two data sets leads the archaeologist back to the archival record in search of a particularistic explanation (e.g., Baugher and Venables, 1987; see also

Cook and Yamin, 1994). As Deetz (1988:363) points out, since we already know, in most cases, the value of an artifact within the cultural context in question, we are left with little more than the "self-evident and expectable relation between affluence and quality of possessions." And, again following Deetz (1988:363), it is difficult to see just how this approach can make fruitful use of the dialectic between archival and archaeological analyses.

Orser's (1987) suggestion that we focus on surplus extraction and distribution may provide a way out of the static artifact-as-reflection concept. Objects can be viewed as active components in the creation and re-creation of social relations. They are the means and the object of surplus extraction. It is through the creation and use of objects that social conflict is fostered and mitigated, and it is through conflict that social life exists. Orser (1987, 1992) regards objects as tools that have symbolic value, rather than as symbols that also may serve some pedestrian purposes. Artifacts mediate between individuals, and between individuals and their attempts to produce their sustenance, and a little bit more. The difficulty with Orser's approach, and one that pervades historical materialism, is the focus on production when our stated interest is in consumption. Moreover, most of the debris collected from archaeological sites consists of domestic materials used within the household and not in places of direct class conflict (e.g., stores, courts). The relations in which such materials can be expected to have played a direct structuring role are domestic household relations.[34]

Consumption versus Production

Regardless of the theoretical perspectives employed, there is a problem that characterizes all consumer behavior studies in historical archaeology: the distinction made between consumption and production. What, for instance, is a consumer? Henry (1991:3) defines a consumer as "an individual or organization who [/that] acquires goods or services for his [/its] own use or for someone else's use." By her definition, virtually all people are consumers, and the term denotes a status rather than a process or activity. LeeDecker (1991:30) proposes two definitions of consumer behavior: "activities related to the satisfaction of human needs and desires," and "patterns of individual, household, or group expenditures, and specifically . . .the acquisition and use of material items." Both definitions are broad, and while neither distinguishes between productive activities and processes and those that are purely consumptive, in practice such a distinction inevitably is implied.[35]

If LeeDecker (1991) and Henry (1991) implicitly distinguish between production goods and consumption goods, historian Lorena S. Walsh (1983) is explicit: consumer goods are household furnishings. Like most historians of Colonial America, Walsh distinguishes between capital goods and consumer goods, the 'tools' of the plantation representing the former and such household furnishings as pottery, furniture, and clothing representing the latter. This same dichotomy is evident in South's (1977:95–96) widely used taxonomic system, which distinguishes between the Activities Group ('tools' used in farming, fishing, construction, and military activities) and the Kitchen Artifact Group.[36] The latter consists of women's objects that, apparently, do not represent activities; at least not on the order of farming, fishing, building, fighting, or even playing. The implicit and explicit dichotomy of production and consumption, between that which produces wealth and that which reproduces the group through the consumption of wealth, pervades virtually all of the literature on the subject.

Defining production separately from consumption may not mirror categories that were culturally meaningful to the people we are studying, and it betrays certain presentist, and sexist, views of the past. A seventeenth-century colonist choosing a hoe, or a parcel of hoes, from the supplies of a merchant ship probably was not thinking in terms of consumption, but in terms of how well the blade would hold up when the seed beds and fields had to be prepared for the next season's crops. The hoes probably were viewed as means toward certain ends, and not as goods to be enjoyed and used up in the process. Similarly, coarse earthenwares, and possibly finer ceramic wares as well, were purchased for the purposes of producing, processing, preparing, storing, and presenting foodstuffs to the household, a household that may well have included field hands who produced nothing if they went unfed, unclothed, or unhoused.[37] Colonial households purchased goods with which to produce and reproduce. Neither production nor consumption, chicken nor egg, can be given priority. They are indivisible parts of a process.

The indivisible nature of consumption and production, which may have been evident on seventeenth-century tobacco plantations, has been arbitrarily segmented and separated by twentieth-century analysts, just as the work environment (misrepresented as production without consumption) and the domestic environment (usually misrepresented as consumption without production) have been segregated and separated in the twentieth-century.[38] Negative connotations to the term "consumption" also resonate the prejudices of the modern period, and particularly those of certain social groups. Consumption generally is feminized and women's spending is an integral part of the twentieth-century comedic canon; unless, of course, the purchases are of tools that are used within the masculine domains of yard and shop.

NEW PERSPECTIVES ON CONSUMER BEHAVIOR

Beginning in the 1980s, a new literature on consumer behavior emerged in the fields of anthropology and history, with varying influence in historical archaeology. McKendrick, Brewer et al. (1982) have had the greatest influence, situating the origins of consumerism in late eighteenth-century England. Not only is the eighteenth century prominent in the literature of American historical archaeology, but the authors use the production and distribution of pottery (historically the most important object domain for historical archaeologists) as one line of evidence for the development of consumerism. The authors' emphasis on Thorstein Veblen's (1934) concepts of status and emulation has been especially attractive for archaeologists, as the literature review in the previous section indicates. One of the drawbacks to this landmark study, apart from its simplistic and unarticulated theory of material culture, is its focus on the production and advertising of consumer goods, rather than on their uses and meanings.

Daniel Miller's (1987) work on a theory of material culture holds promise for dealing with consumer behavior, although to date his work appears to have had little impact in American historical archaeology.[39] Miller views material culture not as a by-product or residual of social behavior, but as culture itself. Drawing from Hegel's concept of alienation (objectification) and Piagetian psychology, he views the artifact as an object created by and from a social group (the subject).[40] Through consumption, or what Hegel termed *sublation*, that object is reincorporated into the subject (reappropriated by the subject, in Miller's terms), and the subject in turn is changed. Cultural change is thereby viewed as an ongoing, positive process of production (self-alienation) and consumption (sublation), in both physical and metaphysical senses. The subject projects an aspect of itself upon the material world and, through reappropriation of the object, re-creates itself. Historical circumstances arise in which one social group attempts to mask or deny that the object so created is part of the subordinate group, but Miller is confident that such events can be overcome or circumvented through new objects created in new domains and through the process of creative recontextualization (i.e., interpretation).[41]

Miller eschews the moral judgments of social critics against consumption, and views late twentieth-century mass consumption as healthy and integral to social development. Although he makes much of his theoretical antecedents in Hegel, Georg Simmel, and Jean Piaget, his intellectual roots are far more familiar to American archaeologists in the works of the Cambridge School anthropologists (e.g., Ian Hodder, Christopher Tilley) and several historians studying consumerism (e.g., McCracken [1988], Appadurai [1986], Kopytoff [1986]).[42] Miller's theoretical perspective is related to the contextualism that has been developing in archaeology during the 1980s and 1990s, much of it emanating from Great Britain. He differs from many of the contextualists in his very positive characterization of material culture and its role in social development, particularly in terms of creative interpretation. As a theory of material culture, and of culture in general, objectification (in Miller's rather than Marx's sense) potentially

is a powerful concept that could break us loose from such culture-bound correspondences as *artifact = status* (a taken-for-granted equality, muddled by such
definable variables as ethnicity and age), *women = consumption* (a necessary if not
entirely laudable relationship), and *men = production* (a truly right and just relationship upon which moral and civil society are founded).[43]

This brief summation of Miller's aproach suggests a reason for the limited
influence of objectification theory in archaeology. The theory is rooted in arcane
philosophical concepts with which few archaeologists are familiar and fewer still
are prepared to use. Fortunately, theoretical work along very similar lines has
been published by Grant McCracken (1988), and in much clearer terms, to which
we can append Miller's concern for interpretation. McCracken (1988:xi) examines the relationship between consumption and culture. He defines culture as
"the ideas and activities with which we construe and construct our world." Consumption includes those processes by which goods and services are created, acquired, and used. Goods are charged with cultural meaning that is used to express
"cultural categories and principles, cultivate ideals, create and sustain lifestyles,
and create (and survive) cultural change" (McCracken 1988:xi).

Using Chandra Mukerji's (1981) *From Graven Images: Patterns of Modern
Materialism* as a point of departure, McCracken suggests that consumerism predates, and gave rise to, capitalism in the fifteenth and sixteenth centuries in
Europe, and that goods became a medium for expressing, transforming, and in-
novating cultural ideals. In short, material culture is instrumental in social life.
Consumer choice is situated in the household, which—through its acquisitions—articulates a sense of itself. The objects with which a household surrounds
itself are a direct statement of what that household believes itself to be, or what it
hopes to become. Artifacts are imbued with meaning. Meaning is historically
derived, but—unlike language—not wholly arbitrary. The physical nature of the
objects, the manner and contexts in which they are used, contributes to their
significance.

Material culture is conservative in its expressiveness, making public those
things—those ideals—that the community does not want to change. The physical
nature (relative immutability and durability, relative to language) of artifacts contributes to this conservatism, and it conveys cultural messages indirectly and
inconspicuously, insinuating values and beliefs into everyday acts.[44] Material
culture "speaks *sotto voce*" (McCracken, 1988:69) about those things that might
otherwise evoke controversy, discord, and outright rejection. McCracken acknowledges that material culture is subject to interpretation by different groups
within a society, but it is here that we might interject Miller's concern with conflicting interpretations of various groups, and his stress on the deliberate attempts
by individuals and groups to manipulate meaning through their use of artifacts.
Finally, McCracken notes the expressive limitations of material culture and the

very limited combinational freedom and generative potential that is given wider scope in verbal language. These limitations set off material culture from language (which often has been used as a metaphor for material culture), but they also invest material culture with greater symbolic value because of the apparent naturalness and immutability of material symbols.

Material culture also provides a bridge between the reality of an individual's or a group's situation, and the ideals for which they strive. Goods give physical form to the abstractions of culture, mediating the contradiction between the real and the ideal, by providing stability and convincing arguments for the reality, validity, and achievability of those ideals. The constellation of artifacts in the possession of a household thereby represents the household's vision of itself, forming what McCracken calls a Diderot unity, a material environment that provides stability and resists change through balance. Earthenware and hoe purchases by a colonial Maryland household, for example, reinforce the household's commitment to specific goals and strategies. Making exceptional acquisitions creates the illusion that the subject is achieving an ideal, reinforcing the premise that the ideal is achievable. But such acquisitions could disrupt the unity, or balance, and lead to additional exceptional acquisitions that lead to a new unity and, perhaps, a new self-definition and ideal. The purchase of silver plate or a plow by the same hypothetical Maryland household, for example, could mark a change in strategy and a redefinition of household relations and identity.

Such a theory of material culture accounts well for the apparent homogeneity that archaeologists find within and among artifact assemblages, as well as for unexpected finds. Artifacts of similar form and function are found among households that are similar in terms of the self-perceptions of those households, measurable in terms of economics, ethnicity, nationalism, and religion. An artifact, the value of which is not in accord with the unity of its associated assemblage (as defined within that cultural context), represents an effort at redefinition, a striving from one state to an ideal state, as perceived by the subject. For example, a glass wine bottle found within a midnineteenth-century slave house assemblage could be interpreted as a symbolic bid by slaves for rights to what they produced on the plantation. That interpretation must be based on contextual evidence for the enslaved Africans' association of such products with the results of their labor as slaves.

The application of McCracken's theory of consumption to the analysis of archaeological assemblages presupposes that systems of meaning, or a symbolic context, can be reconstructed from available archival and archaeological data. Past meanings are notoriously difficult to discover. But McCracken provides some assistance by pointing out the inadequacies of the language metaphor for material culture, as discussed above. Meanings of objects are not like words strung together in sentences. The meanings are not constructed serially, but are read simultaneously as *spectacles* (*sensu* Barthes, 1972 [1957]). And those meanings are not arbitrary, but are based in the physical properties of the object, the manner in which it has been used, and the prior meanings ascribed to the object. These properties are what allow twentieth-century EuroAmerican scholars to identify, analyze, and interpret flaked stone Paleolithic scrapers, Neolithic coppers, Egyptian pyramids, and seventeenth-century Rhenish stoneware jugs.

SUMMARY

Although far from being a definitive critique of the application of social theories to archaeological data, this chapter reconstructs the "climate of opinion" in which consumer behavior theory has been borrowed and applied in historical archaeology since the early 1980s. The principal strengths of the consumer behavior approach are its suitability for placing the small pottery sherds that we work so hard to wrest from the ground into contexts of increasingly larger, nested social formations (i.e., households, communities, ethnic and class formations). Consumer behavior theory allows, and encourages, the interpretation of material culture patterns in an appropriate historical context and it "recognizes" variability in material culture patterning. Deficiencies include the view of material culture as something that is static and reflective rather than active and equivocal, and the separation of consumer behavior from the context of production. The first problem pervades the field, and as has been discussed above in terms of the work of Miller and McCracken, is not a necessary component of consumer behavior theory. The second problem, however, has been integral to consumer behavior studies, conveying late twentieth-century Western prejudices to earlier societies with very different systems of meaning.

Regardless of theoretical or methodological leanings, most if not all of the scholars whose work has been discussed in this chapter would agree that the cultural contexts in which artifacts are made, used, and discarded must be reconstructed as part of the interpretive process. Indeed, the reconstruction of cultural contexts—the identification and modeling of systems of meaning—is the interpretive process. In the next chapter, I construct a model with which we can analyze and interpret the artifacts and cultural contexts of the Anglo-American colonies during the seventeenth and early eighteenth centuries.

NOTES

1. Substantive critiques of the various schools of thought current in American archaeology can be found in Hodder (1991), Leone and Potter (1988), Leone (1982), and Kohl (1981).

2. Although the term *evolution* often is used in the context of South's theoretical work, and by others purporting to use evolutionary models (e.g., K. Lewis, 1975; H. Miller, 1984), functionalism better characterizes these attempts at explaining cultural process. They generally downplay "descent with modification" (i.e., gradual changes in custom and tradition) in favor of "adaptation" to immediate environmental forces, and functional integration. The cultural evolution theories (metaphors?) tend to be teleological and fail to specify the locus of adaptation and selective pressures; namely, nonadaptive behaviors are excluded, *a priori*, and it is unclear at what level of social organization adaptation occurs—the individual, household, extrahousehold organizations, the community, nation, or "society."

3. Historians Guelke (1976) and Harris (1977) similarly adopt adaptationist/functionalist approaches in their explanations of frontier patterning, although Guelke's discussion of *trekboeren* in the South African interior draws a very hazy line between adaptation and economics.

4. It is difficult to integrate published how-to books of the seventeenth century into an adaptationist paradigm. The settlers, to a certain extent, adapted to an environment that they had not yet encountered. Hartley (1989) examines the application of Elizabethan colonization theories to the successful settlement of South Carolina and the eastern seaboard of North America. Perhaps the promotional tracts, Baconian aphorisms, and political treatises constitute preadaptations, as described by Gosden (1992), for the prehistoric settlement of the western Pacific.

5. See Warfel (1982), Forsman and Gallo (1979), Benson (1978), and various other papers in *The Conference on Historic Sites Archeology Papers* for examples.

6. World systems theory, like evolutionary theory, can be characterized as ahistorical in the sense that specific historical conditions do not alter the fundamental causal relationships, only the products of the process.

7. Mrozowski (1987) suggests that the expansion of certain plant communities, as represented by botanical samples from urban sites, was related to developing market forces in Boston and Newport. His data also suggest, however, that not all urban residents altered their land-use practices in the face of these growing market forces.

8. Deetz (1977:5) defined American historical archaeology in similar terms, albeit from the perspective of common practice and not theoretical justification.

9. For a promising early statement on individual decision making within a global context, see Starbuck (1980).

10. See also Orser (1988) and Wolf (cited in McGuire, 1992:88) for the distinction that they draw between Marxist political practice and Marxian analysis. For an example of the Marxist anthropologist as advocate, see the preface in Meillassoux (1981).

11. Cameron (1985:22) addresses the problem somewhat. He characterizes the role of individual capitalists in the construction of new productive forces and property relationships as that of ants, "albeit ants with consciousness." See also Abercrombie et al. (1980).

12. Hodder (1991:70) criticizes Leone's failure to address the context of garden use in eighteenth-century Annapolis.

13. I have found nothing in Defoe's writings to suggest that he would have agreed with Leone's Marxian analyis and interpretation of the Paca garden.

14. This observation also has been made by Carr and Menard (1979:237), and may be equally valid in a critique of Shackel's (1992a,b) studies of "modern discipline" in the purchase of matched ceramic tableware sets in eighteenth-century Annapolis.

15. Becker (1932), in his study of *les philosophes* of the Enlightenment Period, suggests that their break with the ecclesiastical mind-set of the past was more propagandist than real.

16. Leone (1988a,b) accounts for the Georgian worldview from a materialist perspective, attributing it directly to the emergence of the bourgeoisie and their ideological machinations. He does not examine the reality of the Georgian mindset, only one possible cause for its emergence and persistence.

17. Nicholls (1991), in his *Investigating Gunpowder Plot*, describes a government investigation and prosecution in the first few years of the Stuart period that is greatly at odds with what we might expect of a "medieval mindset." Divination is replaced by rational investigation and relatively restrained interrogation; that is, little use was made of torture or tests of faith. Worsley (1984) puts the emergence of England from peasant society at the end of the sixteenth century, later than Macfarlane (1978), but still well before the patterns described by Deetz were supposed to have existed. When speaking of Georgian architecture, we are referring to English Renaissance interpretations of the classicism of Andrea Palladio (1508–1580)—interpretations manifested in the architecture of Inigo Jones (1573–1652) during the early Stuart period.

18. Structuralist analyses in archaeology are based on the concept of binary opposition, each dyad serving as an analogy for every other dyad (e.g., Yentsch, 1991b). There is seldom, if ever, any attempt to demonstrate that the subjects assigned the same meanings to these dyads as those employed by the analysts, much less that there was any historical continuity in such meanings.

19. Recent writings of Bourdieu (1977), and particularly his concept of *habitus*, transcend some of the inherent problems of structuralism by interjecting 'disposition' and strategy between structure and action. His work, however, has had little direct influence on the practice of historical archaeology; due in large part to the highly abstract—one might say mystifying—quality of his writing.

20. Olive Jones (1987) lists only "consumption patterns," and that followed by only three entries, in her index for volumes 1 through 20 of *Historical Archaeology*.

21. Note that Deetz's *In Small Things Forgotten* and South's *Method and Theory in Historical Archeology* both were published 10 years earlier, in 1977. Neither work deals with interassemblage variability nor, by extension, social variability.

22. The indecision as to the nature of the consumer behavior approach—theory, paradigm, model, or middle-range theory—is somewhat unsettling, betraying a high degree of uncertainty as to how it should be used. As discussed, consumer behavior approaches appear to be closely related methods that function outside of a clearly expressed theory of material culture.

23. Notably, Goodenough's (1965) landmark work on the relationship between status and role is rarely cited in archaeological writings that use the concept of status. Keesing (1972), in his study of the Kwangafi, suggests that kinship terms denoting a particular kind of status are too accessible to cultural anthropologists, lending themselves to formal patterning and modeling when decontextualized. A kinship term

represents many statuses that are highlighted or ignored depending upon social context. His argument applies to the concept of socioeconomic status.

24. Wilk (1990), in his analysis of Kekchi Maya consumer behavior, suggests that such a pattern of reinvestment in the homelot may have circumvented the problem of evaluating individual contributions to the wealth of the household. All could share equally by shifting consumption from the individual to the group. Gasco (1992) also notes the low value of even the most expensive ceramics relative to other kinds of household equipment in the province of Soconusco, New Spain [modern Mexico], during the colonial period.

25. Historian Beverly Lemire (1990:270), in an examination of the relationship between crime and consumerism in early modern England, identifies clothing as the most sought after and most easily disposable commodity, through which people could appear "in the guise of neighbours, acquaintances, or even family members."

26. Yentsch (1991a) appears to accept this reflective quality as well, but only in terms of purchase, which she takes as a brief phase in an artifact's existence. See Kopytoff (1986) for a discussion on the phases through which an artifact passes in the course of its 'social life.'

27. Cf. Gasco, who states: "The most obvious use for household inventories is simply to *compare the wealth of individuals* [emphasis added]" (Gasco, 1992:83). Winter (1976) coined the term 'household cluster' to refer to the archaeological remains of household activities as represented by houses, storage pits, graves, ovens, and middens occurring in sufficiently close proximity to warrant the assumption of association and functional integration. As a unit of analysis, the household cluster links disparate archaeological features with the larger community of the Early Formative period of Oaxaca, Mexico.

   "Homelot" bears some of the ebullience of twentieth-century realtors committed to selling "homes," rather than houses. Both "homelot" and "houselot," however, appear in early Colonial period tracts and legal documents. "Homelot" is the term most widely used in historical archaeology, particularly of the Chesapeake Bay region, and it will be used throughout this work. The term "home plantation" is far more common than either "homelot" or "houselot," although it referred to the entire tract, of which the dwelling lot was but a part. The legal term "messuage" is synonymous with "home plantation." "Quarter" refers to a dwelling lot that is part of a larger plantation, but not the residence of the planter, only of the plantation workers.

28. See Beaudry's (1987) comment on the symposium "The Problem of Scale in Urban Archaeology" and M. Brown's (1987) rejoinder.

29. Meillassoux (1981) makes a similar case for hunter-gatherer bands, the memberships of which are determined through political action and individual choice, not kinship. Production and distribution are the principal integrative forces in bands, and these, he argues, are discrete activities of short duration.

30. For an earlier use of this concept, see Winter (1976).

31. This is particularly true for writings on the archaeology of seventeenth-century sites in the Chesapeake Bay region (e.g., Gibb and King, 1991; Keeler, 1978; King, 1988). For instance, a succession of households occupied the St. John's site (18ST1–23) in St. Mary's City, Maryland, between ca. 1638 and 1725. The demographics of those house-

holds are poorly known. Elements of some of those households are known to have occupied dwellings beyond the St. John's homelot. The demographic structures of forts and trading posts are more difficult to reconstruct due to the fluidity of "household" membership and frequent entertaining of trading partners (e.g., Baker, 1985; Cranmer, 1990; Faulkner and Faulkner, 1987; Kenyon, 1986). The range of domestic activities usually can be ascertained, but the household demographics during the occupation of a site invariably are unknown.

32. Gehring's (1987) data from Colonial-period documents in New York State suggest that roemers were not very expensive and, in fact, were used in local taverns.

33. McKendrick's (1982) study of eighteenth-century English consumerism explicitly employs this concept. His work is cited by many archaeologists working with eighteenth/nineteenth-century consumer behavior (e.g., Martin, 1989).

34. For example, Little (1993) examines how nonelite groups simultaneously embrace and resist dominant ideologies through their choices in ceramic wares. While differences between the ceramic assemblages of elite and nonelite households from late historic Annapolis, Maryland, and New York City can be documented, it does not follow that consumer differences represent outward expressions of those class differences.

35. By extension, "consumer good" is redundant since all goods are acquired for use.

36. Toys, and aboriginal-made pottery and pipes, also are included in the Activities Group, although the pottery and pipes appear to be misplaced in their implicit trade (i.e., acquisition) rather than use associations.

37. Schumpeter's (1961:15–16) distinction between products and means, low-order and high-order goods, overlooks the cyclical nature of production and consumption, although, upon reflection, he no. doubt would have acknowledged the arbitrariness of the distinction, as he had done for all economic concepts.

38. Although he does not question this dichotomy, per se, Daniel Miller (1987) does reject the tendency to examine each in isolation, a critique primarily aimed at Marxian scholars, but equally pertinent to the above-cited works.

39. See Cook and Yamin (1994) for a notable exception.

40. Although he appeals to Hegel for the theoretical relationship between subject and object, Miller's concept of objectification bears little relationship to Hegel's "alienation," and we should consider Hegel in this context as a source of inspiration and not as mentor. Miller describes a process akin to art, wherein an idea—expressed in words, physical form, or musical notes—is presented, examined, modified, and then restated. Effective art transforms artist and audience. (Miller's approach to material culture is more fully explored in the next chapter.)

41. Architecture, for example, is one domain particularly subject to control by dominant groups due to the scale of investment necessary to construct a building. But architecture is only one of an infinite variety of domains through which social groups can create and re-create themselves. Even architectural settings are subject to alteration and reinterpretation.

42. Kopytoff's (1986) paper on commoditization and singularization/decommoditization appears in the edited volume by Appadurai (1986) but is inexplicably absent from Miller's book.

43. Pendery's (1992) discussion of the consumer strategies of emulation, innovation, and patina marks an important step in operationalizing objectification theory and in rejecting the simple relationships ironically referred to in this passage. It is hindered somewhat by the questionable nature of his data—200+ ceramic vessels from a Charlestown, Massachusetts, sea captain's cellar, purportedly representing some 20 years' accumulation. Piles of domestic refuse accumulating within a building during its occupation raises questions regarding the depositional history of the deposit and the analytic value of the artifacts recovered.

44. The artifact is anything but inconspicuous, but its conveying of cultural values is often inconspicuous, camouflaged in a setting of seemingly static and natural objects.

Chapter 3

Modeling the Consumer
Behavior of the Colonists

INTRODUCTION

Despite the plethora of papers on consumer behavior recently published by historical archaeologists (e.g., Spencer-Wood, 1987b; Klein and LeeDecker, 1991; and various papers in Little and Shackel, 1992), and the frequency with which such papers are presented at national and regional conferences (e.g., Lees and Majewski, 1993; LeeDecker, 1993), few scholars have attempted to integrate interests in consumer behavior patterns with theories of material culture.[1] Indeed, many of those works examine the effects of one variable, or the interactions of several variables, on the acquisition of certain kinds of material culture by individual households (e.g., Seifert, 1991).

Henry (1991) incorporates many of those variables into a single model, but without the benefit of an explicit theory of material culture. There is within that model, however, the germ of just such a theory. From that germ, we can move into a wider realm of material culture theory that addresses the issue of "why we need things"(Csikszentmihalyi, 1993). This chapter culminates in a model constructed for the interpretation of seventeenth-century Anglo-American archaeological remains. The model accepts all nondiscarded material culture as wealth. Wealth is situated in the household where it is used to re-create household relations on a daily basis.

MODELS OF CONSUMER BEHAVIOR

Henry (1991) provides us with a model of consumer behavior that is general and universal. Consumer choice is embedded within larger social and economic contexts, as are use, lateral cycling and recycling, and discard. The household substitutes for the individual, since archival and archaeological data are rarely appropriate for analyzing and interpreting individual behavior.[2] Henry points out the value of her model for understanding broad patterns in consumerism, the reduction of the work week and increase in leisure time, and the development of new goods and services. Her model, perhaps fortuitously, is a metaphor for the human body, with decision making (intellectual processes), and by extension social forms, given priority. Acquisition and use are analogous to such activities as seeking, collecting, and consuming goods. Discard equals evacuation.

The weakest aspect of the model is the "black box" of internal influences on decision-making, those ineffable processes rooted in the individual psyche and as varied as the experiences, needs, fears, and motivations that constitute each individual. The interactions of 'external influences' (social class, ethnicity, family, marketing efforts) are equally uncertain, although each can be examined in isolation. The interactions between internal and external influences are accessible only insofar as patterns based on large samples can effectively control for, or eliminate, 'internal influences' from the calculus of consumer behavior. Only income is easily identified, controlled, and quantified.

All of this brings us back to the basic relationship between overall wealth and the ability to consume. Actually, Henry's (1991) model involves just a little bit more. She does not explicitly address a theory of material culture, but assumes that the selection and acquisition of goods in some way reconciles the needs, motivations, and abilities of the subject, and the various external influences acting upon the subject. Henry implies that artifacts are mediators in this process. Each acquisition and use of an artifact is a solution which, in turn, defines new problems.

Henry did not pursue the logical ramifications of her model and may not have recognized them at the time that she wrote the piece. Still, whether by intent or accident, she has hit upon a fundamental aspect of material culture theory, one overlooked or avoided by many who have been dealing with consumer theory (see Orser, 1987 and 1992, for exceptions). Henry raises the issue of artifacts as mediators, objects that lead to change in social forms through their creation, acquisition, and use. It is ironic that in the very issue of *Historical Archaeology* in which her paper appears, there is a review of Daniel Miller's (1987) *Material Culture and Mass Consumption* (McCarthy, 1991), a work dealing with the relationship of material culture to society, and that neither she, nor her co-contributors, address.

The limited impact in historical archaeology of postprocessualism in general, and Miller's (1987) objectification theory in particular, can be attributed to two factors: jargon-laden texts that are difficult to relate to material things, and a lack of empirical studies that use the kinds of data ordinarily recovered from archaeological sites. Jargon merely impedes understanding and application, but the lack of in-depth empirical analyses that can serve as models dissuades most researchers from attempting such applications. Both Miller (1987) and Hodder (1992), however, provide us with some basic concepts upon which to build.

First, a name. Postprocessualism is ambiguous, cumbersome, and—since there is a lot of good processual archaeology being done—a misnomer.[3] Objectification theory, as defined by Miller, is subject to misinterpretation due to the different meanings ascribed to the term by Marxian theorists, and it entails a complicated philosophical grounding that is not altogether necessary for its application.[4] The unifying concept and principal contribution of postprocessualism is a concern for historical context, namely, examining objects, actions, and concepts within frameworks of historically constituted ideas and values. Hodder calls this approach 'contextual archaeology' (Hodder, 1992).[5]

Contextual archaeology treats groups of objects as literary texts in the sense that the meaning of each object can be understood only relative to the meanings of associated objects, much in the same way that a word derives its full meaning only within the context of other words. While material culture often is viewed as language with discernible if mutable grammars (e.g., P. Lewis, 1993), Miller suggests that the metaphor is overdrawn and that objects lend a sense of objective reality to the realm of social behavior that is not inherent in the spoken word. Objects embody assumptions about relations between people, although those assumptions are subject to manipulation and negotiation. The meanings of objects—their *signification* (*sensu* Barthes, 1972 [1957])—are neither arbitrary nor simply historical, as in the signs of language, but are based at least partly in the physical qualities of the objects (Csikszentmihalyi, 1993:21; McCracken, 1988).[6]

Paramount in contextual archaeology is the concept of recursivity, wherein objects are regarded not as static phenomena, but as both product and medium of behavior.[7] Social forms are not privileged relative to culture (material and nonmaterial), but exist in a dialectical relationship with material culture that is continually redefined through social practice, namely, through the use, rather than strictly through the creation, of objects as has been the analytical focus of functionalists and Marxian scholars alike:

> We must not forget that an object is the best messenger of a world above that of nature: one can easily see in an object at once a perfection and an absence of origin, a closure and a brilliance, a transformation of life into matter (mat-

ter is more magical than life), and in a word a *silence* which belongs to the
realm of fairy-tales. (Barthes, 1972:88)

Barthes understood that the user of an artifact does not necessarily see the forces
or relations of production underlying its creation, but rather the cultural and
social reality of which both actor and prop are a part.

Miller brings two useful concepts to contextual archaeology: creative recontextualization (both interpretation and consumption) and objectification (production). Objectification is the process whereby an individual or group attempts
to represent or create itself through actions that include the production, acquisition, use, and disposal of material culture.[8] For example, an ethnic parade could
be an attempt at recognizing or objectifying ethnic diversity and the peaceful
coexistence and cooperation between the various ethnic groups of a community.
To the extent that those groups cooperate in assembling and performing the
parade, there is a degree of reality in the expression. However, the participants—
performers and observers—may recontextualize (i.e., interpret or appropriate)
the meaning of the performance as a competitive display between the group with
which they are associated and the other participants.

Those who identify with groups that are not formally recognized or who
have been excluded from the parade (e.g., homosexuals in Boston's St. Patrick's
Day Parade in the 1990s) may regard the performance as exclusionary and political, and appropriate the meaning of the performance as an expression of "them"
as opposed to "us." Disenfranchised groups appropriate the meaning of the ethnic
parade, even though they do not participate in its organization. They need only
have "participated" in the parade by recognizing it as an event.[9]

Objectification is not confined to ritual performances. Quite to the contrary,
objectification—as conceived by Miller—pervades all of human action and all of
the physical world perceived and modified through human action. Indeed, objectification is not only a particular view of culture, it is culture. The image of an
individual or group projected through the production, acquisition, use, and disposal of material culture is not simply perpetuated. Those images are constantly
reinterpreted (Miller's creative recontextualization) and the social form is redefined as a result of interpretation.

The notion that objects and actions are constantly reinterpreted sets Miller's
approach apart from the Marxian Critical Theory perspectives of Leone (1988a)
and Potter (1988). The ability of individuals to interpret objects and actions does
not preclude the ideological machinations of dominant over subordinate groups,
but it does provide a theory of resistance (e.g., McGuire, 1992; Paynter and
McGuire, 1991; McGuire, 1992). Miller acknowledges that in some instances a
dominant group can alienate the creations of a subordinate group, namely, they
can attempt to deny the relationship between a subordinate group and the objects
and institutions that it creates. The subordinate group has the ability, through its

individual constituents, to reject this denial, or to reassert itself in another object domain.[10]

Miller uses *Bauhaus* architecture as an example of elite efforts to deny the heterogeneity of peoples living in the London Council estates during the 1980s.[11] He demonstrates that heterogeneity persists behind the regular, featureless, homogeneous facades of modernist architecture in terms of variability in household formations and the objects that the members of households own. Miller could have made a far stronger argument for recontextualization/interpretation in this respect by detailing the ways in which the estate occupants reinterpreted modernist spaces through the arrangement of furnishings, and through window dressings, outdoor plantings, and fixtures. The important point, however, has been made: the occupants need not understand, nor accept, the meaning that the architects and social planners intend.

The key concept underlying Miller's view of material culture is that the consumption of material goods is a positive rather than a negative process. Acquisition of material goods is not simple fetishism and alienation, nor is it placation and distraction of the poor and middle classes through industrial production and commercialism. Consumption is self-creation. It is creative and liberating. Although Miller is a bit sanguine in his portrayal of people as effective resisters to elite domination and as perpetual and positive re-creators of themselves, determining their own destinies, he does provide some balance for the generally negative interpretations of the critical theorists. Nonelites are not powerless through ignorance or inability to exercise direct control over material and symbolic production. Elites may be able to control the production and distribution of material goods, but they retain limited control over how those objects are used and interpreted.

McCracken (1988) develops the concept of self-creation at greater length. Meanings embodied within an object may represent community ideals, but they are products of individual interpretation, constrained—but not predetermined—by those ideals. McCracken views consumption as a process by which an individual or group creates and re-creates its identity. Csikszentmihalyi (1993) takes this concept a step further in his conception of material culture as a source of sensory input that reminds us of who we are as individuals; props reinforce our sense of identity in the face of "psychic entropy."

If these concepts, and other aspects of contextualism, seem opaque and abstract, it is because they are poor expressions of the patently obvious: individuals and groups acquire and use objects as declarations of identity, goals, and values. Still seem abstract? Actually, these concepts are far less abstract and arcane than assertions that artifacts reflect status or class relations. Young people paying large sums for certain brands of blue jeans and athletic shoes may have a greater understanding of how things are used in self-definition than do university ascetics. Assertions that material culture is central to status display touch on only one aspect of the important role played by material culture in creating self-image.

For purposes of illustration, let's look at a hypothetical example of ethnic culinary practices and choices in dinner services. Excavators recover large quantities of chicken bones and porcelain sherds from deposits around a dwelling known to have been occupied by Chinese émigrés. They take this as evidence of the occupants' Chinese heritage, a surmise supported by archival data. But do these bones and associated porcelain sherds represent the material remains of symbolic expressions? If so, to whom were these messages directed if the meals were eaten within doors and if the participants in the meal were all family or friends? Did the owners and users of these items intend to draw a clearly visible distinction between themselves and others, and was that statement directed at the larger, ethnically mixed but Anglo-American dominated community? Or did the foods and dinner services convey a message directed by the household toward itself; a mythic representation of itself drawn from a multitude of historically constituted signs that echoed Taoist beliefs, Confucian doctrines, immigration history, and the concept of family as lineage with roots in the distant past and in a distant place?

Similarly, the ownership and use of a matched creamware dinner service by a household in eighteenth-century Annapolis, Maryland, had meaning for that household. But was that meaning necessarily one of self-discipline in the emerging capitalist system (Shackel 1992a,b), or might it have had more to do with the household's perception of itself, an expression of unity and harmony that varied with the manner in which specialty ceramic forms were used or not used? The production of matched dinner services no doubt created a need for order, discipline, and hierarchy in British potteries, but it is unclear how those concepts were exported along with the dinnerwares. Not only were the means for informing prospective buyers of this meaning very limited (etiquette books and limited advertising), but there is no motive on the part of the manufacturer to manufacture such meanings for export. On the contrary, there are strong economic incentives for producing goods and services that conform to existing values. Those values need not be held by a majority within the community if the manufacturer can find alternative markets.[12]

Josiah Wedgewood and other British potters used notions of fashion and emulation of social superiors to market their wares, not to promulgate an ethos of self-discipline. Precisely how those wares were used and whether or not those 'in the American colonies' accepted or even recognized the tenets of modern discipline are issues that were remote, and perhaps invisible, to the potters.[13] In short, whether we are discussing chicken bones or sherds of creamware plates, we may be missing the obvious by relating household consumption patterns directly to the community and world systems in which households participated. The household, the family, speaks to itself first. And one of the principal means by which it speaks to itself is through consumer choice.

CONTEXTUALISM AND THE ARCHAEOLOGY OF DOMESTIC SITES

The recent surge of interest in consumer behavior in historical archaeology represents a reaction against the concern for production and the relations of production that figure so prominently in Marxian analyses and, to a similar if less explicit degree, in processual analyses. Contextualism furthers that interest insofar as it draws attention to the full context of material culture—use as well as production of material goods. Miller's (1987) twin concepts of objectification and recontextualization lend greater analytical strength in that they provide a theoretical basis for linking objects to behavior, and for addressing variability among assemblages composed of the same mass-produced objects. The contextualists, however, may be addressing contexts that are somewhat removed from the contexts of use: the emphasis is still, to an extent, on acquisition within the public arena rather than use within the household (e.g., Miller and Tilley, 1984; Yentsch, 1990b). It remains to be seen how this approach to material culture can be used in the analysis and interpretation of domestic sites, the principal analytical units of historical archaeology.

In general terms, the location of a domestic site and its architectural and landscaping features represent the remains of the occupants' material expressions of how they perceived themselves in a physical and social world. The broken bottles and crockery, and the discarded faunal and floral materials, are the residues of their attempts to define and assert themselves as a group. Equally evident may be the construction of the farmstead, attempts at building expansion or simple maintenance, active modification of the landscape, or passive alteration through decay and erosion (e.g., Wilk, 1990). In this sense, every domestic site represents a change in how its occupants perceived themselves: at one time people lived there, and now they don't. In a more subtle vein, we can see the creation, maintenance, and modification of household relations through the material evidence of food-related activities, recreation, and ritual. Patterns in the spatial distributions of drinking vessels, tobacco pipes, and gaming pieces serve as evidence of household relations recreated outside the realm of work. The treatment of the dead could represent efforts to re-create a social whole, rent apart by death, and to further define and naturalize household relations.

In and of themselves, these lines of interpretation do not differ significantly from those employed by Marxian theorists, nor are they wholly alien to scholars undertaking any number of processualist and "preprocessualist" analyses. A contextualist approach differs in that the analyst explicitly attempts to identify culturally meaningful categories, and to relate those categories to cultural–historical developments. Disposal of the dead may or may not be related to the reconstitution of the household, particularly when the decedents are interred in public cemeteries. For example, the burial of veterans in military cemeteries in the United States has no direct bearing on the family. Social scientists can infer this because they are familiar with the rituals and meanings surrounding burials in late nineteenth- and twentieth-century U.S. society. Military cemeteries (and those of some utopian communities such as the Old Salem Moravian cemetery at Winston-Salem, North Carolina) emphasize uniformity, unity, and simplicity, and explicitly reject individualism. Loyalty is to the larger social formation represented by the cemetery, while family, gender, ethnicity, and other social characteristics of the individual decedents are ignored or downplayed.

Similarly, the meanings of certain foods and the paraphernalia with which they are presented may vary depending upon the contexts in which those foods are served and consumed. Tobacco pipes and drinking vessels can be used in an analysis of recreation only if there is contextual evidence to indicate that smoking and drinking meant group recreation to the people who used those objects. Those same objects could have been imbued with sacred meanings manifested in religious ceremonies. How we interpret spatial distributions of tobacco pipe fragments and sherds of drinking vessels will depend upon other contextual evidence as to what these objects meant to those who discarded them. Archival sources can be 'interrogated,' eliminating some assumptions and facilitating the identification of varied meanings for the same phenomenon. Most important, interrogating documents is akin to the ethnographer's questioning of an informant: we do our subjects the courtesy of asking them what happened and what it meant to them.[14]

In short, contextual archaeology is an attempt to discover what specific objects, in specific contexts, meant to the people who used those objects. In historical archaeology, we ask our subjects what they thought they were doing, why, and what it meant to them through the documents and other material remains that they left behind. Based on these data, we undertake analyses that seek the dimensions and ranges of variability underlying cultural change. The discussions about land, labor, commodity, and wealth in Chapters 4 through 6 represent the first steps in developing contexts for the production and consumption of goods by British colonists during the seventeenth and early eighteenth centuries.

A MODEL

One point developed in the next chapter is that wealth, in its seventeenth-century English sense, did not consist solely of precious metals and gems, although in such terms it was often discussed by political economists and satirists. Wealth included all objects that were deemed to have market value, namely, anything that was, or had the potential to become, a commodity. Land occupied an ambiguous status in the object-as-wealth equation, possibly because the nature of land ownership was not clearly defined or agreed upon. Labor, in contrast, constituted wealth in the colonies, prompting one observer to state that "most of the wealth consists in slaves or negroes, for if one has many workmen, much foodstuff and tobacco can be produced" (Michel in Hinke, 1916 [1702]:116–117). More accurately, labor produced wealth, building and clearing, planting and harvesting, and otherwise producing all that was needed, or whatever was needed to procure commodities.

Wealth, in effect, consisted of the total inventory of an individual's material goods that were commodities, *or had the potential to become commodities.* Also, wealth was centered in the household, not in bank accounts, stock certificates, or real estate. Wealth could be tied up in trading goods and ships, letters of credit, or mortgages; but the principal forms of wealth appear in period inventories as household goods, and the home was the repository for household wealth.

The specific forms in which household wealth was manifested varied among colonial households. The Reverend Thomas Teackle, an Anglican clergyman from Virginia's eastern shore, left an estate in 1697 that ranked within the top 10 to 15 percentile for Northampton Parish, Accomack County. Among his possessions: 333 books, covering religion, classical literature, geography, grammar, hieroglyphics, history, mathematics, rhetoric, law, medicine, and navigation (Butler, 1992). Lacking were books on such practical arts (in the context of a plantation economy without direct access to services and manufactured goods) as surveying, cattle raising, and domestic sciences. Teackle's inventory differed from those of his neighbors, both in terms of the number and value of books owned and the subjects covered by those books. Likewise, if perhaps less dramatically, we can expect each household in Northampton Parish to have possessed wealth in different forms from its neighbors. The kinds and relative proportions of materials, and the ways in which they were used, represent efforts by each household to define itself to itself, as well as to the larger community.

Consumer behavior in the seventeenth and early eighteenth centuries involved the acquisition of goods, not consumption in the narrow, twentieth-century sense of that term; viz., to expend through use. That is not to say that earthen pots were not expended: archaeologists find precisely those things that have been expended. But pots, and other manufactured items, were acquired to be used in the production of new wealth. They were not acquired to be enjoyed and then discarded. Few things were actually "consumer goods" in the sense that they were intended to be expended through use. These include foods, drink, and tobacco. Interestingly enough, the ethnohistoric record suggests that these "consumables"

were generally expended in contexts of sociability: family meals, acts of hospital-
ity, and comensality in such ritual contexts as holidays and funerals.

Most objects were acquired as forms of wealth with which new wealth could
be generated or acquired, and with which wealth could be shared among household members, and transferred from one generation to the next. For example:

> Clothing in pre-industrial and early industrial England had a multitude of
> purposes not sufficiently recognized by historians. A good wardrobe could be
> the equivalent of a savings account, as articles of clothing were commonly
> used as a ready source of cash in emergencies. (Lemire, 1990:270)[15]

Clothing, not uncommonly, was bequeathed to one's descendants, not necessarily for purposes of wear but as objects of value that constituted a portion of
the decedent's estate. Notably, seventeenth-century graves are known for their
dearth of grave furniture. Coffin nails or a few pins that held together the ends of
a shroud are usually found with the body, but rarely are there articles of clothing
or any other objects associated with the body.[16]

The notion that wealth was situated in the household and invested in the
household is best illustrated by the seventeenth-century term "estate." In its
twentieth-century sense, this term refers to the total wealth left by a decedent and
to which the decedent's heirs hold certain legally defined rights. In the seventeenth century, however, estate usually referred to an individual's total wealth,
inclusive of all such possessions of his or her household and immediate family
over whom legal guardianship was maintained. Estates were both cumulative and
active: one "adventured" one's estate in the hope of profit. An estate was not held
in escrow, curated by an executor, until its disposition could be determined by the
courts. An estate was a person's wealth, used for the purposes of enlarging itself
and advancing its master, and over which the master's family held only indirect
rights as appointed agents.[17] Upon the master's death, the estate passed, ideally, to
the eldest son. The heir's responsibilities were twofold: to maintain his father's
family in a manner appropriate to their social station and increase the estate to his
father's honor, his own honor, and the advancement of his male heirs. He was
expected to expend wealth, but only in the process of increasing it.[18]

A review of seventeenth-century English court documents, literature, and
political and religious tracts confirms this concern for investment and projected
returns, at least among those groups of people likely to have been represented in
those documents (see Chapters 4 and 5). Care must be taken, however, that the
pitfalls of economic reductionism are avoided. How individual heads of household decided to allocate resources may have differed from cultural ideals. Participation by other members of the household in consumer choices varied
considerably, and while certain goals were widely pursued in the English-speaking community, it does not necessarily follow that everyone adopted identical

means for achieving those goals. Moreover, it would be unwise to assume that everyone who controlled wealth used it exclusively to produce new wealth. Wills excluding prodigal individuals from rights to an estate, or containing language protecting estates from the wasteful depredations of stepfathers, are numerous among seventeenth-century English legal documents.

From these various ideas, we can construct a model with which we can evaluate and interpret archaeological remains from seventeenth-century colonial sites. All material culture is, or was, wealth. The particular forms of wealth at any one domestic site represent the efforts of the household to create and assert its identity on a daily basis. Certain general values for seventeenth-century English colonists can be identified through a variety of legal and literary sources. Among these are concerns for perpetuating patrilineal groups, both in terms of progeny and honor; expressing the personal power, honor, and social position of the male head of household and the virtue of the women in his care; providing for the financial future of sons and daughters, albeit in different ways; perpetuating ideal family relations in a hierarchy consciously analogous to that of the English monarchy of old;[19] achieving self-sufficiency and control over the land; and committing the household to a form of agricultural economy that may or may not have been modeled on familiar practices in England and Ireland. Each of these concerns, and others besides, was acted upon—and, in some instances, realized—through the manipulation of the physical environment, namely, through consumption and production, or through the use of wealth. Those efforts and, by extension, those concerns are accessible for study through their material residues: the homelot site locations, architecture, trash, and grave sites that we recover archaeologically.

SUMMARY

The worn and broken bits of pottery, axes, hoes, bottles, buttons, and buckles recovered from archaeological sites represent expended wealth. They were discarded because they no longer had any value as wealth: they no longer could produce wealth, nor could they articulate the identity and values of their owners. Animal bones and carbonized corn represent expended wealth, expended in the process of reproducing the household, physically and ideologically, and generating new wealth. The bones of a deer or a cow might represent a feast, served with the best tableware, to which friends and neighbors were invited; but the food and the table service and the pots in which the food was cooked all represented the household and the image of the household that was shared by some or all of its members. They represented what the household was and what it would become.

In analyzing and interpreting seventeenth-century British colonial remains, it is necessary to focus on the household and on the household's pursuit of wealth. Specifically, it is necessary to understand how the colonists organized their households and how they perpetuated and altered household organization through architecture and the uses of various forms of manufactured goods and food sources. We must examine the specific forms of wealth represented in the archaeological deposits of a site and determine how the occupants used those objects.

Throughout the remainder of this work, I focus on the household's production, acquisition, and use of material culture as a means of reproducing itself in its own image, and the changes in household organization and perception that flowed from this process. There is no assumption of functional integration or adaptation: given the short-term occupation of the sites discussed in the remaining chapters, such perspectives are doomed to contradiction from the outset. Nor do I assume that the households in question were competing for status or locked in class struggles: the focus on the homelot peripheralizes organization and conflict within the community in favor of organization and conflict within the household. There can be no doubt that the developing world capitalist system constrained and directed household decision making, but we must not lose sight of the fact that households reacted to their perception, and not to a perfect understanding, of larger events. They acted as individual households, and not as basic social units within a periphery.

Four kinds of evidence are examined for the Compton and Patuxent Point sites in southern Maryland, and compared to sites elsewhere in the Chesapeake Basin and New England:

1. Plantation siting.
2. Homelot organization.
3. The production, processing, preparation, storing, and presentation of food.
4. The treatment of the dead.

I selected these categories based on the evidence of seventeenth-century Anglo-American attitudes discussed in the following chapters, the kinds of data recovered from seventeenth-century colonial sites, and the corpus of analytical techniques available and commonly used by historical archaeologists. The next four chapters explore in greater detail some of the issues broached in this chapter. The concepts of wealth, property, land, labor, and environment are examined with reference to English conceptions and debates of the early Modern period, contributing to the construction of a larger cultural–historical context to which this chapter only hints. Much of what follows is based on my research in the

Chesapeake Bay colonies of Maryland and Virginia, but is largely applicable to the Carolinas, the Delaware Bay colonies, New York, and New England.

NOTES

1. See Cook and Yamin (1994), Little (1992a, 1993), and Shackel (1992a,b) for important exceptions.
2. That is not to say that individual behavior is not discernible in the archaeological record, but therein lies the next great challenge in the development of archaeological theory and method.
3. Postprocessualism, like postmodernism, is an ironic phrase that represents a rejection of the concept of progress as improvement and departure from the past. In this sense, "process" and "modern" refer to values and not temporal distinctions.
4. There is much in Miller's (1987) work that parallels that of McCracken (1988), albeit with less clarity. The strength of his work is in its thorough philosophical grounding and its explicit rejection of the priority of social form.
5. See also Yentsch's (1990a) "interpretive archaeology," an approach that emphasizes the pivotal role of the socially positioned interpreter.
6. Obviously, the meanings of words also are historically derived; however, those meanings rarely are based on the physical qualities of sound. Chinese calligraphy and other ideographic systems are most akin to artifacts in the sense that meaning derives to some extent from form.
7. Miller uses the terms *self-creation* and *sublation*, but these terms are unnecessarily arcane, their importance deriving from a specific philosophical argument that is not integral to the application of the theory. The more widely used and inclusive concept of recursivity is used in their stead.
8. Recontextualization is part and parcel of objectification, but is treated separately here for purposes of exposition. Refer to Chapter 2 for the place of objectification theory in consumer behavior studies.
9. Ryan (1989), in her study of the nineteenth-century American parade as a ritual that united society by emphasizing some differences to the exclusion of others, does not address the observer as participant, and by resorting only to newspaper copy (and that largely for descriptions of parades in major cities), she privileges her interpretations over those of the participants. It is important to recognize that an artifact may convey multiple meanings to socially positioned actors, and that those actors could be an important source of information on meaning.
10. By object domain, I refer to a group of related artifact types within their contexts of use.
11. The term "International" style leaves little doubt as to the intentions of such *Bauhaus* gurus as Le Corbusier and Gropius. Diversity is denied in favor of commonalties.
12. I am unaware of any direct connection between British potters and the writers and purveyors of etiquette books. Late eighteenth- and early nineteenth-century transfer-printed earthenwares unabashedly promoted republican and nationalistic values through illustrations of political and military heroes in the garb of ancient Rome.

British potters, however, capitalized on the republican and nationalistic sentiments of colonies that were once subject to the English Crown.

13. Interpreting the popularity in the United States of mass-produced Staffordshire earthenwares in terms of republican and democratic sentiments is more consistent with late eighteenth- and early nineteenth-century developments in politics, art, and literature than is the notion of self-discipline in an industrializing nation.

14. The metaphor 'interrogation' is useful for characterizing the manner in which documents are analyzed. As with all metaphors, however, it mischaracterizes as well: documents do not respond to the interrogator.

15. Lewis (1970) noted a similar phenomenon among the poor of Mexico City during the 1960s, with manufactured goods purchased on credit, used for several months to several years, and then repossessed for nonpayment or pawned to cover other expenses.

16. Most, probably, were buried with a nightshirt or gown (Gittings, 1984), but there is little archaeological evidence in the forms of buttons, buckles, or clothing hooks to indicate burial in full dress.

17. In his speech nominating Sir Thomas Crew as Speaker of the House of Commons (1625), Sir Thomas Edmondes anticipated Crew's (formalistic) refusal on the grounds of the "weak estate of [Crew's] body" (Jansson and Bidwell, 1987:194). This, and similar uses of the term, should be regarded as metaphorical.

18. For example, Cecil Calvert defended before Parliament his prerogative of enacting laws in Maryland by claiming that such an extraordinary power was necessary to protect his estate in that distant colony. Parliament was well aware that Calvert had come by much of this estate by bequest of his father, the First Lord Baron of Baltimore, and that Calvert's estate, in turn, would descend to his eldest male heir, Charles. The rule of primogeniture was recognized by most of England's elite, and few questioned its legitimacy, only the Lord Baltimore's powers vis-à-vis Parliament.

19. It is not at all clear that average folk valued the *constitutional* monarchy as the ideal structure for a household, most especially, if most ironically, among the Puritan parliamentarians. The Tudor form of monarchy, or King Charles I's "personal rule," might be more appropriate analogies than the forms of the late Stuart and Hanover governments.

Chapter **4**

Wealth, Property, Land, and Labor

INTRODUCTION

[O]ur practical philosophy was overwhelmingly shaped by [the Machine Age]. Novel notions about man and society became current and gained the status of axioms. . . . As regards *man*, we were made to accept the heresy that his motives can be described as "material" and "ideal," and that the incentives on which everyday life is organized spring from the "material" motives. . . . As regards *society*, the kindred doctrine was propounded that its institutions were "determined" by the economic system.

Under a market-economy both assertions were, of course, true. *But only under such an economy*. In regard to the past, such a view was no more than an anachronism. In regard to the future, it was a mere prejudice. Yet under the influence of current schools of thought, reinforced by the authority of science and religion, politics and business, these strictly time-bound phenomena came to be regarded as timeless, as transcending the age of the market. To overcome such doctrines . . . may require no less than a reform of our consciousness. (Polanyi, 1971a:61)

Some of the works cited in Chapter 2 embody these "doctrines," not just in terms of their theoretical perspectives, but in their nearly universal acceptance of such undefined terms as 'consumer' and "consumer good," and in the distinction made between "consumer goods" and "producer goods." Even the term "economy," frequently heard in 20th century news broadcasts, political speeches, and over–the–backyard–fence debates, is a cultural construct, the meaning of which may have been lost on seventeenth-century colonists.[1] The definitions of such key concepts as wealth, property, land, and labor are the substance of this chapter.

The goal is to develop some working definitions that take into account seventeenth-century English views of what constituted wealth, property, land, and labor, that is, to develop culturally meaningful contexts in which to interpret seventeenth-century practices.[2]

WEALTH AND COMMODITY

"A wealth of facts," "She is very wealthy," and "The wealth of a nation" are common phrases in academic and popular literature. The fact that such phrases are used in common parlance—that the definition of "wealth" is taken for granted—suggests that wealth should be examined with a little more care before we accept it as a valid scientific concept.

Having at hand a wealth of data or facts does not necessarily lead to fame, fortune, and academic honors, not, at least, if wealth is taken to be a measure of quality as well as quantity. Wealth must imply value for its possessors and those that witness its possession; otherwise it can mean a valueless pile of junk. In practice, at least among historians and economists, wealth implies measurable worth, usually of a range of objects that have little else in common other than the fact that they retain some value that can be measured in the same terms, namely, their individual values can be expressed by a single unit of measure (price) and, therefore, they are mutually exchangeable.[3] For example, a Sarakastani shepherd may be regarded as a man of great honor and wealth, but he could neither buy nor sell his honor. Only his family's herds, home, and furnishings can be enumerated as things of value, constituting the wealth of his estate and contributing to his prestige and honor, and to that of his family (Campbell, 1964).[4]

Wealth, as a term employed both formally and colloquially, also implies accumulation, a sum total of values (e.g., Smith, 1937 [1776]). Again, the idea that these values can be summed implies a measure of equivalency. In compiling an estate inventory, therefore, one can assign a common measure to pots and pans—of both clay and metal—bedsteads, cattle, 'looking glasses,' lumber lying about the yard, and even money. The appraisers then calculate the total value of the estate, as expressed as a total price, namely, the wealth of the individual who owned the objects, measured in terms of what others are willing to pay for those objects. Hobson (1919:9) refers to "things capable of [read *subject to*] being bought and sold, measuring the amount of wealth they represent by the quantity of money they would fetch in the market. . . . All have their market value and . . . '*wealth' is the sum of those values* [emphasis added]." A more recent definition of the term by Alice H. Jones includes the same basic elements:

Wealth is anything that has market value. It is usually measured in stock, rather than a flow. It includes such physical assets as 1) land, 2) tangible, man-made goods used both for production and final consumption, and 3) intangible assets such as good will or claims against others. Its value is determined by what it brings on the market. (Jones, 1980:15)[5]

Adam Smith (1937[1776]:418) defined wealth as constituted of land, houses, "consumable goods of all different kinds," and gold and silver. These also constitute stock, which is further divided into "stock reserved for immediate consumption" and capital. Smith divides the latter into fixed and circulating capital and the former into that portion originally reserved wholly for consumption, income, and such durables as clothing and furniture that are not immediately consumed (Smith, 1937[1776]:260–264). All of these forms of wealth are acquired for purposes of consumption or for the production of consumables. For Smith, "consumption is the sole end and purpose of all production" (Smith, 1937[1776]:625)[6]

Although the formalist definition of wealth may be appropriate for market economies (by no means a certitude—see Kopytoff [1986]), it is inappropriate for those societies lacking market economies, or for those societies whose members do not wholly participate in market economies.[7] For example, it is unlikely that anyone would take the position that precontact Tongan Islanders did not have wealth; but did they participate in a market—a system in which the exchange of goods and services was unrestricted and governed by the principles of supply and demand? The concepts of *mana* and *tabu* precluded pure market exchange. Clearly, goods and services can have use and exchange value, and the sum total of those values can compose "wealth," even if their respective values cannot be expressed in terms of a common denominator.[8] Assigning of cash values to decedents' estates is a convenience insofar as it facilitates taxation and equitable division of inheritances, but those practices have not been present in every society, nor are cash evaluations necessary to calculate taxes or estate divisions.[9] The only common denominator that is required is that at least one segment of the society in which those objects are produced or used recognizes them as desirable things (i.e., things with use or exchange value) that can be used or exchanged, even if the nature of the exchange does not conform to market economy principles.

There is one other quality of wealth that is implied or explicitly addressed in every definition of wealth: possession. Wealth exists in the possessions of an individual or group. The relationship of possessor to possessed, however, is problematical. Schneider (1974) suggests that ownership is never complete and, like the concept of property, refers to the rights to use wealth, and not to wealth itself (cf. Aceves and King, 1978:129-130). Meillassoux's (1981) Marxist perspective, although diametrically opposed to Schneider's formalism in many respects, also expresses ownership and property in terms of alienation of rights:

Property, which in its full meaning contains the rights of *usus*, *fructus*, and *abusus*, is linked to the market economy which allows products to be alienated and transformed into commodities, i.e. which draws it into contractual relations of production different in kind from those prevailing in the domestic community. The term "property" is thus inappropriate [in terms of "domestic societies"] even when it is said to be "common," which in this respect does not alter the meaning. The most relevant category, to be substituted for "property" is that of *patrimony*, that is to say a good which belongs indivisibly to members of a community and is transferred by inheritance, gift or donation between its members. (Meillassoux, 1981:36)

The concept of property as a set of rights of an individual or group to material wealth, in part, stems from the concepts of ownership developed in Roman law and European feudal law. Aylmer (1980) notes that English legal writers in the sixteenth century did not define property, only possession. The following definition, cited by Aylmer, appears in only slightly modified form in subsequent legal texts throughout the seventeenth century, and into the first quarter of the eighteenth century:

Propertie signifieth the highest right that a man hath or can have to any thing; which in no way depending upon any other mans courtesie. And this none in our kingdom can be said to have in any lands, or tenements, but onely the king in the right of his Crowne. Because all the lands through the realm, are in the nature of fee, and doe hold either mediately or immediately of the Crowne. This word nevertheless in our common law, used for the rights in lands and tenements, that common persons have, because it importeth as much at *utile dominium* though not *directum*. (Cowell, 1607, cited in Aylmer, 1980:89)

By this definition, the king held full dominion (*plenum dominium*) over all nonmovables, namely, landed property. Other individuals and institutions could hold real property in fee (*feudum*) only.[10]

If this deconstruction of the term "wealth" seems to obfuscate a fairly simple, straightforward concept, it should be pointed out that those qualities greatly affect the utility of the term. Wealth, like any other concept used to represent social behavior, imposes a degree of cultural uniformity and continuity that may not exist. The familiarity and simplicity of the term creates a false sense of understanding, taking for granted those relationships that may be true for the scholar's society (and social position), but that must be demonstrated for the society to which they are applied.

Allied with the Western concept of wealth is that of commodity. Commodities are goods or services that are produced expressly for exchange, the prices expressed in terms of some medium or media. Wealth in a capitalist society, according to Marx, consists of the accumulation of commodities, with the single commodity being its smallest unit (Marx, 1906:45). Commodities do not necessarily include all of the material culture of a society, only those products of labor intended for exchange in the market. All commodities in a market economy have value, the measure of which might be the labor invested in their production (Marx's labor cost theory of value) or the supply of similar objects relative to demand (Smith's liberal economics and the exchange theory of value). But objects and services that are not produced for market exchange are not considered to be commodities, although they may provide a critical role in commodity production (e.g., child-rearing in the household has use value, but not exchange value, in late twentieth-century Western society).

This concept of commodity, based largely in theoretical interests in production and the conceptual separation of production and consumption, is questionable. Kopytoff (1986) recognizes that artifacts have "social lives," the biographies of which can be traced and analyzed. He attributes no agency, no quality of sentience, to artifacts. Kopytoff does explore the different phases through which artifacts pass, from commodity to potential commodity that retains exchange value to the singularized, decommoditized object that has been denied exchange value. Commodities, for Kopytoff, exist only in exchange and he prefers to emphasize commoditization as process, rather than commodity as status. As we shall see in the ensuing chapters, Kopytoff's conception of commodity is of greater utility than that of Marx or of Adam Smith in dealing with the objects recovered from archaeological contexts. The objects archaeologists extract from the ground are not commodities, nor are they necessarily wealth. They were wealth as long as people used them, and as long as the objects retained use or exchange value. The sherds of ceramic and glass vessels were commodities, but only in trade. Probate inventories, in effect, list recommoditized objects.

THE SEVENTEENTH-CENTURY ENGLISH PERSPECTIVE

The terms "wealth" and "commodity" were current in seventeenth-century England. Colonial political tracts and legislation, for example, make frequent reference to "the commodities of the country." The meaning of commodity, however, is not altogether clear. Cecil, Lord Baltimore, in his instructions to Leonard Calvert and the "adventurers" to Maryland, stipulated that

> they cause all the planters to imploy their servants in planting of sufficient quantity of corne and other provision of victuall and that they do not suffer them to plant *any other commodity* whatsoever before that be done in a sufficient proportion which they are to observe yearly. [emphasis added] (Calvert, 1988 [1633]:23)

Did Lord Baltimore include "provision of victuall" among the commodities that the colonists were to produce, or were commodities those things other than the foods produced for immediate consumption. The ambiguity revolves around the phrase "other commodities," and an analysis of Cecil Calvert's writings would be necessary to ascertain precisely what he meant, or to determine if he in fact drew a sharp distinction between the two. In 1625, Francis Bacon (1955a:114) wrote of the "commodity of navigable rivers, or the discommodity of their over-flowing" in a brief discourse on house siting. The twentieth-century term "convenience" is an appropriate translation for Bacon's "commodity."

In 1635, one of the "adventurers," perhaps one of the governor's privy councillors (Jerome Hawley), authored a promotional tract for the Maryland colony. The fourth chapter of the work is entitled "The Commodities That May Be Procured in Maryland by Industry," the meaning of which is elaborated in the first paragraph:

> Hee that well considers the situation of this Countrey, and findes it placed between Virginia and New–England, cannot but, by his owne reason, conclude that it must needs participate of the naturall commodities of both places, and be capable of those which industry brings into either. (Hawley, 1988:81)

Among these commodities, the author lists various indigenous grains, legumes, and tobacco, as well as a wide range of legumes, tubers, vegetables, and fruit imported from Europe; wood for potash, barrel staves, wainscotting, and ships; hemp, flax, silkworms and mulberry trees for fibers; grapevines for wine; and iron.

> In fine, Butter, Cheese, Porke and Bacon, to transport to other countrys will be no small commodity, which by industry may be quickly had there in great plenty, etc. And if there were no other staple commodities to be hoped for, but Silke and Linnen (the materialls of which, apparantly will grow there) it were sufficient to enrich the inhabitants. (Hawley, 1988[1635]:82–83)

The first quote suggests a meaning of commodity that is as ambiguous as those of Cecil Calvert and Francis Bacon. "Naturall commodities"—natural resources in twentieth-century parlance—are not distinguished from the products of labor destined for long-distance exchange. Bacon's use of the term implies convenience and not, necessarily, product. The second quote clearly refers to products of labor created for exchange. An analysis of the many promotional and political tracts of the period probably would reiterate that ambiguity, with some distinguishing between "provisions" and commodities (e.g., Hammond, 1988 [1656]:286), and others using a less rigid or clear definition (e.g., C. Calvert, quoted above).

While the term "commodity" may have been used in an informal manner in seventeenth century English, that of "wealth" is much clearer in meaning. Hammond (1988[1656]:285–286) wrote of the Virginia colonists after the Indian war of 1622/23 as "they again began to bud forth, to spread further, to gather wealth [in a metaphorical, rather than a literal sense]." Wealth consistently was used to refer to goods—both "stock intended for immediate consumption" and "capital" (*sensu* Smith, 1937 [1776])—by an individual for his or her satisfaction. Defoe's Moll Flanders appears to be on a lifelong search for sufficient wealth to maintain herself in a life of virtue, even though she invariably finds herself in the position of being less than virtuous in order to attain that end. What a twentieth-century reader might easily interpret as avarice or pathological insecurity fairly drips off of the pages of Pepys's (1923 [1660–1669]) *Diary* as he accepts "gifts" from those seeking favor in the early Restoration government. Jonson's "Old Fox" entertains us with his view of acquisition and wealth:

> Good morning to the day; and next, my gold!
> Open the shrine, that I may see my saint. . . .
> Riches, the dumb god, that givest all men tongues,
> That canst do nought, and yet mak'st men do all things;
> The price of souls; even hell, with thee to boot,
> Is made worth heaven. Thou art virtue, fame,
> Honor and all things else. Who can get thee,
> He shall be noble, valiant, honest, wise—[11]

But Volpone derives his wealth in "No Common Way":

> . . . I use no trade, no ventur;
> I wound no earth with plough-shares, fat no beasts
> To feed the shambles; have no mills for iron,
> Oil, corn, or men, to grind them into powder;
> I blow no subtle glass, expose no ships
> To threat'nings of the furrow-faced sea;
> I turn no moneys in the public bank,
> Nor usure profit. (Jonson, *Volpone* 1.1.1, 22–27, 33–40)

Volpone's wealth derives from his attempts to defraud those of equal greed, but of lesser guile. Composed in verse in the first decade of the seventeenth century, Jonson's play *Volpone* (and *The Alchemist*) caricatures those possessing great wealth, and those aspiring to it. He does not belittle the possession of wealth, per se, only the obsession and devious means by which some sought riches. And, if we take Volpone at his word, wealth meant more than things: it meant honor, prestige, nobility.

By the time Lord Baltimore's first group of colonists set sail from "the Cowes," near Yarmouth, for the shores of the Chesapeake Bay, Jonson's plays had become part of a foundation for a genre of literature that parodied and satirized the social mores and practices of the day.[12] The 'gentlemen' who were among the first English colonists to arrive in Maryland, and those who followed, undoubtedly were familiar with this literature. But theirs was not an attempt to gain wealth (and honor?) through chicanery, but through the conventional means of agricultural production and trade.[13]

> The ways to enrich are many, and most of them foul. . . . The improvement of the ground is the most natural obtaining of riches; for it is our great mother's blessing, the earth's; but it is slow. (Bacon, 1955c [1625]:93)

An assortment of tools was required to plant and cultivate tobacco, the increasingly valuable commodity exported by Virginia. But land and labor figured most prominently, and it was for these two resources that the settlers competed, although not always in the "Christian spirit" most of them publicly embraced. Efforts at extending the contracts of servants beyond their customary lengths were not unheard of, and the sale of land to which the seller held no legal right also occurred, although with what frequency is difficult to determine.

LAND

> The first man who, having enclosed a piece of land, thought of saying "This is mine" and found people simple enough to believe him, was the true founder of civil society, . . . the idea of property, depending on many prior ideas which could only have arisen in successive stages, was not formed all at once in the human mind. It was necessary for men to make much progress, to acquire much industry and knowledge, to transmit and increase it from age to age, before finally arriving at this final stage of the state of nature. (Rousseau, 1984 [1754]:109)

Disagree though we might with Rousseau's primitive evolutionism, it is important to examine the issue of land as property, not as the basis of "civil society," in the abstract, but as one feature of English society of the seventeenth and early eighteenth centuries. Private ownership of land, and perhaps ownership in general, did not burst forth on the civil scene in its late twentieth-century form. In this section, the concepts of land and labor as property are examined. Was there 'the first man' in England who said 'this is mine,' and were there simple people around who believed him?

Ownership of land in the seventeenth century was by no means a clear-cut issue. Nor was labor simply a question of who was available and at what price. World capitalism was developing in Europe during the seventeenth century, and during preceding centuries, but a consensus as to who could own land and to what extent labor was "free" had yet to be achieved. Understanding the roles of land and labor, and the nature and degree of controversy surrounding them in

England and the colonial world, is important if we expect to appreciate the political and economic tensions that surrounded colonial production and exchange of goods.

Land ultimately was owned by the English Crown, or so thought the Crown. The history of the Stuart dynasty (1603–1689) easily could be related—without doing too much violence to British history—in terms of the conflict over the source of the Crown's power and the extent of its prerogative in the disposition of lands and offices, and in the Crown's responsibility to finance itself and its government. For example, Cowell's (1607, cited above) definition of property explicitly addressed land and tenements, recognizing the Crown as the ultimate and indisputable owner. Aylmer notes that Cowell's law dictionary, *The Interpreter*, was "violently attacked" by Parliament, but such definitions as Crown, Parliament, subsidy, and prerogative were at issue, not property per se (Aylmer, 1980:88).

John Rastell's law dictionary of 1624 retained the essence of Cowell's definition, distinguishing only among three kinds of rights in property: "propertie absolute," "propertie qualified," and "propertie possessorie."[14] That definition remained unchanged in the editions of 1629, 1671, 1685, and 1721 (Aylmer, 1980:91). We should not take this to mean that the Stuart definition of property, particularly insofar as it relates to landed property, remained unchallenged.[15]

William Shepard, legal advisor to Oliver Cromwell, published *An Epitome of All the Common and Statute Laws of this Nation, Now in Force* in 1656. Shepard dropped all of the qualifications and restrictions on "propertie absolute," as defined by Rastell. William Style's *Regestum Practicale: or, the Practical Register* (1657; cited in Aylmer, 1980:93–94) supported Shepard's definition by citing a precedent regarding the king's highway that vests no interest of the king in the soil of the highway, only in his right-of-way and that of his subjects.

The Crown, reasserting itself with the restoration of Charles II to the throne, invoked the concept of *plenum dominium*, although as Aylmer (1980:94–95) notes it is uncertain to what extent this, and prior definitions, affected legal decisions. It is notable, for instance, that both Parliament and the exiled King Charles II recognized Lord Baltimore's rights to the lands of Maryland, disputing only his right to rule there—Parliament because they believed Calvert's manorial rights to be inconsistent with parliamentary government, and the king because of Calvert's alleged support of Parliament.[16]

Dissension over royal prerogative soon lead to the downfall of the House of Stuart, and the legal redefinition of property appears to have been achieved by the end of the first quarter of the eighteenth century. Borrowing unabashedly from Locke and citing Interregnum precedents, John Lilly proposes:

> An absolute proprietor hath an absolute Power to dispose of his Estate as he pleases, subject only to the Laws of the Land. . . . Every man (unless he hath forfeited it) hath a Property and Right which the Law allows him to defend his

Life, Liberty and Estate; and if it be violated, it gives an Action to redress the
Injury, and Punish the Wrong-doer (Lilly, 1719, cited in Aylmer, 1980:95)

Insofar as it pertains to landed property, the logic of the Stuart definition of
property requires the Crown to take 'an Action to redress the Injury' should an
individual trespass or seize the land in the possession of another, the affront being
against the Crown, true and unequivocal owner of the land. Under the Hanover
statutes, the Crown defends the property rights of its subjects.[17]

Ambiguity over precisely who owned land in England, "in no way depending upon any other man's courtesie," did not spring forth *de novo* during the reign
of King James I. Macfarlane (1978) makes his case that the country folk of England were not peasants, holding only usufruct and not 'propertie absolute,' as far
back as the thirteenth century. The use of the will as a legal instrument of inheritance dates back at least that far in England, and the rural folk used wills to convey
land. Macfarlane asserts that these people were not peasants, insofar as they held
land and other materials as individuals and not as corporate entities. Although he
never succeeds in uncovering the origins of English individualism, Macfarlane
does demonstrate that patterns of ownership in England were individualistic and
true property rights in lands and chattels were divisible and partible.[18] Were the
monarchs of England from the thirteenth century onward living in a fantasy,
incognizant of the fact that their subjects were openly flaunting the Crown's
claims to the land and prerogative to dispose of it in a manner that the sovereign
deemed appropriate? Or did they construe such conveyances as transfers of usufruct, the right of use and profit. Rather than dally longer in English legal history,
a field in which there are many more qualified to pursue this issue, let it suffice
that there was no clear consensus in the matter.

This dissension over property rights and royal prerogative played itself out
in the colonies as well, particularly in proprietary colonies such as Maryland. The
lords Baltimore held the lands and resources of Maryland by virtue of a charter
prepared for George Calvert (and eventually granted unto his son, Cecil), the
First Lord Baron of Baltimore in the Kingdom of Ireland, by King Charles I in
1632.[19] George Calvert's heirs were given wide-ranging powers by the charter, the
powers of a sovereign, subject only to the king and the "laws, statutes, customs
and rights" of England (Greene, 1966:27). Principal among those powers, of
course, was the right to grant land patents in Maryland.[20]

That the Calvert charter was far from secure is evidenced by the correspondence of Cecil Calvert, the second Lord Baltimore, and his need to remain at court
in England to protect the charter. Calvert and the succeeding lords Baltimore
required the colonists to swear an oath of fidelity, upholding the charter and the
rights of the proprietary.[21] Each demand for compliance on this issue from the
Proprietor was greeted by dissension in the Lower House of the General Assembly, the "representative" body of the bicameral legislature, bringing forth claims

of "enslavement" in at least one instance (*Archives of Maryland* [Arch. Md.], I:262–272 [1638]; see also *Arch. Md.*, I:304–306, 316 [1650]). Colonists asked by what right the Lord Baltimore held proprietorship over lands that he had never seen. When the proprietor appealed to his charter from the king, the populace—fully cognizant of political developments in England and Scotland—retorted, by what right had the king granted these lands? While it is tempting to attribute civil conflicts in Maryland during the mid-1640s, 1650s, and 1680s to political upheavals in England, we should not lose sight of the fact that the basic issues of sovereignty were as debatable in the colony as in the homeland: the focus was simply on a more immediate sovereign—the lord proprietor.

Issues of legal proprietorship aside, the colonists were involved with the quotidian tasks of producing their livelihood, and that required land. "The Conditions of Plantation," promulgated by Cecil, Lord Baltimore, granted a warrant (an assurance or guarantee) for 50 acres of land to any individual transporting himself or herself to the colony, and for each person similarly transported.[22] The individual demanded a warrant for each person transported and, once he or she found a suitable tract, requested a survey of the parcel. Rents were due at an annual rate of 2 shillings sterling per 100 acres, deliverable in cash, or its equivalent in commodities. Tracts were granted:

> In Free and Common Soccage *by Fealty only* for all Services Yielding and Paying therefore yearly unto us and our Heirs at our receipt of St. Mary's [City]. At the two most usual Feasts in the Year, vizt., At the Feast of the Annunciation of the Blessed Virgin Mary and at the Feast of St. Michael the Arch-Angel by even and equal Portions the Rent of . . . [emphasis added] (example drawn from *Land Patents*, Q:96–97, 05 August 1658)[23]

In a legal sense, a planter who held a patent was a tenant. That status was reaffirmed through a nominal, semiannual payment of a quit-rent. That this ritual coincided with important Catholic holy days probably was not a coincidence, although historians have not examined the symbolic aspects of quit-rent payments. On the other hand, in the tradition of medieval and early modern England, planters conveyed their lands along with their chattels to their heirs (Macfarlane 1978). Not only was the practice approved of, but the lord proprietor required registration of sales and bequests with the secretary of the colony—for a fee, of course.

Available evidence indicates that the colonists were essentially tenants enjoying usufruct by virtue of their letters patent, and that while they recognized their status as tenants, they did not necessarily accept it. This ambiguity was played out in religious rituals, political forums, and courts of law. It is very curious that with all of the historical research conducted on the colony over the past 150 years this issue has not been addressed, or even publicly recognized.

The symbolic, ritualistic aspects of land acquisition and rent payment warrant further study.

LABOR

Acquiring land was only the first step in the process of building a plantation from which one could expect to earn a subsistence and, hopefully, much more. The soils of Maryland were generally fertile, but they produced little more than a subsistence for a planter or a household unless a significant amount of labor was applied in clearing the land and planting it with the principal cash crop, tobacco. Labor was not freely available, the European population of the colony being small and unable to reproduce itself, and Native Americans being somewhat reluctant to work for the Europeans. Little labor in the colony existed that was not imported.[24]

The principal means by which laborers entered the colony was by voluntary immigration. As an extension of the increased internal migration in England (Horn, 1979), thousands of individuals set sail for the colonies. Some contracted with specific planters directly or through their agents, but many were transported by ships' captains, supercargoes, and merchants who paid the £6 costs of transport with the intention of selling the immigrants' indentures to the planters (e.g., Michel in Hinke, 1916 [1702]).[25]

Terms of servitude ranged from three to seven years or more, depending on the age of the servant and his or her agreement with the transporter. The average term of servitude was from four to five years, as established by the colonial governments for those adults arriving in Maryland without formal indentures (Carr and Walsh, 1977:542). Those who fulfilled their contracts, and those who paid their own transportation and thereby remained free, could bargain with planters to sell their labor on an annual basis.[26] Task-specific contracts, for other than specialized services such as house building or brick making, appear to have been rare. The planter who purchased an individual's indentures could claim the 50-acre "headright,"[27] as well as whatever labor could be extracted from that individual during the term of his or her indentures (Menard, 1973:324). Upon fulfillment of the terms of indenture, a freed servant was entitled to "freedom dues," payable by the master or mistress, and consisting of two suits of clothes, some corn, and tools.

Whether or not a warrant for 50 acres of land constituted a portion of the freedom dues was a point of contention in Maryland for a number of years. Warning prospective servants in 1656, Hammond describes the general conditions of servitude:

> The usual allowance for servants is (besides their charge of passage defrayed) at their expiration, a years provision of corne, dubble apparell, tooles necessary, and land according to the custome of the Country, which is an old delu-

sion, for there is no land accustomary due to the servant, but to the Master, and therefore that servant is unwise that will not dash out that custom in his covenant, and make that due of land absolutely his own, which although at the present not of so great consequence, yet in a few years will be of much worth. (Hammond, 1988[1656]:289)

Since most of the prospective servants who might have benefited from this caution were illiterate, and did not sign their indentures until they arrived in the colonies, it is uncertain for whom this advice was intended and how effective it was in warning the unwary.[28]

The confusion over what was due a servant upon the fulfillment of his or her contract probably emanated from the original "Conditions of Plantation" (Hawley, 1988[1635]:91, 99). This document stipulates a 100-acre warrant for each servant transported to the colony and, in a sample of an indenture, a 50-acre tract to be given to the servant *by the master* upon completion of service. By this arrangement, 50 of the 100 acres warranted by the transporter would, in effect, be held in trust for the servant. That arrangement, if ever practiced, was no longer tenable when the proprietor reduced the premium for transportation to 50 acres.

Clearly, there was some foundation for land claims against planters because the General Assembly addressed the issue in 1663:

An Act for the Repeal of a Clause in an Act made the 23rd day of October, 1640, by Leonard Calvert Esqr., Lieutenant General of this Province, Entitled an Act for Servants Clothes:

The Burgesses in this present General Assembly taking into Consideration the great Vexation and trouble which the Inhabitants of this province are liable unto by reason of the Clause of an Act touching the Fifty Acres of Land, five whereof at Least to be plantable given by virtue of the said Act unto all Servants brought into this province whether men or women at the expiration of their Service And the inhabitants aforesaid not being in Capacity to perform that which the said Act does enjoin as to the Fifty acres of land due and no more for their Transportation hither by virtue of his Lordship's Conditions of plantation now enforced ... [be it enacted that the] Clause enjoining fifty Acres of Land to be allowed to Servants at the end of his or their service be and is hereby Repealed. And that for the future there shall be nothing allowed to any Servant at the end or Expiration of his or their Service more than their Clothes, Hoes, Axe and Corn as is prescribed in the same Act. (*Arch. Md.*, I:496 [1663])[29]

This act of the General Assembly, of course, refers only to the repeal of a provision of the 1640 act and should not have affected the stipulations of individual contracts drawn up in England (see Hammond, 1988[1656]:286).

Repeal of this provision left most planters with the obligation of providing a few necessities with which a freed person could establish his or her own household. Even with a 50-acre tract, however, it is difficult to see how many freedmen could have established their own farmsteads. Most probably found employment on established plantations as either domestics or field hands, freeing the planter for more social activities, at least according to Durand of Dauphinè.

> The land is so rich and so fertile that when a man has fifty acres of ground, two men-servants, a maid and some cattle, neither he nor his wife do anything but visit among neighbors. Most of them do not even take the trouble to oversee the work of their slaves, for there is no house, however modest, where there is not what is called a Lieutenant, generally a freedman, under whose commands his two servants are placed. This Lieutenant keeps himself, works and makes his two servants work, and receives one-third of the tobacco, grain, and whatever they have planted, and thus the master has only to take his share of the crops. If he commands three or four, his share is proportional.... When a freedman has served his indenture, he will serve no longer, no matter what the salary you offer him, for he can find as many situations of Lieutenant as he wishes. (Durand, 1934 [1687]:111–112)[30]

Keeping in mind that Durand was a refugee Huguenot with little, if any, command of the English language, and his descriptions are of Virginia and not Maryland, it is apparent from his account that wage labor did exist to a certain extent (although he may have confused overseeing with tenantry, and servants with slaves). Michel, a Swiss investigating the possibility of establishing a Swiss settlement in Virginia in 1701, is more definite on this point: "If one wants to hire out, as there are some who do so, he can get annually from 4 to 6 pounds [per annum] from merchants; the wealthiest gentleman do not pay more than 10 pounds" (Michel in Hinke, 1916[1702]:125).[31]

Michel's observation may lead us to believe that labor was free, namely, able to negotiate its own price, subject to the laws of supply and demand. Michel also notes, however, that

> wages are fixed, namely, according to law each workman [read *indentured servant*] must pay his master for his board and lodging annually 400 lbs. of tobacco and three barrels of corn. Whatever he can raise above that amount, he can sell, so that within a short time he can pay his passage money. (Michel in Hinke, 1916[1702]:288)[32]

Colonial legislation discouraged free negotiations between prospective employers and employees. For example, the General Assembly of Maryland passed an act in 1661 establishing the maximum terms of servitude (exempting the terms of enslavement), this in partial response to the large number of immigrants arriving without formal indentures. That act was amended in 1666, extending the maximum limits by one year for all those arriving without indentures (*Arch. Md.*, I:409 [1661]). The justification for doing so was that "it is considered the Master and owners of such servants cannot receive their reasonable satisfaction for the charges, trouble and great hazard which all masters and Owners of Servants are and must of necessity be at with their Servants" (*Arch. Md.*, II:147 [1666]).

The Massachusetts Bay Colony took similar action in 1670 to mitigate the effects of falling market prices and the high costs of labor. Prices were established for laborers' day rates, certain commodities, and services, all of which could be purchased with merchantable corn, the price of which was set by the General Court on a yearly basis (Anonymous in Demos, 1972a:251–254). Maryland's colonial legislature periodically passed acts establishing prices at ordinaries, or inns, as well.

> Whereas diverse Ordinary Keepers within this Province do frequently exact and charge excessive Rates for their drink, victualling and lodging, . . . be it enacted . . . that from and after the publication hereof no Ordinary Keeper, Innholder or other person keeping a Victualling house or house of Entertainment shall for the future sell or be allowed for: French brandy above 120 lbs Tobacco per gallon, French wine 40, . . . Strong Cider 20, . . . for diet 10 [per meal], [and for] Lodging with bed 4" (*Arch. Md.*, V:148–149 [1666]).

Governmental control of wages and prices was not new to the seventeenth century, and Adam Smith continued to rail against such actions more than a century later. Labor, as with land ownership, occupied an ambiguous position in seventeenth-century colonial society.

This interpretation of labor in the seventeenth century is somewhat at odds with Menard's (1973) observation that the importation of servants was proportional to the price of tobacco. Menard responded to Craven's (1970) assertion that one ought to emphasize the individual choices of prospective immigrant servants rather than treating indentured labor as a commodity.[33] He did so by counting the number of servants brought before the county courts of Charles County, Maryland, and Northumberland County, Virginia, where their ages and consequent terms of indenture were established, and comparing the trend in appearances with that of the average annual price of tobacco for the years 1662–1706.

While Menard did not intend for this relationship to be the definitive word on the subject, he did point out that the correspondence between average tobacco prices and the importation of indentured labor was close. Precisely how close that relationship was for the years in question was not immediately evident since he provided no quantitative description. For purposes of illustration, Menard's original data are transformed into three-year running means and graphed in Figure 4–1. The transformed data more clearly illustrate the relationship, addressing Menard's (1973:329) caveat that the intensity of peaks and troughs in the immigration data could not be explained simply in terms of fluctuating tobacco prices. The anomalies virtually disappear when the data is smoothed, that is, when short-

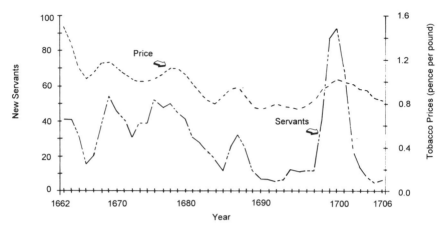

Figure 4–1. Servant indentures and tobacco prices, 1662–1706. (Source: Menard, 1973)

term variation is minimized. With the exception of one dramatic peak in the number of new servants during the last two years of the seventeenth century, the dependent variable (labor) appears to be highly correlated with movements of the independent variable (tobacco prices, expressed in pence per pound).

While it is true that the supply of labor, as provided by merchants and ships' captains, does appear to have been determined by the price of tobacco, it also is true that the "wages" of labor remained constant, as decreed through the acts of the General Assembly of Maryland establishing the terms of indentures. The price of labor, in contrast, varied with the price of tobacco; the average amount of tobacco that could be raised by one adult male servant, once tobacco culture had become established, remained constant regardless of the market price of the product. Tobacco prices were determined on the other side of the Atlantic.

The wages that planters paid their servants, expressed in terms of food, clothing, shelter, and 'freedom dues,' remained stable, with the possible exception of imported clothing. Moreover, servants were not able to move to a different plantation, even if higher wages were offered, until the terms of their indentures had been satisfied. Only freedmen could move from one employer to another and, as illustrated by the price and wage legislation passed by the Massachusetts Bay Colony Court (cited above), their wages were not necessarily determined by the principles of supply and demand.[34]

Planters may have had some flexibility in determining the wages of their servants. For example, it is evident that some permitted their servants to raise pigs. A bill was introduced by the Lower House of the Maryland General Assembly in April of 1666 entitled, "An Act prohibiting all Masters from suffering their Servants to raise any hogs or pigs to their proper use" (*Arch. Md.*, II:18, 30). I have been unable to find specific references to indicate what prompted this action. At any rate, the Upper House rejected the bill:

> It being in the power of every Master not to do it if not obliged by Indentures [signed in] England, and diverse Masters being obliged by Indentures to allow Servants to raise hogs against any that are free, this [Upper] House do think it Unnecessary to pass this Law and in the second part [it is] injurious [to the colony]. (*Arch. Md.*, II:30)

Swine required little or no maintenance, as they were allowed to roam free in the forest, and they provided a source of food and revenue (Beverley, 1947[1705]:318; Hawley, 1988[1635]:79). Francis Bacon (1955c [1625]:90) recommended them, along with goats and a variety of fowl, for colonial plantations in that they are "least subject to diseases, and multiply the fastest." By raising swine, servants could accumulate wealth in advance of their freedom. Selling surplus stock provided the servants with credit that could be used to purchase food and clothing in addition to that supplied by the planter. Servants also could accumulate surpluses with which to purchase or rent a plantation and tools.

> Those Servants that will be industrious may in their time of service gain a competent estate before their Freedomes, which is usually done by many, and they gaine esteeme and assistance that appear so industrious. There is no Master almost but will allow his Servant a parcell of clear ground to plant some Tobacco in for himself, which he may husband at those many idle times he hath allowed him and not prejudice, but rejoyse his master to see it, which in time of Shiping he may lay out for commodities, and in Summer sell them again with advantage, and get a Sow-Pig or two, which anybody almost will give him, and his Master suffer him to keep them with his own, which will be no charge to the Master, and with one or two years increase of them may purchase a Cow Calf or two, and by that time he is for himself, he may have Cattel, Hogs and Tobacco of his own, and come to live gallantly. (Hammond, 1988[1656]:292)

Permitting—and indeed encouraging—servants and slaves to raise their own meat and vegetables divested planters of their responsibility to adequately feed their laborers, thereby lowering the overall costs of producing tobacco.[35] Durand (1934 [1687]:116–117) and Michel (in Hinke, 1916 [1702]:31, 114) both note, albeit briefly, the importance of maize in the diets of laborers in Virginia. That it was acceptable to provide one's laborers with little else to eat—provided some effort was made to enlarge on their diet—is made clear in a court case from Calvert County, Maryland.

In 1663, Richard Preston and six of his servants filed cross-charges against one another. The servants refused to work because Preston did not given them "flesh" to eat. Preston claimed that they usually had meat at least twice, and sometimes three times, each week, but at the time he had none to give them. Preston offered to drop his suit if the servants returned to work, and he promised to give them the use of a boat and credit with which three or four of them could seek out and purchase meat. The servants claimed that

> Mr. Preston doth not allow your petitioners sufficient provisions for the enablement to our work, but straitens us so far that we are brought so weak [that] we are not able to perform the employments he puts us upon. We desire but so much as sufficient, but he will allow us nothing but beans and bread. (Anonymous in Demos, 1972b:135–137)

Preston stated his case as follows:

> [I] am constrained to address myself to this the court, that according to equity and their demerits they may receive such censure as shall be judged equal for such perverse servants, lest a worse evil by their example should ensue by encouraging other servants to do the like. (Anonymous in Demos, 1972b:136)

The court found for Preston, and ordered "two of the mildest" to administer 30 lashes to each of the other servants. Sentence was suspended for all when they asked for forgiveness and promised good behavior for the future. A reasonable effort to adequately feed the servants was clearly expected of Preston; but the court, perhaps responding to Preston's ominous forecast, upheld the rights of the master over those of the servants. Such rights, and the reciprocal relations between master and servant, were likened to that of a king and his subjects (Alsop, 1988[1666]:354–355).

Of course, not all labor in colonial Maryland was contractual. Enslaved Africans played an important role in the agricultural economy of the seventeenth-century Chesapeake Bay colonies, although that role has been neglected in the archaeological and historical literature (as has conflict in general).[36] The reasons given for this neglect are that slaves constituted only a small percentage of the labor force until the end of the century, and most of the slaves were held by the wealthier planters, particularly those in Virginia.

Whether one can calculate the number of slaves in the Chesapeake Bay region for this period with any accuracy remains to be demonstrated. As taxables, they were likely to have been underreported, and lists of taxables for the counties in Virginia and Maryland are few and far between; nor do they necessarily specify whether or not a taxable is a slave or a servant (Carr and Menard, 1979:210).[37] Main (1982:102) provides the ratios of slaves to servants for six Maryland counties for the period 1674 to 1700, based on probate inventories. Those ratios swing wildly from 0.28 in 1674–1676, to 0.18 in 1677–1679, to 0.51 in 1680–1682, to 0.31 in 1683–1685, and so forth. There was little official notice taken of the deaths of enslaved Africans and there certainly were no inventories taken of slaves' estates: as property, slaves did not have estates.[38]

Morgan (1975) suggests that the number of enslaved Africans residing in Virginia remained relatively small until the last quarter of the seventeenth century, at which time the importation of slaves increased to supplement, and eventually replace, a sagging servant "market." Walsh (1977:128) provides statistics from a 1704 census of the population in Charles County, Maryland: 578 enslaved Africans distributed among 408 households and representing 19% of the total population of 2,989 individuals.

Deetz (1988), citing Morgan (1975:155) and archaeological data from Flowerdew Hundred in Virginia, suggests that increased segregation and separation of slaves on plantations occurred during the last two decades of the century. Deetz quotes Morgan: "there is more than a little evidence that Virginians during these years (before 1660) were ready to think of negroes as members of or potential members of the community on the same terms as other men and to demand of them the same standards of behavior" (Morgan, 1975:155, as cited in Deetz, 1988:366). Such sentiments would account for otherwise contradictory attitudes, and provide a strong contrast with the subsequent spatial segregation of Europeans and Africans hypothesized by Deetz.

Perhaps the transition came earlier to Maryland, or perhaps the Maryland colonists felt differently about Africans, for they passed an act of the General Assembly that represents a very different attitude:

> [A]ll Negroes or other slaves already within the Province [of Maryland] and All Negroes and other slaves to be hereafter imported into the Province shall serve *Durante Vita*. And all Children born of any Negro or other slaves shall be slaves as their fathers were for the term of their lives. And forasmuch as diverse freeborne English women forgetful of their free Condition and to the disgrace of our Nation do intermarry with Negro Slaves by which also diverse suits may arise touching the Issue of such a woman and a great damage does befall the Masters of such Negroes for prevention whereof for deterring such freeborn women from such shameful Matches. Be it enacted . . . That whatsoever free born women shall intermarry with any slave from and after the Last day of this present Assembly shall serve the Master of such slave during the life of her husband. And that all the Issue of such freeborn women so married shall be Slaves as their fathers were. And . . . all the Issues of English or other freeborn women that have already married Negroes shall serve the Masters of their Parents till they be Thirty years of age and no longer. (*Arch. Md.*, I:534[1664])

These are not the attitudes of a people harboring good will toward their African neighbors. Nor does the very fact of the legislation indicate an insignificant African population. This piece of legislation remanded a number of people to lifelong servitude. Enslaved Africans and their luckless offspring and mates did not represent free labor.

LAND, LABOR, AND MERCANTILISM

Ownership of land by the monarch and tight restrictions on labor were not alien concepts to the English of the seventeenth century, even less so to the French and Spanish of that period, although the Dutch may have regarded them as archaic and inconvenient legalisms.[39] They can be regarded as part of what has been called the mercantilist system, a socioeconomic form that Adam Smith (1937 [1776]) roundly criticized in Book IV of *An Inquiry into the Nature and Causes of the Wealth of Nations*. Although Smith characterized mercantilism as a system, Cole (1964:23) notes that mercantilism was not a coherent theory in the early seventeenth-century, but instead consisted of "a loose aggregation of more or less related concepts lacking any close, logical relation." Indeed, he suggests that

> the term is unsuitable, since it implies that mercantilism was a well-formulated economic philosophy like other *isms*, such as communism or socialism; and this mercantilism was not, until it was formulated into a too-logical, too-narrow, and unhistorical system by its enemies in the eighteenth century. (Cole, 1964:20)

No doubt Cole ranks Adam Smith high among these enemies.

Mercantilist philosophy clearly developed during the seventeenth century, and Cole's assessment that it was an ex post facto theory imposed by liberal economists, perhaps, should be taken as an overstatement. Cole does identify three assumptions, however, that seem to have pervaded mercantilist thinking— in whatever stage—throughout the period: self-sufficiency, bullionism, and the monarch's responsibility to protect and promote trade through government regulation. A nation increased its wealth by acquiring the wealth of other lands and other nations. This was accomplished through self-sufficiency in all necessities, encouraging exports of surpluses in exchange for gold bullion, and discouraging the importation of goods except for those that could not be produced at home (and, consequently, discouraging the export of bullion). The monarch promoted these goals through the imposition of duties on imports, providing a strong navy to protect shipping, and encouraging colonization for purposes of securing raw materials and markets for manufactured goods.

The Reverend Hugh Jones provides us with a matter-of-fact understanding of mercantilism when, in 1724, he noted that improved husbandry in Virginia might improve the quality of wool produced:

> But to do this, would be of little Use, since it is contrary to the Interest of Great Britain to allow them [the Virginians] Exportation of their Woollen Manufactures; and what [unmanufactured] Woollen is there might be nearly had as cheap, and better from England. (Jones, 1724:41)

Alsop (1988 [1666]:361–363) noted that commerce of all sorts was "the very soul of the kingdom."

Historian John Demos (1972:250) states that the American colonists assumed "that wealth was essentially a fixed quantity and that economic activity should be governed by principles of orderliness and stability." It was the right and duty of the state to intervene to maintain stability and balance. Government—within certain bounds—controlled wages and prices, required all men to work, and established standards for measurement and trade, including stringent prohibitions against engrossment, or monopolization. Lord Baltimore, for example, legislated against engrossment of imported manufactured goods and 'price-gouging' in taverns. Engrossment of land was discouraged through a law that required the 'planting' of tracts within three years of award of patent, and instructions to the surveyor general were explicit in limiting the amount of water frontage that a patentee could claim per 50 acres of land.

The English Crown was particularly active in protecting traditional land and labor relations during the Tudor and early Stuart periods as it battled mercantile interests through the poor laws and antienclosure acts. In the long run, those efforts were ineffectual, and relations of land and labor were altered, both beginning their transformation into what Polyani called "false commodities." Ambiguities regarding the ownership of land and the status of labor continued throughout the seventeenth century. The concept that government should actively control economic forces continued as well, although there was a great deal of debate regarding in whom those powers should be vested. In effect, there were two economic systems developing: a maturing market system in Europe in which the value of tobacco was determined by supply and demand, and a modified feudal system re-created in the colonies wherein the prices of labor and rent were established by custom and—to a certain extent—by decree.

SUMMARY

Quibble over the number of slaves though we might, the vast majority of laborers in the Chesapeake colonies were not free. Either they were permanently enslaved or they entered into indentured servitude for several years. A few—

probably a very few—individuals who did not own or rent a plantation, or belong to a family that did, sold their labor upon the market. Wage and price legislation in some cases established maximum limits on their wages. These were the conditions of labor in the Chesapeake colonies: free, and yet not free, much as the land was both owned and not owned. Servants' indentures were purchased in Europe under conditions that may have resembled those of a capitalist labor market: that market was poorly developed, at best, in the colonies.

The contradictions in land tenure were even more pronounced than those in the nature of labor. One did not purchase land from the colony's proprietor. There were fees due to the surveyor general for surveying a patent and to the Provincial and County Court clerks for registering warrants, patents, and conveyances. Tenure, however, was based upon fealty to the lord proprietor and an annual quitrent, payable in two installments. The Maryland colonists were renters, a fact reinforced by the omission of land from their probate inventories. But lands were conveyed by will and by "alienation." Testators and sellers of land may have thought they owned the land outright, and those to whom the land was conveyed may have thought themselves to be owners, free and clear; but the lords proprietary did not share in that illusion, and it is not clear how the colonists reconciled the ritual of semiannual rent payments with outright ownership.

The perspective adopted in this work is that the colonists, by and large, did not and could not reconcile that contradiction. They recognized that they were renters, despite the improvements that they made to the land, and they resented it. Such resentment can be seen in the political tensions that pervaded the Maryland colony throughout most of the seventeenth century. Carson et al. (1981) attribute the impermanent nature of colonial Chesapeake architecture to swidden-style tobacco agriculture practiced at the time, and they undoubtedly are correct to a large extent, but we can but wonder what effect the tenuous nature of land ownership in the colony might have had on whether those simple, frame structures were maintained or allowed to deteriorate.

The seventeenth century in Western Europe and in the European colonies is not a cultural-historical period suited to simple characterization (as if any were). Undoubtedly, the difficulty lies in approaching a culture from an entirely different ethos, from a Weltanshauung that omits the basic assumptions and tenets necessary to completely understand the goals and motivations of the people of that culture.[40] Not insignificant, however, the basic concepts of property and the rights of labor were debated throughout Europe and the colonies during the seventeenth century, and those debates have continued to the present. No accord was reached, despite the impeachment and decapitation of one king, the ousting and abdication of another, and the mutilation and deaths of thousands of English, Scottish, and Irish people.

Wealth and commodity had meaning to the colonists, although it is unlikely that the meaning of the latter term was any more specific than creature comforts, whether products of nature or labor. The meaning of wealth, on the surface, was less ambiguous. Accumulation of wealth appears to have been sufficiently important to enough people to attract the barbed quill pens of Jonson, Defoe, Swift, and a spate of other great wits. Many colonial officers may have borne a close resemblance to Pepys's self-portrait, scrambling to acquire more tobacco, more "commodities," and more land. Whether or not theirs was a consuming interest in wealth (pun intended) remains to be seen.

Before returning to the archaeology of consumption, we should backtrack for a moment and fill out some of the early colonial history of Maryland, particularly in terms of household formation and organization on the Chesapeake frontier. Incorporating the concepts explored in this chapter, Chapter 5 develops a cultural context in which household decisions were made and enacted.

NOTES

1. While the terms "commodity," "profit," and "riches" occur with some regularity in seventeenth-century tracts and other documents, the term "Œconomick" is relatively rare and signifies household management (e.g., Gainsforth, 1995 [1616]; Griffith, 1995 [1633]). Apropos Polanyi's statement, the conceptual removal of economy from society may be a recent phenomenon, a concomitant or necessary feature of a market economy (see Dalton, 1971).

2. Although England maintained economic and political hegemony in the North American colonies, other than Canada, for most of the Colonial period, the reader should keep in mind that the colonies consisted of individuals from many European and non-European cultures. Van der Donk (1968[1655]), for example, describes a heterogeneous community of Dutch, French, English, Scots, Algonkians, and Iroquois in New Netherland. The Chesapeake colonists came from England, Ireland, France, Sweden, Norway, Denmark, Portugal, Spain, Bohemia, the Netherlands, Germany, Switzerland, Poland, parts of Africa, and the Caribbean (e.g., *Archives of Maryland* [*Arch. Md.*], V:205–206 [1669]). Differences in cultural meanings arising from ethnic differences await further study.

3. Goods and services have value insofar as they fulfill human needs. Prices are assigned to objects through market mechanisms, but not necessarily on the basis of the human labor expended in creating them, some objects existing without benefit of labor.

4. The U.S. Internal Revenue Service allows for the amortization of something called "good will," that which one purchases along with tangible assets when buying a company, the value of which equals the purchase price of the company minus the fair market value of its tangible assets. Franchises are based on the concept that one can buy reputation.

5. Jones (1984:240) also defines wealth as product accumulated beyond consumption, but does not elaborate on that point.

6. Note, however, that Smith did not dismiss the possibility that consumables could be reallocated as capital, and his phrase "reserved for immediate consumption" implies a degree of arbitrariness in determining what is to be consumed and what is to be redeployed as capital.

7. Notably, Schneider (1974) does not mention market exchange in his glossary definition of wealth—no doubt a product of his anthropological training.

8. Barth (1967) recognized nonequivalencies in his work "Economic Spheres in Dar-Fur," as did Bohannan (1955) among the Tiv. One might argue that a bit of a "straw man" is being set up here in that pure, unrestricted market conditions are unknown in world history. By the same reasoning, however, it is equally true that wealth and commodity can exist outside of pure market conditions.

9. "Equitable" and "equity" are relative terms that do not necessarily imply absolute, abstract sums that can be divided into identical portions through the application of arithmetic and higher mathematics. This one concept comes as close as any to the heart of Polanyi's (1971a,b,c) thinking.

10. *Plenum dominium:* literally, full dominion, complete ownership and unrestricted use. It combines the concepts of *dominium directum*, or the power inherent in the original owner, and *dominium utile*, or the control over use inherent in the title of the tenant. By way of contrast, *feudum* refers to realty held conditionally upon payment of homage or services to the immediate lord; hence the term "feudalism," which refers to a hierarchical system in which all but the king hold realty in *fee*. (In one sense, the king also holds his kingdom conditionally upon payment of homage or services to his immediate lord, God.)

11. Bacon (1955b [1625]:75) also recognized that wealth may provide more than material satisfaction, but only by "spending for honour and good action."

12. Jonson died in 1637, approximately 4 years after the *Ark* and the *Dove* brought the first English settlers to Maryland, and 30 years after the settlement of Jamestown Island in Virginia.

13. Prospecting for precious minerals and trade for animal pelts occurred, but having learned from the misadventures of the Virginia Company, and under the conditions of settlement established by Cecil, Lord Baltimore, the colonists almost immediately set themselves to agricultural pursuits (see Hawley, 1988[1635]:79–83).

14. These terms distinguish between the degree to which control is exercised over realty. Qualified property consists of rights that are held conditionally, suggested in the term *feudum*, as defined in note 10. "Propertie possessorie" refers to usufruct, or possession without rights other than those guaranteed by contract.

15. Hobbes (1968 [1651]:367–368), concerned with the weakening of the Common-wealth (in the broadest meaning of that term), supported every man's "Propriety that excludes the Right of every other Subject." Exclusion of the sovereign, however, was rejected as inconsistent with the sovereign's responsibility to defend the rights of individuals from the incursions and injuries of foreign powers and other subjects. Hobbes does not appear to have enjoyed the affections of either party during or after the English civil wars.

16. Calvert defended himself by his assertion that "certainly any Monarchicall Government in forraign parts which is subordinate to, and dependent on, this Common-

wealth, may be consistent with it, as well as divers Kings under that famous Common-wealth of the Romans" (Calvert, 1988b [1653]:173). The exiled King Charles II, perceiving that Maryland sympathized with Parliament, commissioned Sir William D'Avenant in 1650 as lieutenant governor of the colony, "although Wee intend not hereby to prejudice the right of the Proprietary in the Soyle" (King Charles II in Calvert, 1988b [1653]:180).

17. Reeve (1980), in a rejoinder to Aylmer's article, disputes the timing and nature of the redefinition of property, but his critique explicitly recognizes the ambiguity inherent in the debate.

18. Searches for origins invariably are doomed to failure as one must always choose among, and pursue, threads of evidence that extend through time to the point where appropriate evidence does not exist. To portray the general population of late medie-val and early Renaissance England as essentially modern in respect to landholding is an overstatement of the case. Mcfarlane's evidence, however, does point out important inconsistencies in the logic of *plenum dominium* and that of *utile directum*.

19. The patent was issued during King Charles's "personal rule," the 11 years leading up to the English civil wars and during which Parliament went unsummoned. George Calvert died prior to the award of patent and the actual colonization of Maryland.

20. The very term "patent" implies a monopoly held at the discretion of the grantor, and not outright ownership as suggested by the term "deed." By granting patents, the lords Baltimore retained ownership (*plenum dominium*) and the right to charge rent. A deed surrenders all rights of the grantor, and his or her heirs, a point that is made formulis-tically in virtually all American land deeds of the nineteenth and twentieth centuries.

21. "I do swear that I will bear true faith unto his Lordship and his Heires as to the true and absolute Lords and proprietaries of [Maryland] and the Islands thereunto belonging, and will not at any time by words or actions in publick or private, wittingly or willingly to the best of my understanding any way derogate from; but will at all times as occa-sion shall require to the uttermost of my power defend and maintaine all such his said Lordships and his Heires Right, Title, Interest, Priveliges, Royal Jurisdiction, Pre-rogative, propriety and Dominion over and in the said province . . . and over the people who are or shall be therein for the time being" (Hall, 1988[1655]:214).

22. Initially, the warrants were issued at a rate of 100 acres per poll, but the proprietor reduced that to 50 acres out of a concern for the rapid depletion of desirable lands (*Arch. Md.*, I:331 [1651]). The headright system was abolished by Charles, the third Lord Baltimore, in 1683, the lands to be had for 100 pounds of tobacco per 50 acres. Proprietary conveyances still took the form of patents, and the lands remained subject to the annual quit-rent (*Arch. MD.*, V:390-391 [1683]). The quit-rent was a small, largely symbolic, annual fee paid in lieu of services that might be required of the tenant by the lord. In 1667, Cecil Calvert ordered the surveyor general, his nephew Baker Brooke, to limit the amount of waterfront included within a survey to no more than approximately 250 feet per 50 acres, this to allow each planter access to water trans-portation (*Arch. Md.*, V:95 [1667]).

23. Original document on file at the Maryland State Archives, Annapolis, Maryland. Here-inafter cited as *Patents*, liber and page numbers, and date of patent or warrant, if

known. The feast days of the Annunciation and Michaelmas were celebrated on March 25 and September 29, respectively.

24. Native Americans were enslaved, first by the Spanish, and then by the English colonists of South Carolina (e.g., Hartley, 1989). Why this practice never took hold in the middle and northern colonies is uncertain.

25. Main (1982:45 fn) estimates that an able-bodied field hand could cultivate 3 acres of tobacco, producing approximately 1,500 pounds of tobacco per annum. (Late twenteeth-century technologies and practices permit yields upward of 1,800 pounds per acre on the best soils.) With an average value of one pence per pound, a field hand could produce £6 of tobacco per annum, the cost of transportation to the colony.

26. For examples of sharecropper and overseer contracts, see *Arch. Md.*, LXX:86–89 and 237–239 [ca. 1680], respectively.

27. "Headright" refers to the claim for land that an individual could make on the proprietor for transporting an individual to the colony. Some immigrants could afford to transport themselves, and even family members, thereby retaining those headrights. Most, however, essentially sold their headright to their master or mistress for transportation to the colony. An individual could purchase land warrants from others, but it should be noted that all headright warrants were claims for land for which surveying and recording costs would be charged by the colony's secretary and for which a semiannual rent was due. Land was by no means free, although it was generally inexpensive (Beverley, 1947[1705]:273)

28. Bruce (1964) puts illiteracy rates for Virginia men at between 40% to 46%, women at 75%, during the period 1641–1670. Based largely on signature data, these are overestimates.

29. This is a more detailed and explicit enumeration of freedom dues than expressed in the interregnum-period act of 1654 (*Arch. Md.*, I:352–353).

30. In their analyses of the estate accounts of Robert Cole in St. Mary's County, Maryland (1662–1673), Menard et al. (1988) and Carr et al. (1991) effectively confirm Durand's observation.

31. Michel's observations closely mirror some of those made by Durand nearly 15 years earlier, suggesting that the former had read, and was influenced by, the latter's published report.

32. This practice has not been verified by independent sources and, as with much of what Michel reports, it should be accepted with reservations. It is difficult, for example, to see how a planter could gain from such an arrangement, other than by charging interest on the cost of passage.

33. Craven was responding to Abbott Emerson Smith's (1947) characterization of indentured servants as commodities to be bought and sold.

34. A planter (rather than an itinerant freedman) could take advantage of the high price of labor by hiring out skilled and unskilled workers to neighboring planters for short periods.

35. "[The planters] allow them [African slaves] to plant little Platts for potatoes or Indian pease and Cimnells [i.e., squashes], which they do on Sundays or night, for they work from Sunrising to setting" (Grove, 1732, in Stiverson and Butler, 1977:32).

36. As discussed in the next chapter, social historians working with Chesapeake material have focused on demographics and the distribution of wealth, with little attention given to the tensions that pervaded the social and political life of the colony during the seventeenth century. Such conflict that has been addressed generally has been examined as an extension of the religious quarrels occurring in England at the time, or direct economic conflict over a rapidly diminishing resource—arable land along navigable streams.

37. Slaves, male and female, over the age of 10 years were taxable at the same rate as all European males over the age of 16 (*Arch. Md.*, I:449[1662]).

38. In keeping with practices that continued up until emancipation, however, slaves could be convicted and sentenced to death for a variety of crimes, thereby raising the question: How can property commit a crime, much less assume responsibility for criminal behavior?

39. "And they [the United Provinces] still retain that sign of a Commonwealth yet uncorrupted, 'Private property, and public weal'!" (Overbury, 1964 [1626]:215).

40. Carl Becker, in *The Heavenly City of the Eighteenth-Century Philosophers*, states that "no serious scholar would now postulate the existence and goodness of God as a point of departure for explaining the quantum theory or the French Revolution" (1932:16), but those assumptions pervaded the thoughts of most people during the premodern and early modern eras.

Chapter **5**

Maryland in the Seventeenth Century

INTRODUCTION

The colonization of Maryland and Virginia during the seventeenth century has been the focus of intensive historical and archaeological study, particularly since the early 1970s. Studies of demographics and the distribution of wealth have been particularly prominent (e.g., Tate and Ammerman, 1979). This chapter reviews and synthesizes some of this material, particularly that which pertains most directly to a household's ability to produce wealth. A brief historical overview sets up more detailed discussions of population growth and the distribution of wealth.

HISTORICAL OVERVIEW

The English, under the patronage and rule of the Calvert family, conquered and colonized Maryland in the second third of the seventeenth century. The venture was part of a larger process of European commercial expansion in the Baltic, the Mediterranean, Southeast Asia, Africa, South America, Middle America, and the Caribbean. England competed fiercely with the French, Spanish, Dutch, and Swedes in North America. The Swedes succumbed to the Dutch in the Delaware Bay region before midcentury, and the Dutch surrendered to the English in Delaware and New Netherland in 1664, with a brief Dutch resurgence in 1673. The French and English continued battling over coastal Canada and the American interior until the Peace of Paris. England annexed Canada from the French, and Florida from the Spanish, in 1763.

European colonization was guided by a developing mercantilist model, wherein manufactured goods were exported to the colonies in exchange for raw materials, each country struggling to monopolize the trade of its colony while attempting to usurp the colonial trade of its rivals. Maryland colonists engaged in the international fur trade to a limited extent, but settled on tobacco production. Virtually every able-bodied adult was involved in tobacco planting, either directly or in a support or supervisory capacity. Tobacco is a 13-month crop, requiring the raising and transplanting of seedlings, weeding, removing insects and unwanted leaves, cutting, curing, stripping, and packaging. Few other trades were practiced and food crops were limited largely to production for home use and limited inter-colonial trade. The demands of tobacco culture and the policies of the proprietor-ship (see below) dispersed settlement and hindered the development of urban places. The capital was established at St. Mary's City in 1634 and remained there until it was moved to Annapolis in the early 1690s.

The colony suffered from political turmoil throughout most of the seven-teenth century, with Protestant-led insurrections against the Catholic proprietors coincident with major political upheavals in England in the 1640s, 1650s, and 1680s. The 1660s and 1670s—the restoration and reign of King Charles II—were years of relative peace and stability in Maryland, although tensions intensified between the English and their Dutch neighbors and commercial rivals. Proprie-tary rule continued until the abdication of King James II and the appointment of a royal governor by King William and Queen Mary.

POPULATION

In 1689, the Glorious Revolution occurred. James I, King of England, was deposed by Mary, his daughter, and William III of Orange, his son-in-law. The question of who would rule the realm—Papists or Protestants—was resolved. The Protestants were in, the Papists out. That was largely true of the government of Maryland as well. Fifty-five years after the colony's founding, this very basic conflict had been resolved. Power shifted to the Protestant majority who, in dem-onstrating and consolidating their authority, removed the colony's capital in the 1690s from the Catholic (and proprietary) stronghold at St. Mary's City to the established Protestant stronghold at Arundel Town (soon after anointed as the City of Annapolis; Luckenbach, 1995).

Conflict over the sharing of power, and over the proprietor's prerogative, beset the colony since its founding in March of 1634. Colonization occasionally was stalled by the conflict and sometimes, as with the rapid settlement of the eastern shore of the Chesapeake Bay, it was accelerated by the resulting divisions and internal migrations. International conflicts over sovereignty, control over

fisheries in coastal waters, and control over colonial trade often interrupted the
flow of peoples and goods across the Atlantic (Davis, 1975).

> The Quantity of Tobacco does not lessen the Price here but the want of ships
> to fetch it away which are not exported till the Lord pleases to remove the
> Scourges of War and Pestilence from our native Nation of England which war
> and pestilence is the only principal cause not only of the Contemptableness
> of our principal Commodity tobacco at present but of all Commodities in
> America. (*Arch. Md.*, II:44[1666])

The Lower House of the General Assembly protested a stint on the production of tobacco proposed by the Upper House as a means of raising the price of the
commodity.[1] Events in England, and particularly the outbreak of plague and the
second Anglo-Dutch war (1664–1667), were blamed for the fall in exports and
export prices, not the fall in demand in the overseas markets. Plague, war, and
falling commodity prices did little to encourage emigration to the New World.[2]

Outbreaks of plague severely limited emigration to the New World colonies,
insofar as those outbreaks resulted in legal and practical restrictions on internal
migration in England. Using passenger lists compiled in the port towns of Bristol,
London, and Liverpool, Horn (1979) demonstrates that emigration to the colonies was an extension of internal migration within England, itself a product of
enclosure and the growth of the international textile trade. The effects of enclosure were particularly profound, appearing as early as 1518, and documented in
the words of Thomas More's fictional character Raphael:

> Your sheep ... that used to be so meek and eat so little. Now they are becom-
> ing so greedy and wild that they devour men themselves, as I hear. They
> devastate and pillage fields, houses, and towns. For in whatever parts of the
> land the sheep yield the softest and most expensive wool, there the nobility
> and gentry, yes, and even some abbots though otherwise holy men, are not
> content with the old rents which the land yielded to their predecessors. Living
> in idleness and luxury, without doing any good to society, no longer satisfies
> them; they have to do positive evil. For they leave no land free for the plow;
> they enclose every acre for pasture; they destroy houses and abolish towns,
> keeping only the churches, and those for sheep-barns (More, 1975
> [1518]:14).[3]

More than a century of enclosures displaced rural agricultural workers,
some directly through ejectment and many indirectly through reduced demand
for laborers and artisans in supporting trades. Enclosure not only fueled emigration, it determined the character of the èmigrès. Approximately 47% of those
leaving from Bristol (lists of 1654–1686) for the Chesapeake colonies were agricultural workers, nearly double the percentage of those embarking from London
(lists of 1683–1684) (Horn, 1979:58). Bristol and Liverpool (lists of 1697–1707)

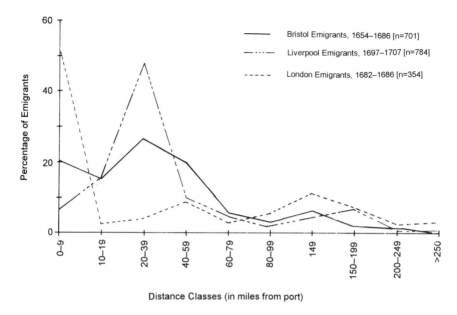

Figure 5–1. Distances traveled to ports by those emigrating to the Chesapeake colonies. (Source: Horn, 1979:69)

drew more than 80% of their departing emigrants from a radius of under 60 miles, whereas London drew more than 50% of its *departees* from a radius of less than 10 miles (Horn 1979:69; Figure 5–1). Many of the èmigrès, therefore, were city dwellers, unaccustomed to rural life and untrained in agricultural pursuits. Horn (1979:65) estimates that half of the èmigrès were unskilled workers, and many of them were under the age of majority.

The immigrants were largely young and male (Figure 5–2). The male to female ratio ranged between 6:1 to 3:1 in the passenger lists of the three principal ports (Figure 5–3). Prohibitions against marriage during terms of servitude, and English Christian prohibitions against procreation out of wedlock, exacerbated the problem of the relative scarcity of women, thereby severely restricting natural increase in the colonies.[4] Population growth throughout the remainder of the seventeenth century, and into the first quarter of the eighteenth century, was largely a matter of recruitment rather than reproduction, a point examined below in connection with households.

Despite outbreaks of plague and civil war, the population of Maryland grew and expanded beyond the pale of the village of St. Mary's City and throughout the coastal lands of the colony. Growth was gradual but steady throughout the seventeenth and early eighteenth centuries. By the second decade of the eighteenth

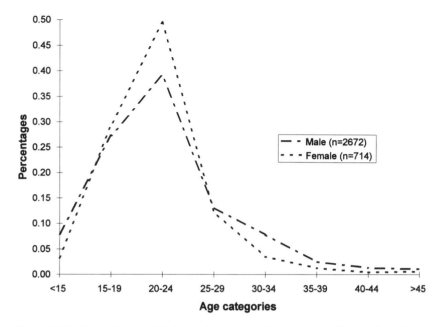

Figure 5–2. Ages and sexes of indentured servants emigrating to the Chesapeake colonies. (Source: Horn, 1979:62)

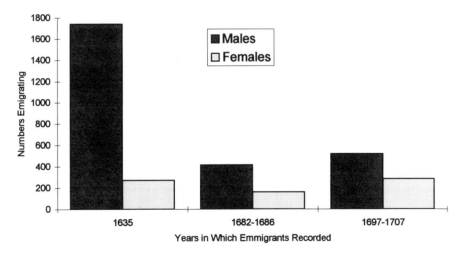

Figure 5–3. Female and male servants emigrating to the Chesapeake colonies. (Source: Horn, 1979:62)

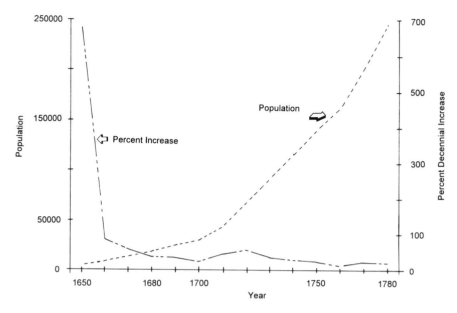

Figure 5–4. Population growth in Maryland, 1640–1790. (Source: U.S. Bureau of the Census, 1970:1168)

century, the population grew at a marked rate (Figure 5–4). Kulikoff (1986) attributes rapid growth throughout the eighteenth century to continued immigration into Maryland (both voluntary and involuntary) and natural increase.

Death rates among the Chesapeake colonists have been considered to be very high, possibly as an indirect result of the high incidence of malaria (Rutman and Rutman, 1979). Hugh Jones described the "seasoning" to those who remained in England:

> At the sudden Changes of the Weather, from Heat to Cold, People are apt to take Cold, often neglecting to shift [i.e., change] their Cloaths with the Weather; which with Abundance of Damps and Mists from the Water, and by eating too plentifully of some delicious Fruits, makes the People subject to Feavers and Agues, which is the Country Distemper, a severe fit of which (called a Seasoning) most expect some time after their Arrival in that Climate; but the Goodness of God has furnished us with a perfect Catholicon [i.e., general cure] for that Sickness, viz. the Bark: which being taken and repeated in a right Manner, seldom fails [to] Cure (Jones, 1724:50).

Rutman and Rutman (1979) suggest that the symptoms enumerated by the Reverend Jones indicate malaria, which, although not in and of itself a fatal disease, sufficiently weakened newcomers and made them more vulnerable to other, more lethal maladies such as dehydration through dysentery. The bark mentioned by Jones may have contained alkaloid salts comparable to those extracted from cinchona bark for the purpose of making quinine, a prophylaxis in the prevention of malaria.

Given the nature of the water supply and the near tropical conditions that persist in the region during the summer, there are a wide range of diseases and parasites that could have been transmitted from microbes to account for the "'Feavers and Agues.'"[5] Analyses are being conducted on human remains exhumed at St. Mary's City to determine whether or not malaria was endemic in the area in the late seventeenth century—this through the attempted extraction of antigens from a preserved cranial blood clot from one of three individuals interred within lead-lined coffins beneath the Catholic chapel (H. Miller et al., 1993).

Malaria and other diseases aside, those who voyaged to the colonies also suffered psychological stress, often without the benefit of family support. Even voluntary relocation could severely disrupt the mental health of immigrants, leading to higher incidences of homicide, suicide, alcoholism, and a general weakness of spirit that is reflected in the ability of individuals to fend off disease. Add to this the unfamiliar climate and surroundings, the change in diet, and the physiological and psychological stresses of the ocean voyage, and it is not difficult to imagine the poor state of health in which many immigrants arrived.

One observer, whose name is lost to us, claimed that the death rate in Virginia in the middle of the seventeenth century was lower than anywhere in England (Anonymous, 1649, cited in Force 1963:7; see also K. Thomas [1971] and Notestein [1954]). The validity of these claims remains to be tested. The tangible nature of surviving letters and published pamphlets (both attacking and defending the colonial situation), and the relative lack of good forensic data from the colonies, can lead to assessments that are based on political rather than medical evidence. Studies of regional mortality patterns have been conducted with reconstructed demographic data (e.g., Earle, 1979; Menard, 1975; Kulikoff, 1986; Rutman and Rutman, 1979), but confirming forensic data are limited to a very few samples, some of which are discussed in Chapters 9 and 10 of this work.

Whether or not the high death rate in Maryland was due to malaria, and whether or not the death rate was higher than that experienced in England, it is clear that life expectancy was short. Men typically lived to between 40 and 45 years of age, 75% dying before the age of 50 (Menard, 1975:182). Women fared even less well (Rutman and Rutman, 1979:177–182), due in no small part to the hazards of childbirth compounded by anemia, and nearly 50% of all children born in Maryland during the seventeenth century died before reaching the age of 20 (Walsh and Menard, 1974:193, 222).[6] Death rates were ameliorated somewhat in the eighteenth century as the population developed natural immunities to local diseases and cultural means of dealing with local climatic conditions.[7] As noted above, natural increase led to a more balanced sex ratio among Europeans and enslaved Africans (Kulikoff, 1986), providing a more stable population and labor force.

Indentured servitude, the unbalanced sex ratio, and high mortality contributed to the creation of novel household forms on the Chesapeake frontier. All male households, consisting of two or more 'mates,' established their own plantations, usually upon the expiration of their indentures, sharing work in the fields and on the homelot. Menard (1975:323–329) estimates that more than one-quarter of all male colonists in Maryland during the seventeenth century died unmarried.[8] High death rates, the lateness of marriage (as indentured servants were prohibited from marrying), and the high incidence of remarriage upon the death of a spouse resulted in mixed households consisting of

> orphans, half-brothers, stepbrothers and stepsisters, and wards running a gamut of ages. The father figure in the house might well be an uncle or a brother, the mother figure an aunt, elder sister, or simply the father's "now-wife"—to use the word frequently found in the conveyances and wills [of Middlesex County, Virginia]. (Rutman and Rutman, 1979:167)[9]

What probably distinguishes this situation from North American households of the eighteenth and nineteenth centuries is the high frequency with which mixed households occurred during the first century of colonization. Also, as illustrated in Figure 5-2, seventeenth-century households were young, with the majority of servants arriving during their midtwenties and death generally occurring by age 45. The above-cited passage omits servants, but they may have been present in the majority of households in seventeenth-century Maryland.

WEALTH-HOLDING

Population growth and mortality monopolize the time of many Chesapeake historians, but those subjects represent only one moiety of a larger interest: the formation of a highly stratified Chesapeake society. The creation and distribution of wealth, and the role of wealth in the formation of Chesapeake society, represents the other focus, and it is to this second moiety that we now turn our attention.

Probate inventories and land records figure prominently in scores of analyses conducted by a relatively small group of Chesapeake Bay regional historians, born and bred into the "new social history." This group focused its research on the social and cultural development of the Chesapeake Tidewater, a region defined by a common history and culture rather than by political institutions. Archaeologists contributed to this work insofar as they have sought to reconstruct the material world of the colonists (e.g., Pogue, 1993). These studies, historical and archaeological, address two processes: the creation of wealth and its distribution among the members of Chesapeake society.

The Creation of Wealth

The discussion in Chapter 4 clearly establishes labor as an integral component in the creation of wealth during the early Colonial period. The role of land in the generation of wealth also has been touched upon and is addressed at somewhat greater length in Chapter 6. At this point, let's explore the actual process of creating wealth, or value, in the Chesapeake wilderness; particularly in terms of social organization and activities. The principal questions are:

1. Where was wealth produced?
2. Who produced wealth and how?
3. How was wealth distributed?

The Production of Wealth

Wealth can be produced in factories. It can be produced in the shops of tradesmen. Wealth can be produced in mines and quarries, and in the banks, brokerage firms, and shipyards of large urban areas. But early colonial Maryland was entirely rural. It had few shops, no factories to speak of (although there were some sawmills and gristmills and several iron furnaces), no banks or brokerage firms, and few shipyards worthy of the name. What Maryland did have was the tobacco plantation: small, family-owned and -operated farmsteads dispersed across the landscape, producing tobacco, and, to a lesser extent, livestock and grains. Production occurred within the household, as did consumption. Wealth was accumulated within the household, with few opportunities for the large scale accumulation afforded by urban life (Leone, 1983).

Households in the Chesapeake Tidewater region consisted of mixtures of near kin, extended kin, half kin, and non-kin, that is, servants and slaves. They did not necessarily share a single roof, the household cluster (*sensu* Wilk, 1991) probably occurring most often. Indeed, the early use of the 'quarter' (a house or homelot for servants or slaves spatially divorced from the house or homelot of the planter's family) segregated the members of a plantation household, sometimes in clusters lying at considerable distances from one another. Nonetheless, household heads, or their appointees, organized all work.

Labor was organized around two basic and, perhaps, structurally analogous categories: gender and servitude. Men and women, ideally, undertook different kinds of tasks. I say ideally because there were texts written in England (e.g., Markham, 1986 [1615]) describing the tasks men and women ought to do and how they should go about doing them. Various court cases, the briefs of which have been preserved in the P*roceedings of the Provincial Court of Maryland* (Arch. Md.), also reflect certain expectations. One such brief, for example, notes that Mary Clocker's husband sued an individual for the fees due Mary for her midwifery services, provided "in the busiest time of her dairy" (Arch. Md., XLI:335 [ca. 1650s]). As part of a sharecropping agreement with John Baker, Nicholas Maneire's wife (name not recorded) was "to Dresse the Victualls Milke the Cowes, wash the servants [clothes] and Doe all things Necessary for a woman to doe upon the sd. [Warners] Plantation" (*Arch. Md.*, LXX:87 [1681]). Hammond [1656] described women's duties as follows:

> Women are not (as is reported) put into the ground to worke, but occupie such domestique imployments and housewifery as in England, that is dressing victuals, righting up the house, milking, imployed about dayries [i.e., making butter and cheese], washing, sowing [read *sewing*], etc. and both men and women have times of recreations, as much or more than in any part of the world besides, yet som wenches that are nasty, beastly and not fit to be so imployed are put into the ground, for reason tells us, they must not at charge be transported and then maintained for nothing, but those that prove so awkward are rather burthensome than servants desirable or usefull. (Hammond, 1988 [1656]:290–291)

Hammond states that women were not expected to work with men in the fields. Only those who were "nasty, beastly and not fit" to be employed about the house were relegated to the fields, although what he conceived to be beastly and nasty is unknown. Hammond tried to persuade his compatriots to emigrate to the Chesapeake colonies,[10] and it perhaps was no accident that he neglected to list gardening and livestock care—manual labor conducted out of doors and in the area of production rather than consumption—among women's chores.

Beverley provides the following observation regarding women's work in Virginia during the first decade of the eighteenth century:

> Sufficient Distinction is also made between the Female-Servants, and Slaves; for a White Women is rarely or never put to work in the Ground, if she be good for any thing else: And to Discourage all Planters from using any Women so, [Virginia] Law imposes the heaviest Taxes upon Female-Servants working in the Ground, while it suffers all other white Women to be absolutely exempted [from the poll tax]: Whereas on the other hand, it is a common thing to work a Women Slave out of Doors; nor does the Law make any Distinction in her Taxes, whether her Work be Abroad, or at Home." (Beverley, 1947 [1705]:272)

While the ideal of women working within the homelot is clear from the above quotes, it also should be clear that some female servants worked out in the fields. What our informants fail to tell us, in a straightforward, unambiguous way, are the conditions under which European women worked in the fields. We might hypothesize that those households suffering from temporary or chronic labor shortages could not achieve the ideal, particularly those with few means with which to purchase the indentures of healthy servants, or those with few or no children or extended kin of sufficient age and strength to assist in the fields (Main, 1982:109). There also is the possibility that some women preferred working in the fields to working in and around the house, although no evidence of such behavior has emerged to date.[11]

While gender provided a conventional means for dividing tasks and responsibilities on the plantation, the statuses of free and unfree also were integral to, and perhaps paramount in, the division of labor.[12] Enslaved Africans of both sexes generally were assigned to work in the fields, and both were counted among the taxables. Male European servants found much of their employments in the fields, and they too were accounted taxable. Beverley, (1947 [1705]:271–272) reports that

> the Male-Servants and Slaves of both Sexes are imployed together in Tilling and Manuring the Ground, in Sowing and Planting Tobacco, Corn, etc. Some Distinction indeed is made between them in their Cloaths and Food; but the Work of both, is no other than what the Overseers, Freemen, and the Planters themselves do.

The ideal work situation for men and women in the Chesapeake colonies during the seventeenth century, as described by contemporaries, has women working in and around the homelot and men working in the fields, on ships and wharves, in taverns, and in any other places in which political and economic business was transacted. Some court records, such as the lawsuit to which Mary Clocker was a party (cited above), indicate that some women were engaged outside of their own homes, albeit generally in the homes of others or in ordinaries. The exchange of homemade goods and services, such as dairy products, also occurred, although on what scale is difficult to determine. Such exchanges were recorded only as incidentals to other events, usually those of direct importance to men.

Women were responsible for reproducing the household by providing for its immediate needs. They produced and processed certain foodstuffs, cooked, laundered, cleaned house, raised and educated children, raised cash crops, and maintained the physical plant of the farm. Men probably arranged most market purchases since such purchases generally were on a credit basis; the credit was issued in the names of the heads of households, the majority of whom were men. Precisely what role women, children, and servants of both sexes had in the purchase of manufactured goods is uncertain.

The realities of the division of labor by sex differed from the ideals in at least two respects, only one of which may be quantifiable. Some unmarried men formed partnerships early on in their agricultural careers, sharing domestic and agricultural duties. The frequency of such relationships can be charted simply by counting the number of unmarried male decedents dying without family, leaving their property to their surviving "mate." Calculating the number of women engaged periodically or regularly in agricultural work outside of the homelot garden is difficult, and may be impossible. The colonial government did not conduct regular censuses, and many European men may have been less than proud of having their female kin working in the fields; hence they were unlikely to record such a practice for their peers, much less for posterity. The colonial government of Virginia discouraged the employment of European women in the fields with a poll tax (Beverley, 1947 [1705]:271–272, quoted above).

The documentary record provides little data on the occupations of women. Architectural remains and the degree of spatial patterning of activity areas at archaeological sites may provide the best evidence of a well-defined sexual division of labor, with larger, wealthier plantations yielding evidence of large labor forces and task-specific activity areas (Gibb, 1991; Gibb and King, 1991).[13]

It is important to point out that the cultural ideal of a rigid sexual division of labor was adhered to imperfectly, with those of lesser means less likely to comply with the moral order. Men and women collaborated in building plantations, and that included production, processing, preparation, and presentation of food as well as clearing arable. It required mending clothes, tending gardens, and minding livestock as much as it did planting and harvesting tobacco and grains. Contracting for labor, generally men's work, was pointless—and perhaps impossible—if women did not produce the necessary domestic services required to feed, clothe, and shelter the servants.[14] In short, both men and women were involved in the production of tobacco, and in the reproduction of the household.

Spatial segregation and the assignment of tasks on the basis of sex may appear to have divorced women from "production" (and there is little enough evidence of that), but their part in household production was of such importance that the noun "contribution" tends to trivialize and peripheralize their role in the agricultural economy. The household economy in the Chesapeake Tidewater region, as in most agrarian societies, was wholly integrated. Extraction for study of a set of activities labeled 'consumption' runs the risk of analytically destroying the very relationships with which we are interested. Production and consumption, and the roles of men and women, within the colonial household should be viewed as complementary and interdependent.

The Distribution of Wealth

Share though they might in producing wealth on the plantation, men and women did not necessarily share equally in that wealth, nor did each household share equally in the net wealth of the colony. Servants received only a small portion of what they produced, and slaves received even less. Historians may disagree on just how unevenly wealth was distributed in colonial Maryland (e.g., Kulikoff, 1986; Carr and Menard, 1979), but all would agree that there were rich persons and poor, free persons and those committed to servitude for a few years or for life. The principal area of concern has been changing opportunities for the accumulation of wealth during the course of the seventeenth and eighteenth centuries and, therefore, in identifying the point at which the hierarchical, autocratic society of the southern colonies emerged and how it differed from the allegedly more egalitarian societies of the north.[15]

Carr and Menard (1979) explored the changing opportunities of ex-servants in the Chesapeake region for the latter half of the seventeenth century, addressing in part Morgan's (1975) surmise that decreased opportunity during this period contributed to a growing threat of impoverished freedmen rebelling against the established order.[16] Although Carr and Menard describe how the downturn in the tobacco market, beginning in the 1660s and accelerating in the 1680s, limited opportunities for the social and economic advancement of freedmen, they conclude their paper on a positive note: a sufficient number of recent successes always were in sight to convince individual freedmen that material success was possible. For those not so convinced, there was the ever-expanding frontier in which to seek opportunity.

Carr and Menard also note that a freedman's ability to achieve material wealth depended upon his ability to form a household through marriage, procreation, and servant recruitment. With the death rate measured at 40% of all servants prior to completion of their terms of indenture (Carr and Menard, 1979:209) and with a male to female ratio of 2.5:1 by the end of the century, the probability of forming a household, and thereby accumulate wealth, begins to look rather bleak.[17]

Historians seem to agree that as late as the 1680s, individuals who arrived in the colonies as servants stood a plausible chance of establishing their own plantations and living reasonably comfortably.[18] Those that paid their own passage and brought families or capital with them to Maryland were more likely to succeed, and to pass the patrimony on to their children.

Women shared in the production of wealth (Carr and Menard, 1979), but shared unequally in it when the head of household died, the land going to the male heirs and only some movables such as cattle, some servants or slaves, and interior furnishings going to the daughters (Norton, 1984). Although a woman might be responsible for producing half of the wealth of a plantation, legally she could expect only a life interest in one-third of her husband's estate, unless he bequeathed the estate to her without entail. The ideal was to pass on the estate as intact as possible to the eldest surviving son, carrier of the family name and vessel of its honor.

Unfortunately, most historical analyses focusing on the distribution of wealth deal with men only (e.g., Menard et al., 1988; Menard, 1973; Carr and Menard, 1979; Walsh, 1977). While modern prejudices play some part in this biased perspective, the skewed nature of the principal data source—probate inventories—is far more pronounced in its influence. Wealth, in most cases, was legally held by the male head of household, or by his wife in trust for their children. Women are most prominent in the wills left by their male kin, often appearing as their husbands' executors and beneficiaries.

Unless a prenuptial agreement was signed prior to remarriage,[19] a woman's property became that of her new husband, the woman retaining rights only to her dower (Prior, 1990:203). For example, Mary Hodges, widow of John, made the following agreement on the day before her remarriage:

> Mary Hodger the present Executrix unto John Hodger deceased being through the permittance of Almighty God intended to mary doth by these presents before the day of Matrimony make over and give unto her Son John Hodges one Complete Suit of bedding that is to Say one feather bed and bolster and rugg and two blanketts with a Suit of Searge Curtaines and Vallence trimmed with Silk frenge as also a fowling piece and an Iron Pott; . . . more to be added one Silver Sack Cup & a dram Cup. (*Arch. Md.*, X:419 [1655])

Mary Prior (1990), in her analyses of sixteenth- and seventeenth-century women's wills in England, found that women increasingly secured rights to property, largely through trusts that guaranteed them incomes and the right to devise an interest in estates.

Wealth distribution among men has been studied primarily using two related means. The simplest technique has been simply to map out the distribution of estates by total value (exclusive of land). Such analyses (e.g., Carr and Menard, 1979) emphasize secular trends in the overall distribution of wealth, and touch only briefly on the forms of wealth involved. Such analyses note the trend toward concentration of wealth into fewer and fewer hands. Gloria Main (1982) pursued the more difficult route in analyzing the contents of probate inventories from six Maryland counties for the period 1656 to 1719 to examine the distribution of forms of wealth. Her analyses demonstrate the limited nature of goods owned by even the wealthiest planters, differences among all decedents characterized as much by quantity as variety of possessions: "The principal differences between rich and poor lay not in the size and quality of housing but in the number of structures" (Main, 1982:148; see also 151ff.).

As with other historical studies relying on probate data, however, Main's results must be used with care. She notes, for instance, that "earthenwares" appear in only 36% of the decedents' inventories (Main, 1982:170). This finding contradicts archaeological findings, where the number of households that owned and used pottery is a consistent 100%. Some earthenware vessels may appear in the inventories as fry pans, skillets, pots, and kettles, all of which Main lists in much higher percentages of the inventories and, apparently, assumes to be metal. Given the lack of familiarity with archaeological findings exhibited in the following quote, it is likely that she overlooked this possibility: "Large drinking vessels, in particular, require a malleable, durable, lightweight material, and useful substitutes for pewter seem to have been lacking" (Main, 1982:171, fn. 10). English and Rhenish stoneware tankards, jugs, and drinking pots were large, but neither malleable nor particularly lightweight. They are common, however, in seventeenth- and early eighteenth-century assemblages. Ceramic skillets and fry pans are also common in some assemblages, a point to which we will return in Chapters 8 through 11.

Of greater import than the occurrence of specific objects in households of varying wealth is the issue broached in Chapter 2. That wealthy people own more stuff, greater varieties of stuff, and stuff of generally better quality is self-evident. After all, that is why some households are considered wealthy and others are not. We still need to move beyond that tautological vortex and begin to examine the meaning of goods. As Main points out, the estates of some of the wealthiest individuals in early colonial Maryland consisted of modest quantities of goods of inconspicuous value, with most of their wealth invested in lands, livestock, and labor (Main, 1982:148, see also 151ff.). The critical difference is in how those goods—those items of wealth—were used.

SUMMARY

Throughout the seventeenth century, the population of Maryland was diffuse, small, and virtually incapable of reproducing itself. It consisted of people coming from very different cultural backgrounds including those of provincial and urban England and Ireland and, to a lesser extent, various parts of the African and European continents. Life was brief and health appears to have been generally poor. Most productive and consumptive activities occurred within households, which varied greatly in size and constitution. Wealth was unevenly distributed among and within households, but the nature of the market (foreign manufactured goods on a nonindustrial scale) and the limited access that the colonists had to that market (cargoes transported by tobacco merchant ships) restricted the range of goods that any one household could acquire. Differences among households were largely quantitative rather than qualitative.

Although there has been a tendency to regard most domestic materials as evidence of consumption (i.e., the discretionary expenditure of profits from the sale of tobacco), domestic artifacts played an important part in the production of the colonists' livelihoods. The designation of certain goods, particularly those employed in and around the homelot in women's activities, as "consumer goods" is a manifestation of late twentieth-century prejudices that undermines our ability to examine the creation of colonial life and its development in subsequent centuries. The arbitrary assignment of certain objects to production and others to consumption defines and "explains" consumption and its relationship to production *a priori*. Consumer behavior theory, thereby, is given little opportunity to explain the unequal and varied distributions and uses of wealth.

Labor has been identified as one of the principal means by which wealth was created on the colonial Chesapeake frontier. Labor cleared land and planted and harvested "provisions of victuall," as well as cash crops. Labor produced, processed, prepared, stored, and presented food, and labor built and improved the plantations and moved the household when the plantation was no longer tenable. Land distribution was an important factor in determining how much wealth a household could produce through its labor, and it is to that issue that the next chapter is devoted.

NOTES

1. The Upper House proposed a prohibition on the planting of tobacco during the 1666/1667 season in order to reduce supply and increase the price. Given the centrality of tobacco to household economies and to the regional economy, this proposal was ill-conceived and destined for outright rejection by the Lower House. Arguments in support of the stint also betray a high degree of naïveté on the part of the members of the Upper House regarding market mechanisms and their continued adherence to mercantilist principles, the notion of demand inelasticity not least among them. This concern for "overproduction" continued among Western nations throughout the eighteenth and nineteenth centuries.
2. Cole (1964:555) notes that most commodity prices declined during the second half of the seventeenth century after decades of rising prices attendant upon the large influx of precious metals into Europe via Spain. Economic circumstances affecting emigration to the American colonies were not confined to the ebb and flow of the tobacco market.
3. Beresford and Hurst (1990) report 40 years of archaeological research at Wharram Percy, Yorkshire (UK), complementing More's parable with tangible evidence.
4. Childbearing during the term of indentures confused the issue of "ownership" of labor: was a child born under these circumstances indentured as well, and thereby required to serve until his or her attainment of majority? Were the reproductive abilities of women servants part of the "package"?

5. Negative archaeological evidence suggests that water was drawn from surface springs, rather than from wells, in the Chesapeake region. Shallow barrel-wells have been discovered in Virginia.
6. Ubelaker, et al. (1993) also point out the ubiquity of malnutrition, as evidenced in the skeletal remains of some colonists. Unfortunately, nutritional stress suffered prior to emigration is indistinguishable from later stress without supporting biographical data. To date, none of the individuals excavated in the region can be identified by name.
7. Deep wells laid up with fired brick were common in the Tidewater region in the eighteenth century.
8. Based on analyses of wills, this estimate underestimates the number of dual-sex households. Nonsanctioned cohabitations between Europeans and Native Americans, between Europeans and Africans, and between unmarried European men and women are unlikely to be recorded among legal records, particularly conveyances of property rights. Mixed, and other unconventional marriages, may be counted among the defining characteristics of European colonial frontiers.
9. Based on their analysis of a 1687 census compiled in neighboring Delaware, Grettler and Seidel (1993) report a remarkably low average of four individuals per household, with only 20% having three or more children in residence.
10. See Holifield (1989) for a discussion of the literature of persuasion that characterizes the period.
11. Could it have been these women to whom Hammond referred to as "nasty and beastly"?
12. Servitude, of course, also existed in Europe: it was not a novel institution confined to colonies.
13. For example, Neiman (1980) uncovered evidence of a dairy area at the late seventeenth/early eighteenth-century Cliffs Plantation in Westmoreland County, Virginia. Dairying in Anglo-American culture—outside of commercial dairying—was generally women's work (e.g., Markham, 1986 [1615]; Hammond, 1988 [1656]:290).
14. As part of his contract, planter Hugh French was supposed to provide his overseer, Thomas Swaney, with "sufficient diet, washing and lodging" (*Arch. Md.*, LXX:237 [1680]).
15. See also Fischer (1989) for a folkways approach to this same problem.
16. The leaders in "Bacon's Rebellion" in Virginia in the 1670s, however, were not impoverished freedmen. They were moderately well-off planters seeking social and political, as well as economic, advancement.
17. Taking the 60% survival rate reported by Carr and Menard (1979), and multiplying it by the 75% marriage rate reported by Menard (1975:323–329), yields a 45% rate, or a less than even chance of survivorship and family formation for men, not particularly good odds given the stakes. The odds of successfully forming a family were better for women who could use the unbalanced sex ratio to advantage.
18. Grettler and Seidel (1993) are far less sanguine in their characterization of late seventeenth-century colonial life in central Delaware. Debt and an inability to retain ownership of their lands were two of the three "facts of life" with which Delaware colonists (most of whom were ex-servants from Maryland) contended.

19. The prospective groom usually contracted with a third party, since marriage nullified contracts signed by the prospective bride. The object was to preserve the family estate for the decedent's male heirs. For example, Martha Ashcomb protected her deceased husband's estate through a contract between John Dansey, her intended husband, and Major Dent (see *Calvert County Wills*, 11:266 [16 November 1702]; 14:150 [27 September 1716]; and 18:256 [22 April 1724]).

Chapter **6**

Land and Settlement Patterning in the Pursuit of Wealth

INTRODUCTION

Europeans settled in the Chesapeake colonies for a variety of reasons. Durand of Dauphiné described Virginia as a refuge for those "unable to earn a livelihood in England," as well as a place of exile for those felons transported from England.[1] "Persons of quality," disenfranchised from family estates through the rule of primogeniture, also emigrated to the New World where they might "live in high state on little wealth" (Durand, 1934 [1687]:109–110). Beverley recognized the opportunities for these dispossessed worthies, as well as the haven that Virginia provided for those "persecuted for their Principles of Religion, or Government" (Beverley, 1947 [1705]:286–287; see also Milton, 1950 [ca.1645]:509-519). Those and, perhaps, other reasons account for why certain individuals emigrated to the colonies. But why should the colonists invest limited resources in bringing others over?

The reason for the large number of indentured servants imported by established settlers into Maryland, and neighboring Virginia, is simple enough. Extensive tracts of land in the colony were relatively easy to come by, through land warrants from the land office, or through purchase or rent from other colonists (Michel, 1916 [1702]:116–117, 124); but the land had little value without having people to clear and plant it. Labor applied to land produced wealth. The amount and quality of land to which a household had access, and its proximity to waterborne transportation, determined the household's potential to produce wealth.

As discussed in Chapter 4, the precise nature of land ownership was a point of some debate. Much of that debate, however, was legalistic and, as Aylmer

93

(1980) pointed out, the degree to which ambiguity in the meaning of ownership affected the outcomes of legal disputes remains to be studied. One point, however, should be kept in mind: Maryland planters paid rent. Trifling though that rent might have been—2 shillings, or about 24 pounds of tobacco per year per 100 acres—it was still rent, and that indicates tenancy rather than outright ownership. Concern for who owned land and who rented the land of others through sharecropping or annual leases diverts scholarly attention from the obvious fact that no one in Maryland, or anywhere in English America, owned land. That point always must be kept in mind as attitudes toward the land and the built environment are examined.

The more pedestrian aspects of landholding practices are equally important. How much land did planters, on average, have access to? To what extent did the natural advantages of tracts vary? Lacking access to land and labor—the basic materials whence wealth derives—the issue of consumer behavior is moot: One could produce wealth or appropriate wealth produced by others. Most planters in Maryland did both. Patterns in the distribution of land provide a basis for examining variability in consumer behavior, as well as household strategies in producing wealth. Variability in tract size and quality are analyzed in this chapter.

VARIABILITY IN TRACT SIZE

Compiling data on landholding patterns from Maryland's colonial land records is a substantial undertaking, the investment in time of which would be out of proportion with the principal subject of this work—the application of consumer behavior theory to seventeenth-century archaeological assemblages. Fortunately, a body of sample data already exists. During the 1930s, Vertrees J. Wyckoff, professor of economics at St. John's College in Annapolis, compiled data on seventeenth-century land sales and prices in the colony (Wyckoff, 1937, 1938). These data are presented and reinterpreted in this section. The specific questions addressed include the following:

1. How was land distributed among plantations?
2. Did the nature of that distribution change during the course of the seventeenth century?
3. Were attitudes toward land and land tenure reflected in the distribution of land among the colonists?
4. Did land values change during the course of the century?

Wyckoff drew his data from the land records of seven eastern Maryland counties (Figure 6–1): Anne Arundel (AA), Baltimore (BA), Charles (CH), Dorchester (DO), Kent (KE), Somerset (SO), and Talbot (TA). Wyckoff omitted Cecil

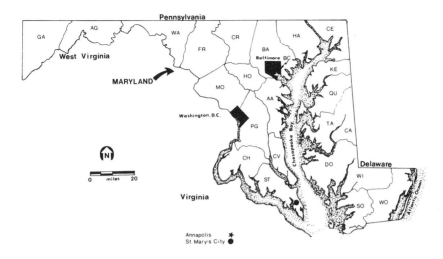

Figure 6–1. Sample counties in tract size analysis.

(CE) and Prince George's (PG) counties because of the late dates at which they were erected (1674 and 1695, respectively). He omitted St. Mary's (ST) and Calvert (CV) counties, the two earliest, because he thought that most of their early land records had not survived. Wyckoff chose 1663 for his beginning date (the year in which recording of land conveyances became mandatory) and 1699 as an end date.[2] He selected a maximum of 10 nonproprietary (i.e., private) land sales for each county for each of the sample years, drawn in the order in which they were recorded. Conveyances that did not reveal the value of the sale, or that concealed the price in a patently nominal charge, were omitted from the sample. The total sample of nonproprietary land sales for the period 1663 to 1699 amounted to 1,683 individual conveyances.

Wyckoff recorded five variables for each of the sales in the sample: date of conveyance, places of residence for buyer and seller (not addressed in this analysis), acreage, land price, and whether or not the land was improved (i.e., whether the land had been cleared and built upon; also omitted in this analysis).[3] Wyckoff defined acreage classes arbitrarily by 100-acre intervals, except for the first class, which includes tracts of 1 to 49 acres. Lacking the original raw data, it is impossible to redefine the classes with greater statistical rigor. In order to mitigate the sampling bias created by the patenting of land in multiples of 100 acres (initially, the basic unit for headrights), Wyckoff made multiples of 100 the central numbers in each class (Table 6–1). He then lumped these data together by decade, without regard to county, assigned the values to acreage classes, and converted them into percentages.

Table 6-1. Non-proprietary Land Conveyances for Seven Eastern Maryland Counties, 1663–1699

Class	1660	Proportion	1670	Proportion	1680	Proportion	1690	Proportion	Total
1–49 acres	0	0.00	1	0.00	13	0.02	12	0.02	26
49–149	30	0.27	205	0.40	200	0.38	237	0.45	672
150–249	30	0.27	147	0.29	170	0.32	153	0.29	500
250–349	20	0.18	87	0.17	64	0.12	61	0.11	232
350–449	12	0.11	23	0.05	28	0.05	26	0.05	89
450–549	7	0.06	22	0.04	23	0.04	20	0.04	72
>550	11	0.10	24	0.05	35	0.07	22	0.04	92
Total	110	1.00	509	1.00	533	1.00	531	1.00	1683

Source. Wyckoff, 1937.

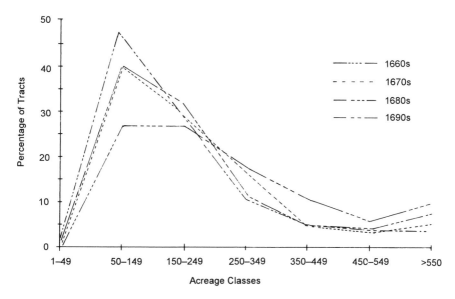

Figure 6–2. Distribution of tract sizes by acreage class, 1663–1699. (Source: Wyckoff, 1937)

The distribution of tract sizes, as represented by a sample of private, nonproprietary conveyances, was remarkably uniform throughout the last third of the seventeenth century. The broken-line graph in Figure 6–2 illustrates the distributions. Only the trend line for the 1660s differs, and the distribution of frequency data for that decade is significantly different from that of succeeding decades.[4] This anomaly can be attributed to a period of accommodation wherein the colonists were just beginning to become accustomed to filing their patents in the wake of new legislation. Given the costs involved in alienating a tract of land, the fees in filing the patent, and the annual quit-rent due on the land, purchasers may not have been inclined to formally record such transactions, particularly when only small tracts were involved. The distributions may underrepresent tracts under 149 acres.[5]

Wyckoff (1937) suggested that there had been a decrease in tract size over the latter third of the seventeenth century, based on his visual inspection of the percentage data. He attributed this trend to partible inheritance, the sale of portions of tracts by land speculators, and the demand for land occasioned by the increase in the colony's population. The graphic analysis of the growth in population presented in the previous chapter (see Figure 5–4), however, suggests that the increase in demand would have been gradual and might not have dramatically affected the distribution of tract sizes.

Male decedents, insofar as it was possible, tended to bequeath land to each of their sons, their daughters usually receiving cattle and other movables (Norton, 1984). A perusal of the abstracts of wills in the Maryland State Archives, however, suggests that men attempted to buy several tracts to provide for their sons: they tended not to divide existing tracts. Again, the costs of transferring land combined with the costs of resurveying a tract may have discouraged subdividing. Menard et al. (1988:189) note an instance of this practice wherein an estate administrator purchased tracts of 200, 210, and 115 acres for three of the decedent's sons, the eldest inheriting the 300-acre home plantation upon his achieving the age of majority.

Purchasing land for one's sons was a simple matter. Through headrights or purchases from other colonists, planters could acquire sufficiently large tracts to get each of their sons started. A tract might not be optimally located in terms of access to navigable water or to high-quality soils, and it might be located farther from the home plantation than the parents might like, particularly given the possibility of shared labor among kin. The principal stumbling block to acquiring land for one's sons, however, was the "Conditions of Plantation," wherein the lord proprietor stipulated that the land must be cleared and a house built upon it within three years of award of patent. A planter, therefore, had to time purchases of land very carefully to avoid the problem encountered by William Stephens:

> Uppon ye Pet[ition] of ye [plaintiff, Thomas Trueman] concerning a Parcell of Land Surveyed by ye [defendant, William Stephens]; and forfeited by ye Condicions of Plantation of which the [plaintiff] having notice procured with lawful warrant & took up the same land.—the [defendant] (although forewarned by the pltf) hath seated and built upon the said land, and disturbed ye pltf. And the deft appealing to the Court in Equity It is Ordered ye pltf satisfy ye Deft what he payd to the Carpenters for building, and satisfaction also for the nayles. (*Provincial Land Records/Judgments Records*, S:109, 1658).

Evidently, upon learning that his tract was patented to Thomas Trueman, William Stephens built a house on it to satisfy the "Conditions of Plantation" and nullify the escheatment, or forfeiture, of patent. The ruse did not work, and Stephens still had to provide land for his two sons.

Land speculation did occur, as evidenced by some individuals on the proprietor's council (a.k.a. the Upper House of the General Assembly) who had patented tens of thousands of acres.[6] This, of course, was far more land than was necessary to provide for one's children. In many cases, speculation took the form of land leasing, the tenants required to improve the land as well as to share some of their produce with the patentee. This arrangement was common in the region in the eighteenth century (Stiverson 1977). Whether or not speculation, combined with increased demand, raised the price of land can be determined using Wyckoff's land price data (Table 6–2).

**Table 6–2. Median Land Prices in Pounds of Tobacco per Acre,
1663–1699**

Year	Median	Year	Median	Year	Median
1663	15	1675	29	1687	31
1664	16	1676	31	1688	32
1665	17	1677	28	1689	35
1666	18	1678	29	1690	32
1667	16	1679	32	1691	49
1668	28	1680	27	1692	39
1669	19	1681	34	1693	40
1670	28	1682	28	1694	41
1671	19	1683	29	1695	43
1672	25	1684	30	1696	31
1673	30	1685	25	1697	37
1674	27	1686	31	1698	44
				1699	37

Source. Wyckoff, 1938.

Wyckoff's median land prices are plotted in Figure 6–3 against Menard's (1973) median tobacco prices. Transforming these data with three-year running means smooths the peaks and valleys in the distributions, thereby facilitating comparison. The three-year running mean attempts to account for farmers' decisions, averaging the past year's experience with current conditions and projected conditions for the following season.

The patterns are unmistakable: while tobacco prices dropped, land prices increased. This relationship may come as no surprise if tobacco is seen as a stand-in for money. One needs more money/tobacco as its value is deflated in order to purchase the same amount of a commodity/land that one could have purchased when the money/tobacco was of a higher value. In a market economy, wages must rise in order to meet rising costs without curtailing sales; otherwise demand drops, eventually leading to a drop in prices. But tobacco was not money: it was, and is, a commodity. The only way to get more is to grow it, and that takes a great deal more effort than programming a machine to print additional certificates of tender.

Where land values doubled during the seventeenth century as a result of the fall in tobacco prices, households had to produce twice as much tobacco to purchase land. That required twice as much labor. The fall in tobacco prices throughout the seventeenth century must have had a debilitating effect on the ability of most households to expand production and to purchase goods. Given the vital importance of acquiring sufficient land for producing tobacco,[8] we might expect purchases of imported goods to decline across the colony while land prices rose.

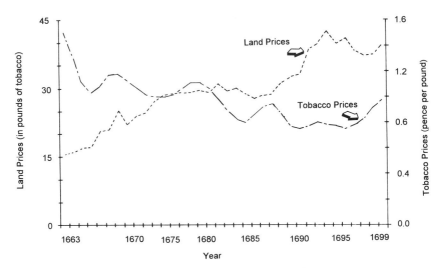

Figure 6–3. Tobacco prices and land prices in seven Maryland counties, 1663–1699; expressed as three-year running means. (Sources: Menard, 1973; Wyckoff, 1938)

Also, we might expect a proportional increase in credit sales of land and other goods, and a concomitant rise in indebtedness and foreclosures.

Land was instrumental in tobacco production. In the face of declining tobacco prices, households were forced to increase the amount of land under intensive cultivation to maintain their income. In the absence of intensive agricultural practices (manuring, crop rotation), the chemical composition and drainage of the soil determined the quantity and quality of the crop. Those households with access to high-quality tobacco soils were likely to get the best prices from visiting merchant ships: those producing small yields of indifferent or poor quality might gain little, and perhaps nothing, for their efforts. Understanding the variability in productivity of soils is essential to understanding the variability in income that characterized colonial households, and their ability to procure manufactured goods.[9] Toward this end, we must examine patterns in plantation siting.

VARIABILITY IN PLANTATION SITING[10]

Smolek (1984) and Lukezic (1990) developed predictive models for the seventeenth- and eighteenth-century settlement of the Tidewater region, and Edwards and Brown (1993) have called for the testing and refining of these models with data from recently identified sites. Reps (1972) describes settlement patterning in the region as dispersed, with little aggregation, despite repeated

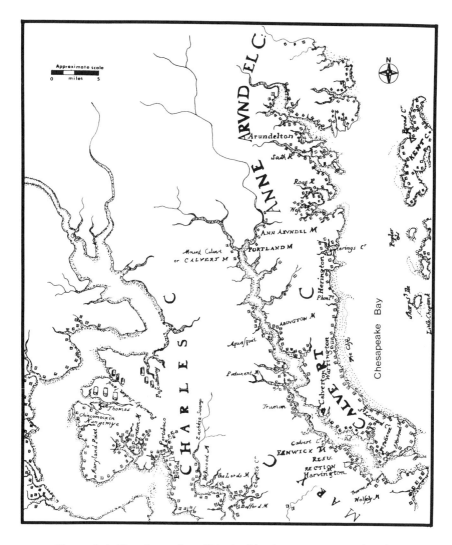

Figure 6–4. Map of a portion of Maryland by Augustine Herrman (1673).

attempts by the lords proprietary to legislate the creation of towns (see also Kelly [1979] for similar developments in Virginia).

The colonists needed large tracts of land to accommodate the long fallow periods required after two to three years of tobacco cultivation. They also chose sites along the shores of the navigable tidewater creeks and rivers to allow for the efficient transportation of tobacco to merchant ships. Francis Bacon recognized the convenience of such a pattern during the early years of Virginia settlement, but recommended that the colonists move their habitations as soon as it was feasible:

> It hath been a great endangering to the health of some plantations, that they have built along the sea and rivers, in marish [read *marshy*] and unwholesome grounds. Therefore, though you begin there, to avoid carriage and some other discommodities, yet build still upwards from the streams, [rather] than along (Bacon, 1955c [1625]:91).

Bacon's advice appears largely to have been ignored until the second quarter of the eighteenth century when large manses were constructed on eminences well above, but still in view of, the principal streams of the region.[11]

The importance of navigable water in selecting a plantation site is nowhere more evident than in Augustine Herrman's 1673 map of the Chesapeake Bay and its tributaries (Figure 6–4). It is a crude map, drawn aboard ship and exhibiting the bias of a coastal survey. Each plantation is represented by a single structure, presumably indicating a dwelling, and all sense of variability is subordinated to the principal statement of the cartographer; namely, Chesapeake settlements were decidedly coastal in nature.[12]

Cecil Calvert recognized the importance of water frontage to the colonists when he ordered Baker Brooke, surveyor general of Maryland (and Calvert's nephew), to

> take special Care that there be not Surveyed for any Adventuror or Planter above fifteen Pole [245.5 feet] of the sides of any Creeke or Rivers of the Said Province [of Maryland] for every fifty Acres due to any such Planter or Adventuror by his Lordships Conditions of Plantation or other warrant and so respectively of Greater Proportions without special and express directions from his Lordship to the Contrary and the rest to be laid forth up into the inland Correspondent to that which each one hath respectively on the water side according to the proportion aforesaid that so Conveniency of Access to the water side be preserved to every planter upon each of their respective Plantations for the better Transportation of their Goods. (*Arch. Md.*, V:95 [1671])

Cecil Calvert also appreciated the importance of towns as loci of trade and services, and their contribution to the self-sufficiency of the colony. That he recognized their role in capital accumulation is less certain, but he did understand the relationship between towns and his ability to regulate (hence tax) trade.[13]

The General Assembly of Maryland, with the encouragement of the lords Baltimore, legislated the creation of towns and tobacco inspection warehouses during the last quarter of the seventeenth century and the first quarter of the eighteenth century (e.g., H. Miller, 1988; Pogue, 1984; Reps, 1972). The proprietary government reserved, not actually purchased, town sites from local planters, and subdivided the sites into small lots for sale to individual residents, reserving lots for such public facilities as chapels, courthouses, jails, and tobacco inspection warehouses (e.g., Hurry, 1990). One such town, Calverton, was platted in 1668 on Battle Creek in Calvert County, and served as the county seat for nearly half a century (Pogue, 1985; Figure 6–5). Its replacement, St. Leonard, was platted in 1706 near the head of navigable water at St. Leonard's Creek (Figure 6–6). The regularity of the lots, imposed on irregular topography (Hurry, 1990), stands in marked contrast to the irregular polygonal tracts patented as plantations. The significance of that regularity, and the placement of such public buildings as churches, court houses, and jails on town tracts, probably did not elude potential lot buyers, or, in this case, nonbuyers.

Most legislated towns failed to materialize. Planters simply refused to buy and settle lots that were distant from their agricultural holdings, and where all their transactions were subject to scrutiny and taxation:

> Neither the Interests nor the Inclinations of the Virginians induce them to cohabit in Towns; so that they are not forward in contributing their Assistance towards the making of particular Places, every Plantation affording the Owner the Provision of a little Market; wherefore they most commonly build upon some convenient Spot or Neck of Land in their own Plantation, though Towns are laid out and establish'd in each County. (Jones, 1724:35)

As Paynter and McGuire note, "An important characteristic shared by all successful revolutions was the ability of the rebels to physically isolate themselves from the central power" (1991:15). The Protestant majority realized this maxim with the establishment of Arundel Town (later known as Annapolis) in the 1650s and their subsequent designation of the town as the colonial capital in the 1690s (Luckenbach, 1995). The average planter recognized its wisdom every day of the seventeenth century in choosing a dispersed form of settlement.

The paradox of the Calverts' dual strategies of aggregating and dispersing the Maryland population is further exemplified in Cecil Calvert promoting the settlement of the eastern shore of the Chesapeake Bay beginning in the early 1660s. Concerned over Dutch infringement on his patent, Calvert proposed easy terms for those willing to settle on what today is referred to as the Delmarva peninsula. Many planters and freed servants accepted the proprietor's terms, patenting and erecting plantations at a great distance from what had been the core of the colony. Whether by happenstance or design, many of those who removed themselves to the eastern shore were Protestant sectaries, particularly Puritans and Quakers. Many came from Calvert County, the seat of the revolutionary government during the Protectorate in the 1650s. One possible by-product of this great migration in the mid-1660s was the lessening of political tensions between Catholic royalists

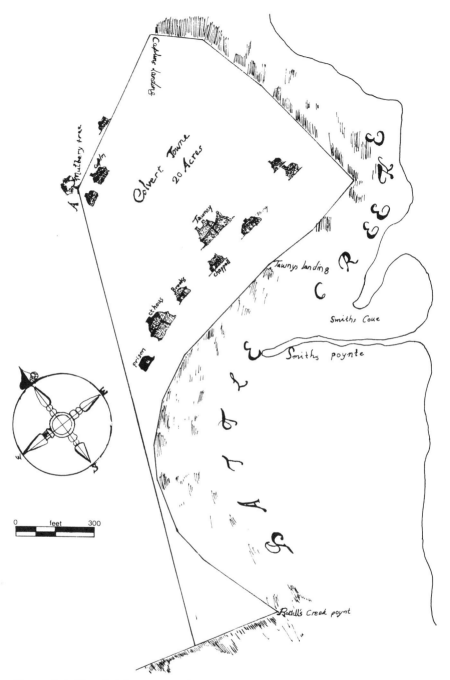

Figure 6–5. Plat of Calverton in Calvert County, surveyed by Charles Boteler, 1668, and resurveyed in 1682. (Source: Robert Jones Survey Book, 1682–1684; Maryland Historical Society, MS 446, volume 1)

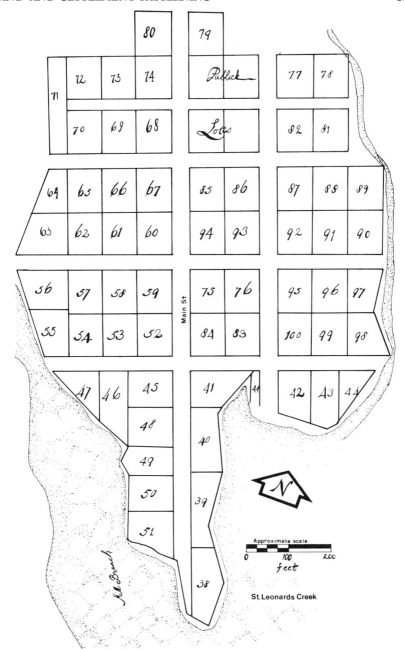

Figure 6–6. Plat of St. Leonard, post-1706. (Source: Hurry, 1990)

and Protestant parliamentarians. Space provided a temporary solution to a political problem.

The apparent contradictions in the actions of Cecil and Charles Calvert may have been products of conflicting goals and realities. Constantly striking a balance of interests on both sides of the Atlantic, the Calverts tried to increase their control over the colonists by mandating the erection of towns, while—purposely or inadvertently—limiting the colonists' ability to organize and express a common interest through the "Conditions of Plantation" by which land patents were issued. Most planters dispensed with the conveniences and investment opportunities offered by town life and maintained direct control over the land and labor that produced their wealth. Urban amenities did not influence plantation siting for most colonists; access to navigable water and productive soils did. The criteria by which planters selected plantation sites affected the politics of space and the potential for accumulating wealth.

Locational Analysis

Smolek's (1984) analysis of seventeenth-century site locations demonstrated that nearly 90% lie within 5,000 feet of the shoreline and 80% could be found within 2,000 feet of the shore. He also demonstrated that 92% of the seventeenth-century sites that had been found in Maryland up until 1984 occurred on, or near, good or prime tobacco soils.[14] Smolek's model appears to be substantially correct in terms of its ability to predict the locations of typical seventeenth-century sites, particularly when complemented by archival data; however, his model does not explicitly address variability. Given the premise that soil quality, tract size, and access to navigable water determine the potential of a plantation to produce wealth, any comparative analysis of wealth-holding among the colonists should address plantation siting. In collaboration with Esther Doyle Read, I have developed and refined a method for identifying and describing variability in plantation siting (Gibb and Read, 1992), the results of which are presented below.

By current standards, the soils of southern Maryland were good for the cultivation of tobacco, but not uniformly so. Using modern soil surveys (Figure 6–7), we can see that between 40% and 60% of the soils in St. Mary's, Anne Arundel, and Calvert counties produce little or no tobacco. Less than 10% produce very high yields, while 30% to nearly 60% produce moderate to high yields. Two edaphic factors have the greatest effect on the quality and quantity of tobacco that a given soil will produce: the composition, texture, and drainage of the soil, and the degree to which it has been eroded. Erosion would have had little part in the decision making of prospective patentees during the seventeenth century since the amount of clearing (and attendant erosion) by Native American groups appears to have been very limited. It was the quality of the soil that influenced plantation siting considerations. Several observers noted that vegetation patterns

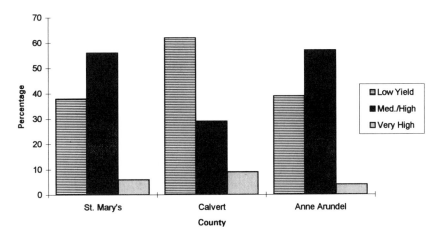

Figure 6–7. Soil regimes of Calvert, St. Mary's, and Anne Arundel counties, Maryland. (Source: U.S. Department of the Interior 1971, 1978, and 1979)

indicate degree of soil fertility, although they provided few specifics (e.g., H. Jones, 1987 [1699]; H. Jones, 1724; see Beverley 1947, [1705]:123–125,129, for the most detailed discussion).

Methodology

Wyckoff's data are useful for estimating variability in the size of Maryland plantations; however, they are unsuitable for determining the potential productivity and monetary value of individual plantations. Data from the colony's rent roles are of little value in this regard since the annual quit-rent on each patent was based on the number of acres patented, and not on the value of the land and improvements.[15] Due to the crudeness of the land surveys and the sketchy manner in which they were described, it is difficult—if not impossible—to locate most patented tracts on the ground with any precision. The following patent description is atypical in the sense that it is relatively rich in detail:

> Laid out for Ishmael Wright of this Province, Planter, a parcel of land lying on the North side of the Patuxent River near to the land of William Stephens, Beginning at a marked Oak and bounding on the River with a line drawn South South West from the Said Oak for the length of Sixty and five perches unto a marked ash on the South with a line drawn East and by South from the said ash for the length of One hundred and twenty perches to a marked Chestnut Tree on the East with a line drawn North North East from the Chestnut unto Stephens Land on the North with the said Land Containing

and now laid out for seventy-five acres more or less (Land Records, AB&H 322, 08 August 1651).

The description for William Stephens Land (*Land Records*, AB&H 354–355, 08 August 1651) is similarly vague, but is not wholly destitute of landmarks. The first course of that survey ran from the northwest corner of Wright's tract ("Compton") for some 80 perches along the river to a marked white oak tree standing near Stephens Creek. Several nineteenth-century deed references identify Stephens Creek as Hungerford Creek, the location of which is clearly noted in nineteenth-century land records. Identifying the location of a single tract appearing in the colony's patents and rent rolls could involve many weeks of piecing together adjoining tracts from such descriptions, often with little else to go on than the surveyor's cryptic notes.

Accurately locating a statistically valid sample of seventeenth-century tracts on the ground would be challenging, to say the least. Moreover, it is clear from numerous lawsuits throughout the seventeenth, eighteenth, and nineteenth centuries that these surveyed tracts were very difficult to identify on the ground at the time of their initial survey. Committees were formed to periodically walk the perimeters of tracts to establish boundaries, indicating that tract boundaries were defined on the basis of custom as much as by formal survey.[16] The precise sizes of tracts were as much at issue as their boundaries. Menard et al. (1988:186), for example, note that a resurvey in 1678 of St. Clement's Manor in St. Mary's County, Maryland, found 11,400 acres rather than the 6,000 acres noted in the original 1641 survey.[17] Given the difficulty in retracing seventeenth-century patents on twentieth-century maps, and the dubious value of such an exercise, patent descriptions have been rejected in favor of the locations of known archaeological sites. In so doing, however, plantation size must be eliminated from the analysis since few rural seventeenth-century sites have been tied directly to specific patents.

Using ceramic assemblages as a guide, all archaeological sites in southern Maryland that could be attributed to the period 1640 to 1725, with a reasonable degree of confidence, were drawn from the site files of the Maryland Historical Trust.[18] Sites found at St. Mary's City, the seventeenth-century capital of the colony, have been eliminated from the sample due to their unique urban setting. A total of 44 sites, spanning five counties on the Chesapeake Bay's western shore, were located on topographic and soils maps. Distance to navigable water and productivity of surrounding soils have been calculated from these maps for each of the sites.

Measuring the distance between a seventeenth-century plantation site and the nearest navigable water is not as simple as it may seem. Headland erosion has pushed the shoreline back hundreds of feet in some places, and centuries of poor farming practices silted up those small creeks that were navigable in the seven-

Figure 6–8. Transparent grid and its placement over seventeenth-century colonial
sites. (Source: Gibb and Read, 1992)

teenth and early eighteenth centuries. Distances to the shorelines of the principal
waterways have been measured as if there had been no appreciable loss of land to
erosion: there simply is no means for identifying seventeenth-century coast-
lines.[19] Deeply cut creeks are assumed to have been navigable, despite the thick
silts that fill them today.

Measuring soils around known sites requires a more complicated procedure.
Noting the kind of soil that a site occurs upon or adjacent to is inadequate, as
those soils may not be representative of the plantation. For example, a site may be
located on a small island of highly productive Matapeake silt loam, only to be

surrounded by a sea of nonproductive (in terms of tobacco) Othello silt loam, or vice versa. Any attempt to compare the potential productivity of seventeenth-century tobacco plantations must involve a standardized technique for quantifying the range of available soils around each site and their potential yields.

Soil surveys provide yield ratings for most of the soils in the five sample counties. Five categories are defined on the basis of late twentieth-century tobacco yields: no or low potential (<700 lb/acre), medium (700–1,100 lb/acre), high (1,100–1,500 lb/acre), and very high (>1,500 lb/acre) potential. Soils around each site were measured with a square transparent grid (Figure 6–8). Each grid is drawn to the appropriate scale for a particular series of soil maps, and includes 25 grid squares encompassing a total of 100 acres. The selection of the 100-acre grid was informed, in part, by the analysis of Wyckoff's tract-size data (see above): it represents a standardized measure of a meaningful size that facilitates intersite comparisons. In cases where a site lies directly on the shoreline, it is centered on one side of the grid; otherwise, the grid is centered squarely over the site and the principal soil in each grid square recorded. Two or more soils may occur in a grid square, but only the most extensive soil is recorded (Figure 6–9).

Current soils ratings take into account the severe erosion that has occurred in the region over the past 350 years. All of the values for each of the sites, therefore, have been recalculated based on the ratings achieved for each soil type in a noneroded condition. For example, Caroline silt loams will produce moderate quantities of tobacco (700–1100 lb/acre) in an eroded condition but high yields (1,100–1,500 lb/acre) on a relatively level, stable surface. The frequency of each predominate soil type is computed and assigned a tobacco yield value of zero to very high. The numbers of grid squares dominated by each yield class are then computed (the total being 25 in each case) and multiplied by four; thereby transforming the data into index values with a maximum absolute value of 100. The resulting values are not, strictly speaking, percentages. The high-yield soil class at the Melon Field site (18CV169; a.k.a. the Roscoe Brown site) dominates in 28% of the grid squares, it does not necessarily constitute 28% of the soils around the site. These are index values, they are not area measurements. A digitizer could be used to calculate precise percentages; however, a standard area still would have to be imposed on each site since the tract boundaries, in most cases, are unknown. Again, the method samples available soils in the immediate vicinity of known early colonial sites, it does not necessarily produce an accurate measure of a plantation's soils.[20]

Each site ($n = 44$), then, bears its own soil signature based on the constellation of soil types in its immediate vicinity. The data are analyzed using Kintigh's (1992) k-means statistical procedure. Although frequently used in spatial analysis, k-means cluster analysis has been used effectively to derive taxonomies (e.g., Doran and Hodson, 1975:218–264; see also Kintigh, 1990). It is a nonhierarchi-

GRID SQUARE	SOIL TYPE	GRID SQUARE	SOIL TYPE
1,1	Tm	3,4	WoB
1,2	SrE	3,5	ReC
1,3	MuB2	4,1	WoA
1,4	MuB2	4,2	MnB2
1,5	M1C3	4,3	WoB
2,1	W	4,4	SrE
2,2	MnB2	4,5	SrE
2,3	MnA	5,1	WuB2
2,4	EvB	5,2	My
2,5	HyD3	5,3	MnB2
3,1	WoA	5,4	ErE
3,2	MnA	5,5	SrE
3,3	WoB		

Figure 6–9. Example of a soil data recording form. (Source: Gibb and Read 1992)

cal, divisive clustering procedure that operates on large numbers of observations with modest numbers of variables (a maximum of 8,000 data values—Kintigh, 1992:1).

The program goes through a two–way process of calculating and recalculating centroids for a given number of observations and variables, always seeking to minimize intracluster variances while maximizing intercluster distances (Kintigh and Ammerman, 1982:39). Means are calculated for each variable for a particular cluster level, while minimizing the squared summed errors (SSE, or the sum of the squared Euclidean distances) for each object from the centroid of the cluster to which it has been assigned:

$$SSE = \sum_{i=1}^{n} \sum_{j=1}^{var} (X_{ij} - XC_{ij})^2$$

where X_{ij} is the value for unit i on variable j and XC_{ij} is the mean of variable j for the cluster including unit i.

The SSE is first calculated for the entire data set. SSEs for successive cluster levels are calculated and compared to the SSE for the entire data set (i.e., for the one-cluster solution). The analyst instructs the program as to the number of clusters to be computed, usually—but not necessarily—based on a hypothesis as to how the data are structured. The resulting values, or their percentage transformations, are then plotted on a two-dimensional trend-line graph. The cluster level at which the line deviates markedly (beyond the second cluster level, which usually shows a marked deflection) generally indicates a potentially meaningful solution. The analyst, of course, determines whether or not the solution is meaningful within the context of the particular problem domain.

Kintigh also developed a subroutine that randomizes the sample data for each variable and allows the analyst to run simulations of chance distributions. Since the randomized data are normally distributed for any given number of runs, a mean and standard deviation can be calculated and the resulting linear trends in the SSEs plotted against those generated from the original data set. Using this procedure, it is possible to determine whether the trend in SSEs derived from the original data could have been arrived at by chance.

Results

The k-means analysis was conducted for 44 sites on the distance of each site to navigable water and the index values for the four types of soils: no potential, low-, medium-, and high-yield potential. Table 6-3 presents the SSEs computed for 10 cluster levels for the original data set and for 100 random runs of the randomized data. The means and two-standard deviation ranges calculated for the randomized data are plotted along with the SSEs for the original data set in Figure 6–10.

Based on the trends illustrated in Figure 6–10, particularly the sharp deviation of the trend line, a six-cluster solution best describes the clustering of observations. The position of the SSE trend line below the randomized data trends, particularly beginning with the six-cluster solution, suggests that the pattern is not a chance occurrence. The six-cluster solution falls well outside of the two-standard-deviation range calculated for the randomized data, with a 5% error.

Table 6–4 provides summary statistics for each of the classes of site, based on the potential of their surrounding soils to produce tobacco. Cluster 2 is an outlier, and has proven to be so at several levels of clustering, with and without the distance to navigable water variable. The site Glenn Wood IV (18ST287) lies within a mosaic of soils of varying productivity. Other sites should occur in similar soil regimes if, following Francis Bacon's advice (1955c [1625]:114), the colonists sought a "mixture of grounds of several natures"; but, then, Bacon had never been in the American colonies, nor did he anticipate the degree of monocropping that eventually characterized much of Maryland's western shore.

Table 6–3. Sum of Squared Errors (SSE) for Original and Randomized Data
for Cluster Levels 1 through 10

Cluster	Data SSE	Percentage of data SSE	Mean of randomized data SSE	Percentage of mean of randomized data SSE	−2 standard deviations	+2 standard deviations
1	225	1.00	225	1.00	225.0	225.0
2	182	0.81	178	0.79	170.9	185.1
3	126	0.56	136	0.60	126.4	145.6
4	87	0.39	102	0.45	92.6	111.4
5	48	0.21	77	0.34	66.7	87.3
6	33	0.15	59	0.26	49.5	68.5
7	26	0.12	49	0.22	41.3	56.7
8	21	0.09	42	0.19	35.4	48.6
9	18	0.08	37	0.16	31.0	43.0
10	14	0.06	33	0.15	27.4	38.6

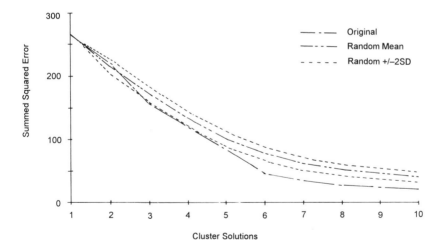

Figure 6–10. Plot of the sum of squared errors for the original data and the mean
and 2*SD* range of summed squared errors for the randomized data.

The two sites of Cluster 3 are anomalous in terms of their distances from
navigable water. Inland sites from the period 1634–1725 are rare and, perhaps, are
different in other respects as well. Middle Plantation (18AN46) was occupied

Table 6–4. Summary Statistics for Soil Regimes Around Seventeenth-Century Sites, by Cluster

	Distance (feet)	No yield	Low yield	Medium yield	High yield	Very high yield
Cluster 1 (n = 14)						
Median	1000	10	0	0	84	0
Range	50–5000	0–36	0	0	48–92	0–28
Cluster 2 (n = 1)						
Observed	3400	12	32	4	48	4
Cluster 3 (n = 2)						
Median	15,500	6	0	6	88	0
Range	13,500–17,500	0–12	0	0	88–88	0
Cluster 4 (n = 6)						
Median	2500	14	0	32	38	2
Range	100–3750	4–28	0–8	24–52	20–60	0–36
Cluster 5 (n = 7)						
Median	200	92	0	0	0	8
Range	50–600	60–100	0	0–20	0–24	0–8
Cluster 6 (n = 14)						
Median	725	20	0	0	20	54
Range	50–1500	0–44	0	0–28	0–52	28–92

beginning in the late seventeenth century and continuing throughout much of the eighteenth century. The Turner site (18CH209) is the only seventeenth-century colonial site reported for Charles County to date, and it—like so many early colonial sites examined in southern Maryland—remains unreported. Its attribution as a seventeenth-century site is based on a large number of terra-cotta tobacco pipes recovered from the surface of a plowed field (M. Smolek 1992, personal communication). It is possible that the Turner site represents a Native American or creole site.

The remainder of the 41 sites fall into four clusters: numbers 6, 1, 4, and 5, in descending order of potential productivity and preferred location relative to waterways. The large standard deviations, relative to their corresponding means, for most of the variables indicate that there is a fair amount of variability within each cluster. Excavated samples from each of the sites, or from representative samples of each cluster, could be analyzed to determine what, if any, relationship exists between locational variability and material culture variability. Unfortunately, few of the sites in the sample have been excavated, and fewer still are sufficiently well reported to admit any comparisons. The point of this experiment, however, is to illustrate the range of variability in tobacco yields and market access that might be expected based solely on plantation siting. It is clear from this analysis that the variability was considerable, even without the inclusion of tract size among the variables.

Interpretation

Choices in plantation siting were constrained by several variables. The quantity of land that could be patented depended upon the headrights one owned, and the number of acres one could improve sufficiently to comply with the proprietors' "Conditions of Plantation." Alternatively, land could be leased or privately purchased. The size and quality of a plantation depended on the availability of unpatented lands and the soil regimes of a particular area. Extensive areas of level to gradually sloped land with high-yield tobacco soils were considered optimal, even if we are uncertain about how the colonists assessed soils. Direct access to navigable water was critical, both for commerce and for communication with one's neighbors.

The cluster summary data presented in Table 6–4 are particularly telling, both in terms of the principal choices and the outcome of those choices. Of the 44 sites 28 (64%), are situated on high to very high yield soils (clusters 6 and 1), and most of those lie within 1,000 to 1,500 ft. of navigable water. These were the preferred sites. Planters occupying such sites—all other things equal—were best able to support and expand their households, and thereby create and accumulate more wealth. Those occupying tracts with mixed soils, such as those represented by Cluster 4, could compete less successfully in tobacco production. The variety of available soils could have demanded or encouraged diversified agriculture, admitting the diversified farmer into the coastal trade in foodstuffs. Given the rapid decline in tobacco prices after 1660, and the general problems inherent in a monocropping economy, the less than optimal mixture of soils may have proven profitable in the long term.

Seven of the 44 sites (16%) are situated on soils that are poor at best. Four (18ST323, 347, 357, and 360) are situated in the midst of Othello silt loams; a soil that is worthless for raising tobacco. Were these poor choices, or were these sites chosen for purposes other than tobacco cultivation? These sites may represent satellite household clusters, housing stockmen, ferry operators, or other specialists. None have been investigated to date, but each may bring a new perspective to Chesapeake archaeology by forcing us to look at non-plantation sites and by reminding us that some households extended beyond the confines of single homelots.

The means, medians, and other values presented in Table 6–4 are convenient measures of variability. Unfortunately, they reveal little of the true nature of variability in plantation siting. They may represent the range of wealth enjoyed by Maryland planters—from great wealth to even greater poverty—or they may reveal a degree of economic specialization that is not well represented in surviving documents. Until those sites are excavated and analyzed, our understanding of plantation siting and its social and economic ramifications will continue to rest on a very poor footing.

SUMMARY

The above analyses demonstrate, and to some extent quantify, variability in the sizes, potential productivity, and transportation access of tobacco plantations in southern Maryland during the latter half of the seventeenth, and first quarter of the eighteenth centuries. Productivity was not simply a matter of plantation size. Whether by chance or design, some plantation sites possessed certain advantages over others in terms of both access to water transportation and potential soil productivity.

The stability seen in Wyckoff's (1937, 1938) data suggests that the colonists generally did not subdivide tracts, but tended to convey them intact. Even the sale of proprietary tracts in the late seventeenth century probably involved lands that escheated to the lord proprietor due to nonsettlement, nonpayment of rent, convictions of treason, or determinations by the Coroner's Court that the owner had committed suicide. Variability in tract size, soils, and proximity to navigable water lay at the heart of a plantation household's ability to produce tobacco, the form and measure of wealth in colonial Chesapeake society. It also suggests variability between households in terms of their strategies in using and producing wealth.

The last major ingredient to this mixture is labor, which has been discussed in Chapters 4 and 5. Unfortunately, the labor forces at most plantations cannot as yet be reconstructed: census and poll tax data simply do not exist in sufficiently detailed form to include labor into the above analysis. The only way to estimate the number of individuals present, hence the availability and organization of labor at a plantation site, may be through analyses of archaeological and architectural data, for example, comparative analyses of interior spaces, homelot size, or degree of spatial complexity.

The economic empiricism of the above experiment should not overshadow the political and symbolic nature of landholding. Conflicting goals and solutions for both proprietor and planter resulted in a highly dispersed, decentralized settlement pattern with very few central places of note. Had Cecil Calvert prized social and political control over his concern for land sales, or had the planters preferred the conveniences and opportunities of central places over their fear of proprietary control, the resulting settlement pattern may have been very different, and we would be dealing with a very different society with a very different culture.

This chapter, along with the previous three chapters, demonstrates several dimensions of variability in seventeenth-century Chesapeake society. Wealth, commodity, land, and labor were not singular concepts to which all individuals subscribed. In the case of commodity, it is difficult to see what, if any, difference a diversity of opinion would have had on the colonists. Perhaps the distinction between natural resource and product of labor had some relevance in disputes over the proprietor's rights to the fur trade and claims to a percentage of any precious metals recovered from the earth. On the other hand, the lords Baltimore appear not to have been interested in controlling the taking of game, oysters, or fishes within their realm, other than by those who were not resident in the colony.

The nature of wealth also may not have affected the ways in which the colonists dealt with one another and their social superiors, but the lack of accord over what constituted wealth is confronted by every scholar who has dealt with the colonial Chesapeake region, and colonial America as a whole. Much of the variability identified in probate inventories may be a result of differing opinions as to what constituted wealth and what did not. Menard et al. (1988) set "tools" apart from "consumer goods" without defining what a tool is and without providing a theoretical justification for making such a distinction, and their study represents but one instance of a general pattern in the scholarship of the region. Is an earthenware pot found within a decedent's kitchen a commodity, a part of his overall wealth?

Yentsch (1990b:30) notes that until 1700, the majority of decedents in the Annapolis, Maryland, area did not own ceramics. Between 1697 and 1723, only about 50% of the inventories listed ceramics despite the fact that every colonial period site that has been subjected to even minimal archaeological testing produced ceramics. Menard et al. (1988:189), in their analysis of probate inventories for decedents on St. Clement's Manor, St. Mary's County, Maryland, for the years 1658 through 1665, found that 11 of the 29 householders did not have tools listed among their possessions; yet they must have had axes and hoes. They suggest, unconvincingly, that such tools may have been included under "old iron" or "old lumber." Are we missing or misidentifying sites and grossly misunderstanding the nature of early colonial society in the Chesapeake Bay region, or are there some fundamental problems inherent in probate inventories as a source of data?

A likely solution to this problem is that not all of the probate enumerators recognized certain objects as things of value or as the property of the decedent. For example, in some cases women may have been regarded—implicitly or explicitly—as the owners of ceramics and other kitchen furnishings, thereby separating those objects from the rest of the estate.[21] Many enumerators may have regarded such mundane items as pottery and hoes as things of little value for which they could not readily assign a price, namely, things that were permanently decommoditized. Unfortunately, no studies relating the social characteristics of executors and enumerators to variability in probate inventories have been published. It is odd, however, that the colonial authorities appear not to have questioned the completeness of most probate inventories, despite the great deal of variability that we can see in surviving inventories.

Ambiguities in the meaning of land ownership and the rights of labor, ironically, are far clearer than what constituted an object of value and who it belonged to. Ownership in general was openly debated in England's Parliament and in Maryland's General Assembly. The rights of labor and the responsibilities and rights of employers were constantly assessed and redefined through civil and criminal court cases. The ambiguous position of enslaved Africans further complicated the issue, requiring legislators to clarify relationships that they may have preferred to leave vague. More important, the conflicts and tensions over land ownership and the rights of labor were played out across the landscape on a daily basis. Indeed, those conflicts and tensions created the seventeenth-century Chesapeake landscape, in terms of both the overall settlement pattern and the spatial organization of individual plantations. In such a context of ambiguity and conflict, consumption of goods was not simply a by-product; it was an elemental force, shaping and re-creating social relationships as much as any land patent or act of the General Assembly. But before we begin to examine how objects, space, and resources were used, it is necessary to explore in greater depth the larger environment in which they were used. Chapter 7 examines the Chesapeake Tidewater environment, and available resources, from the perspective of the colonists, providing the final overlay in this construction of cultural-historical context.

NOTES

1. Hammond (1988 [1656]:285) also notes the transportation of convicts to Virginia during the early years of settlement. That practice continued fitfully throughout the seventeenth and eighteenth centuries. Defoe's *Moll Flanders* conveys some of the flavor of transportation and settlement.

2. "An Act for the Enrollment of Conveyances and Securing the Estates of Purchasers," enacted in 1671, required filing of all conveyances with the secretary of the colony within six months of contract signing and at a fee of 12 pence, plus 16 pence per side of folio sheet in recording the particulars of the transaction (*Arch. Md.*, II:307). Wyckoff refers to acts reprinted in *Arch. Md.*, I:61–62, 159–160, 194, and 487–488 (1663).

3. Wyckoff distinguished between improved and unimproved tracts based upon his reading of the transactions, examining each for evidence of a building having been constructed or the land cleared. This aspect of Wyckoff's data is difficult to replicate. For present purposes, only the land price data are used without modification.

4. The hypothesis that the distributions from the four decades are similar (i.e., the differences are due to sampling error) was tested. Classes I and II were combined to eliminate zero values. The null hypothesis was rejected (chi-square = 35.92, α=.05, df=15, $c.v.$=24.996), but was retained when the 1660s data were eliminated (chi-square = 16.01, α=.05, df=10, $c.v.$=18.307). See also Wyckoff (1937:332).

5. Wyckoff (1937) presented similar tract-size data on proprietary grants (n=910). Unfortunately, the decade distributions are presented as percentages without subtotals, precluding direct comparisons with the private sales and analyses of significance. The raw data provided for the entire period, however, are clearly different from those of private sales insofar as Class I tracts are overrepresented in the former; namely, the proprietorship was more conscientious about recording conveyances than were individuals involved in private transactions.

6. By patenting a manor of 1,000 acres, or more, major land owners circumvented the provision of the "Conditions of Plantation" requiring "planting" of the tract within three years of award of patent (see also Main, 1982:42). One suspects, at any rate, that enforcement was selective.

7. Wyckoff's distinction between improved and unimproved land is on shaky ground. In my experience with seventeenth- through twentieth-century land records, it is impossible to determine whether or not a tract is improved without independent evidence, or a statement within the instrument of conveyance to that effect. The median prices for improved and unimproved lands are provided simply as a reminder of whence the composite data were drawn.

8. Menard et al. (1988:188) estimate 20 acres per field hand for continuous tobacco production, plus 2 acres for corn and an unspecified number of acres in pasture and woodland.

9. Since most plantation households produced their own subsistence, acquiring large quantities of tobacco lands was not integral to a household's physical survival, but it was vital to their efforts to purchase goods.

10. The research for this section was undertaken with the assistance of Esther Doyle Read and Susan C. Buonocore and presented at the 25th annual Conference on Historical and Underwater Archaeology, held in Kingston, Jamaica, January 1992. Their assistance is greatly appreciated.

11. For a description of the perfect site upon which to erect a dwelling, see Bacon's (1955a [1625]:114–117) essay "Of Buildings."

12. Local scholars sometimes refer to the apparent accuracy of the Herrman map, based on the distribution of structures along the coastline in areas where seventeenth-century sites have been found. It should be noted, however, that Herrman's cartographic work spanned the 1660s (Sanchez-Saavedra, 1975:15–21). Given the existing technology and the lengthy period of the survey, it seems unlikely that the small symbols on the map represent anything more than an impression of overall plantation siting. Herrman compiled the map at his own expense for Cecil, Lord Baltimore, possibly to promote colonization. Implying that all settlers had access to navigable water was a powerful, if subtle inducement.

13. See O'Mara (1982) regarding models of town building and the seventeenth-century colonial town as trading station modeled on the Venetian *fondachi* and the Hansa

Kontors of the sixteenth century. Cecil, Lord Baltimore, was familiar with the fortified settlements in Maine (e.g., Cranmer, 1990; Faulkner and Faulkner, 1987). He also benefited from his father's experience in an unsuccessful attempt at colonizing Avalon in Newfoundland. Nevertheless, Calvert's strategy was very different from the strategies of his French and English contemporaries in Canada and New England.

14. Smolek (1984) and Lukezic (1990) both address elevation and proximity to potable water, but these variables are ignored in this study since elevation is largely a function of proximity to the waterways and all early colonial Maryland sites are situated near potable surface water.

15. Large, folio, manuscript ledgers or rent rolls were maintained by the proprietary, with copies in the colony and in England. Copies of the rent rolls, now curated by the Maryland State Archives, Annapolis, Maryland, list plantations by tract name, acreage, original patentee and date of patent, successive patentees, and rents due.

16. The same Ishmael Wright noted above was sued in Provincial Court by his neighbor to the south, John Ashcomb, for cutting trees on what Ashcomb claimed to be part of his plantation, Point Patience (*Arch. Md.*, X:205, 218; 20 January 1653).

17. Clearly, there was a mathematical error, but was it calculated or unintentional? Did the surveyor and/or the patentee deliberately intend to misrepresent the quantity of land patented, and if so why? Perhaps the additional £5.08 (a not inconsiderable sum at the time) annual rent may have had something to do with the reported acreage, particularly over 37 years.

18. Data collection was undertaken primarily by Susan C. Buonocore. The presence of certain ceramic wares (e.g., North Devon earthenwares, Rhenish brown stonewares), and the absence of others (e.g., Buckley earthenware and white salt glaze stoneware), was used to estimate the dates during which each site was occupied.

19. Attempts at reconstructing the Quaternary shoreline succession on Jamestown Island (Edwards, 1994) have been very successful, but utilize resources not currently available in Maryland.

20. Ideally, Lord Baltimore's instructions to the surveyor general (1671) limiting the amount of waterfront per 50 acres also should be taken into account. That would greatly complicate the procedure and, of course, we have not determined whether the surveyor complied with those instructions. Moreover, the lord proprietor issued patents for most of the prime lands in the sample counties before issuing these instructions to the surveyor general.

21. Women's implicit or explicit ownership of kitchen utensils contradicts the legal and customary rights of a husband to his wife's property, unless otherwise waived through a prenuptial contract. But, as we have seen in the foregoing analyses of wealth, land ownership, and the rights of labor, contradictions existed in several fundamental institutions of seventeenth-century English society.

Chapter 7

Environment and History of William Stephens Land

INTRODUCTION

Contextualism, with its emphasis on abstract meanings and systems of meaning, can be misconstrued as a rejection of the material world (e.g., Mrozowski, 1993:106–107). Hodder (1982, 1991), however, has shown that the physical environment is an integral part of meaning. It provides physical and physiological constraints on all living matter, and it provides a material source for the construction of meaning. The environment is an infinitely complex phenomenon, resistant to exhaustive description by the most rigorous and meticulous procedures. It is an artifact of perception. As artifacts of perception, the environments of Compton and Patuxent Point should be described from the perspectives of their occupants.

The Stephens family, like most of the colonists, did not convey those perceptions to us, at least not in any readily decipherable manner. We will have to look to their contemporaries for guidance, much in the manner of the preceding forays into the definitions of wealth, commodity, land, and labor. A general discussion of the Tidewater environment, based on the observations of seventeenth-century colonists and visitors, is presented first, followed by a description and analysis of William Stephens Land in those same terms. The history of the tract is then analyzed with data drawn from surviving documents.

THE CHESAPEAKE TIDEWATER ENVIRONMENT

The newly settled Tidewater region inspired numerous observers to describe the area, through personal letters and promotional pamphlets, to their compatriots in England and throughout northwestern Europe. There are many ways in which they could have described the region, many ways in which they could have organized their observations. But there are two motifs that appear in virtually all period descriptions of the Chesapeake: its appearance and climate relative to that of England, and the natural resources that existed in relative abundance.[1] Insofar as these descriptions generally were designed to persuade people to emigrate to the Chesapeake colonies (only Beverley's [1947 (1705)] and van der Donk's [1968 (1655)] descriptions approaching our sense of scientific objectivity), these emphases should come as no surprise. But seventeenth-century observers also should be credited with an awareness of their compatriots' concerns: the familiarity of the environment and food, but mostly food.

If we follow Defoe on his *Tour through the Whole Island of Great Britain* (1971 [1724–26]), we find numerous similarities drawn between like counties, matter-of-fact descriptions of the buildings and layouts of towns, commercial activities and connections, and references to prominent individuals and histories of specific locales. This kind of description is virtually absent in representations of Maryland and Virginia. By the end of the seventeenth century, there were few places that had any history, so far as Europeans were concerned, and commercial activities were limited and confined largely to the wharves of individual plantations. There were few private buildings and fewer public buildings of note, much less towns in the English sense of that term.[2] There were few, if any, parallels drawn between landscape features of the Chesapeake Tidewater and Great Britain.

The region was described as thickly forested along the shore, such clearings as did exist being the recent products of plantation clearing or the sites of long-abandoned Indian towns:

> The whole Country is a perfect Forest, except where the Woods are cleared for Plantations, and old Fields, and where have been formerly Indian Towns, and poisoned Fields and Meadows, where the Timber has been burnt down in Fire-Hunting. (H. Jones, 1724:35)
> All the low land is verry woody like one continued Forrest, no part clear but what is cleared by the English. And tho we are pretty close seated, yett we cannot see our neighbours house for trees. (H. Jones, 1987 [1699]:39)

Reverend Hugh Jones, the Younger (1724), made his observation after Virginia had been settled for more than a century. The practice of abandoning fields to fallow was beginning to leave its mark on the landscape, and the scars of aboriginal occupation were still evident. Reverend Hugh Jones, the Elder (1987

[1699]), recorded his observations in Calvert County, Maryland, while serving as minister for the parish of Christ's Church. Calvert County had been colonized for a half century at the time.

Plantations, hugging the tidewater shoreline, were tied together by the 200-mile-long Chesapeake Bay and its many rivers and smaller tributaries. Virtually all observers whose writings have survived comment on this immense waterway. Unlike archaeologists and ecologists in the region today who marvel at the abundance and diversity of marine and avian fauna, or the real estate developers and government officials who are entranced by the commercial, residential, and recreational potential of the area, early European visitors were drawn to the Bay's transportation potential (e.g., Hawley, 1988 [1635]:78; Jones, 1987 [1699]:39). Here was a means of ready, inexpensive access to the bulk commodity-producing plantations in a well-sheltered, easily navigable waterway that required no development beyond the construction of simple wharves, and this discovery made upon the eve of Great Britain's canal-building boom.

The principal liability of the Chesapeake drainage was that it left the settlers vulnerable to attack. The settlers at Jamestown in 1607, and to a lesser extent those at St. Mary's City in 1634, recognized this property and accordingly built their settlements in defensible positions. As the Spanish menace abated, and as Native American peoples were either driven further inland or exterminated, the great waterway became an unqualified advantage. Defensibility was no longer an important consideration in plantation siting by the last quarter of the seventeenth century.[3]

The climate was quite unlike that to which people were accustomed in England. It was, and is, generally temperate with short, mild winters and a long growing season. The summers, however, were quite warm and humid, as "hot as in Spaine" (Hawley, 1988 [1635]:77). Colonists arriving with the annual tobacco fleet in the autumn or early winter were probably enamored with the climate. But summer weather arrives in the region by May, and many British colonists must have been unprepared for the oppressive heat and humidity that developed throughout the most active part of the agricultural season. Hammond (1988 [1656]:290) noted that the summers were warmer in Virginia than in England, "but that heat [is] sweetly allayed by a continual breaze of winde, which never failes to coole and refresh the labourer and traveler." Either climatic conditions have changed considerably over the past three centuries, or Hammond was being less than candid about the extreme summer temperatures. Given the promotional nature of his pamphlet, the latter explanation seems the more likely of the two.

Without exception, Chesapeake Bay promoters and explorers of the early Colonial period tell us and their contemporaries of the great bounty of the land. Hammond's description is worth quoting at length, both for its content and for its focus on the ease with which this bounty could be had, a leitmotif in virtually all of the promotional literature of the American colonies and one that reflects upon the motivations of those emigrating to the tobacco colonies:

> The Country is fruitfull, apt for all and more than England can or does produce. The usuall diet is such as in England, for the rivers afford innumerable sortes of choyce fish . . .and that in many places sufficient to serve the use of man and to fatten hoggs. Water-fowle of all sortes are . . .plentifull and easy to be killed . . ... Deare all over the Country, and in many places so many that venison is accounted a tiresom meat;[4] wilde Turkeys are frequent . . ., huge Oysters and store [read *plenty*] [in] all parts where salt-water comes in . . ..The Country is exceedingly replenished with Neat cattle, Hoggs, Goats and Tame-fowle, but not many sheep; so that mutton is somwhat scarce . . .. The Country is full of Gallant Orchards . . .Grapes in infinite manners [read *varieties*] grow wilde, so do Walnuts, Smalnuts, Chestnuts and abundance of excellent fruits, Plums and Berries, not growing or known in England; graine we have, both English and Indian for bread and Bear [beer], and Pease besides English of ten several sorts, all exceeding ours in England; the gallant root of Potatoes are common, and so are all sorts of rootes, herbes and Garden stuffe.
>
> It must needs follow then that diet cannot be scarce, since both rivers and woods affords it, and that such plenty of Cattle and Hogs are every where, which yield beef, veal, milk, butter, cheese and other made dishes, porke, bacon, and pigs . . .these with the help of Orchards and Gardens, Oysters, Fish, Fowle and Venison, certainly cannot but be sufficient for a good diet and wholsom accommodation, considering how plentifully they are, and how easy with industry to be had. (Hammond, 1988 [1656]:291–292)

Such a detailed, and sanguine, description of the colonies must have proven very attractive to certain groups of people in England. Anderson (1971), in his study of seventeenth-century English yeoman foodways, concludes that yeoman and husbandmen did not starve, nor were they malnourished, although the quality of their diet did change through the seasons, becoming most limited in variety and nutrition during the spring. He also notes, however, that cottagers and laborers did not share in that prosperity (Anderson, 1971:271), and those living in London and other cities undoubtedly were hard pressed as well. When we consider the effects of the English civil wars (1641–1660), the Anglo-Dutch wars of the 1650s, 1660s, and 1670s, and the periodic return of plague (e.g., 1665/1666), however, Anderson's conclusions must be qualified. For a lot of people at different times, Hammond's description, and those of his near contemporaries, looked very attractive.

John Hammond, cautious as to painting too rosy a picture of life in the colonies, which might cast doubt on the truth of his portrayal, warned prospective colonists:

> I affirme the Country [of Virginia] to be wholesome, healthy and fruitfull; and a modell on which industry may as much improve itself in, as in any habitable

part of the World; yet not such a Lubberland as the Fiction of the land of Ease is reported to be, nor such a Utopian as Sr. Thomas Moore hath related to be found out. (Hammond, 1988 [1656]:287)[5]

The region had its inconveniences, among which Beverley (1947 [1705]:299) included "Thunder, Heat, and troublesome Vermin," that is, snakes, mosquitoes, chiggers, and ticks. The most inconvenient aspect of the region, however, may well have been the forests that had to be cleared prior to planting.

Beverley (1947 [1705]:124) and Jones (1724:35) both note open, savanna-like lands along the interior drainage divides, places that were lightly wooded and generally level. These areas, however, were distant from navigable water, and the grassy, relatively lightly forested soils were not well regarded by English farmers.[6] Such lands, like the "poisoned Fields and Meadows, where the Timber has been burnt down in Fire-Hunting" (Jones, 1724:36), were deemed suitable for live-stock and little else (e.g., Beverley, 1947 [1705]:124). Fr. Andrew White described the preferred lowland soils as

> Excellent so that we cannot sett downe a foot, but tread on Strawberries, raspires [raspberries], fallen mulberrie vines, acchorns, walnutts, saxafras [sassafras] etc.: and these in the wildest woods. The ground is commonly a blacke mould above, and a foot within ground of a readish [reddish] colour. All is high woods except where the Indians have cleared for corne. (White, 1988 [1634]:45)

Hawley (1988) echoed White's assessment, but provided some additional detail in terms meaningful to prospective settlers:

> The soil generally is very rich, like that which is about Cheesweek [Chiswick] neere London, where it is worth 20. shillings an Acre yeerely to Tillage in the Common-fields, and in very many places, you will have two foote of blacke rich mould,[7] wherein you shall scarce find a stone, it is like a sifted Garden-mould, and is so rich that if it be not first planted with Indian corne, Tobacco, Hempe, or some such thing that may take off the ranknesse thereof, it will not be fit for any English graine. (Hawley, 1988 [1635]:81)

Jones (1724:39) suggested that such tobacco land would produce for several years, "if the Land be good; as it is where fine Timber, or Grape Vines grow." In short, the colonists appear to have preferred those lands that also required the greatest effort to clear.

There are indications that some colonists sought lands that were not only rich and suited to tobacco cultivation, but that exhibited a variety of soils suited to a variety of crops. In Chapter 6, I noted that Francis Bacon recommended seeking mixed soils suitable for growing a mixture of crops. Beverley (1947 [1705]:123) observed in Virginia that "the Soil is of such Variety, according to the

Difference of Situation, that one Part or other of it, seems fitted to every Sort of Plant, that is requisite either for the Benefit or Pleasure of Mankind."

> The Land of these upper Parts [i.e., the headwaters within the interior drainage divides] affords greater Variety of Soil, than any other, and as great Variety in the Foundations of the Soil or Mould, of which good judgment may be made, by the Plants and Herbs that grow upon it. (Beverley, 1947 [1705]:125)

Beverley devoted several pages to describing the lay of the land in Virginia, the different kinds of soils, and their value for different crops, livestock husbandry, and lumbering. As we have seen from the analysis of settlement patterning and soils in Chapter 6, however, the tendency in southern Maryland appears to have been to select relatively homogeneous soils that were particularly well suited to the cultivation of tobacco. This pattern betrays a general, but not complete, lack of interest on the part of colonists in other cash crops.

WILLIAM STEPHENS LAND

The William Stephens Land tract is located on the east bank of the lower Patuxent River, at the mouth of—and on the south side of—what is now called Hungerford Creek (Universal Transmercator coordinates 18.371800.4245350).[8] The Patuxent River opens into the Chesapeake Bay just a few miles to the southeast. The tract, measuring approximately 100 acres, is relatively level, ranging in elevation from 36 to 43 feet above mean sea level. The soils of the A-horizon are deep, light, relatively well drained, friable, moderately acidic, and remarkably fertile. There is very little gravel in the plowzone or the underlying B-horizon (a yellowish brown silty loam), but some deep excavations encountered poorly consolidated, well-sorted sands and gravels. Mattapex silt loam is the principal soil with lesser amounts of Matapeake and Othello silt loams occurring along the riverbank. The tract as whole, consisting of both the Compton and Patuxent Point sites, rated very well in the analysis in Chapter 6 due to the predominance of soils rated as "very high" for tobacco yields, and the proximity of the sites to navigable water.

William Stephens Land is sited in an enviable location for tobacco production; however, it lacks the mixture of soils that might have supported a more diversified agricultural economy. Other available resources included fishes and oysters from the river, and deer from the interior forests. Wild fruits also were available, and there were orchards planted on some of the neighboring plantations.[9] The principal source of food, however, was maize grown on the plantation.

Throughout the twentieth century, William Stephens Land was cultivated, and archaeological and archival research demonstrate continual occupation of the tract throughout much of the historic period, with a gap occurring during the last two decades of the seventeenth century and the first decade or two of the eighteenth century. Intensive occupation for 350 years altered the landscape considerably, clearing and leveling the land, contributing to the siltation of Hungerford Creek, and introducing a wide range of exotic plant species. Both the Compton and Patuxent Point sites have since been demolished during the course of residential development.

Archival Research and Analysis

William Stephens patented his 100 acre tract in August of 1651 and, presumably, settled it soon after with his wife, Magdelen, his sons John and William, and servants Margaret Aylin, William Hardin, Daniel Elsmore, and John Mark (*Land Patents*, AB&H:354–355, 08 August 1651). At that time, there were three trends in the settlement of the colony:

1. Areas beyond the St. Mary's City core were rapidly settled, particularly Calvert County.
2. Many Protestant sectaries (i.e., Puritans and, later, Quakers) arrived from Virginia, where they no longer were welcome.
3. A greater number of immigrants arrived in family groups than had arrived in previous decades or would arrive during the remaining decades of the seventeenth century.

The Stephens family arrived as a family group and they became Quakers, although whether they joined the Society of Friends before or after settling along the Patuxent River is uncertain. No record of their prior settlement in Virginia, nor of their crossing from England, has been found.

Neighboring tracts such as Compton and Hodgkins Neck (Figure 7–1) were settled at the same time, the former by Henry Bullen and Alexander Mayrobe (tenants of Quakers Ishmael and Ann Wright), and the latter by John and Mary Hodges, brother-in-law and sister of William Stephens. The Wrights subsequently sold their interest in the 75-acre Compton tract for 2,500 pounds of tobacco to Antoine (a.k.a. Anthony) LeCompte,[10] a Huguenot from Picardy, France, "with the Dwelling house and all the other houses, edifices, buildings, fruit trees, [and] Timber . . ." (*Land Patents* 3:264–265, 13 January 1656). Upon John Hodges's death, his widow, Mary, and her new husband, Richard Keene (a Quaker; see Carroll, 1970:15), sold the 100-acre Hodgkins Neck to John Obder (*Land Patents*, Q:227, 24 November 1658).[11]

John Ashcomb, arriving in the colony with his family in 1651, patented nearby Point Patience in 1658, a 360-acre tract that eventually became his "home plantation" (*Land Patents*, Q:98–99, 05 August 1658). The Ashcomb family became major landowners in the area during the latter part of the seventeenth century and the first quarter of the eighteenth century, acquiring among other

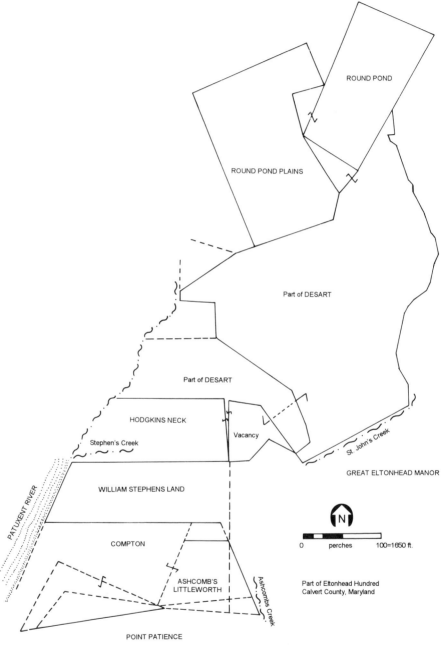

Figure 7–1. Tract map of area around William Stephens Land, reconstructed from surveyors' descriptions.

tracts their "quarter" at Compton (*Wills & Testaments*, 4:65, 16 July 1684; and 11:266, 16 November 1702). The patriarch and his sons appear to have been Protestants, although not members of any splinter sect.[12] Henry Hooper and his family also arrived in the area in 1658, patenting the 550-acre Hooper's Neck tract to the north (*Land Patents*, Q:94, 05 August 1658). The political-religious leanings of this family have not been determined, although it is likely that they were Protestants.

By 1660, much of the premium land in Calvert County had been "taken up." Staunchly Protestant, the community formed one of two centers of Protestant power during the interregnum, the other center being in Providence, where Annapolis is now located (Luckenbach, 1995). A third stronghold was developing on the eastern shore after the Restoration of King Charles II. Not coincidentally, the Stephenses, LeComptes, and John Obder emigrated to the Great Choptank River area on the eastern shore, in what are now Dorchester and Talbot counties, in the early 1660s. It was at Horne Point, on the south side of the Great Choptank River in Dorchester County, that one of the founders of the Society of Friends, George Fox, was entertained by William and Magdelen Stephens in 1673 (Fox, 1988 [1694]:404–405). Fox also visited William, Jr., and Mary [Sharp] Stevens on the north side of the river in Talbot County. A large number of settlers in Calvert County removed themselves to the eastern shore in the 1660s, planting themselves next to one another and carrying with them the names that they and their neighbors had given to plantations on the western shore. Unfortunately, we do not know to whom the Stephens's lands in Calvert County passed, nor by what instruments.

Based on the description of William Stephens's Calvert County patent, his plantation lay on the south side of the confluence of Stephens (now Hungerford) Creek and the Patuxent River. The Compton site, so-called because the original investigators confused the Stephens tract with the Compton land immediately to the south (Louis Berger & Associates, 1989), clearly lies within this tract. Based on temporally diagnostic artifacts recovered from the site, particularly pipestem bore diameter distributions, the Compton site undoubtedly was the home plantation of the Stephens family from 1651 until the early 1660s.

All measurable pipestem bores recovered from Compton and Patuxent Point were measured in the manner described by Harrington (1954), and the resulting frequencies plotted in Figure 7–2.[13] Both distributions peak at 7/64 of an inch, dating the assemblages to the period 1650 to 1680. The Patuxent Point distribution is bimodal, with approximately the same number of bore diameters at 6/64 and 7/64 of an inch. Given the overall reduction in the size of pipestem bores (correlating with an increase in pipestem lengths), the Patuxent Point assemblage appears to be later than that recovered from Compton. Other temporally diagnos-

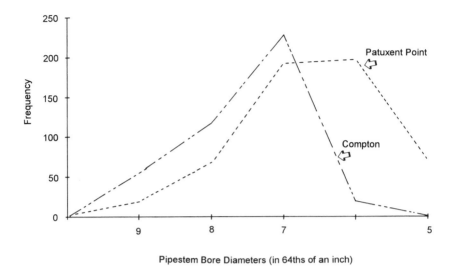

Figure 7–2. Distribution of pipestem bore diameters from pipestems recovered from Compton and Patuxent Point.

tic artifacts place the Compton occupation in the 1650s (Gibb and Balla, 1993), and the Patuxent Point occupation in the 1660s (see Chapters 8 and 9).

Patuxent Point, named for the townhouse development occupying the site, lies 800 feet to the east of Compton, and approximately 400 feet south of Stephens Creek. We do not know who lived at this site, although it almost certainly was not the tract owner. There has been speculation that it lies on the adjoining Hodgkins Neck tract (King and Turowski, 1993), and that is a possibility since the reconstructed tract lines in Figure 7–1 are only approximations. However, for chronological reasons discussed below, it is unlikely that the excavated homelot had anything to do with John Obder. Obder moved to the eastern shore by 1661, at which time he was appointed a commissioner by the governor: occupation of the site appears to date several years later. Moreover, both sites were located on the same 94-acre tract as early as 1883 (*Land Records*, SS6:70–72, 08 November 1883; Figure 7–3). Property bounds change, particularly over 200 years, but continuity in the ownership of adjacent tracts lessens the likelihood that the configuration of the Stephens tract changed significantly.

The names of the occupants of Patuxent Point continue to elude us, despite intensive archival research and analysis. Rent roll entries that probably date to the first and second decades of the eighteenth-century state, in connection with "William Stephens Land," that "none claims this land" (*Land Records*, Rent Roll #3:23, ca. 1706–1716). Edmund Hungerford acquired "Hodsons Neck" as his "home

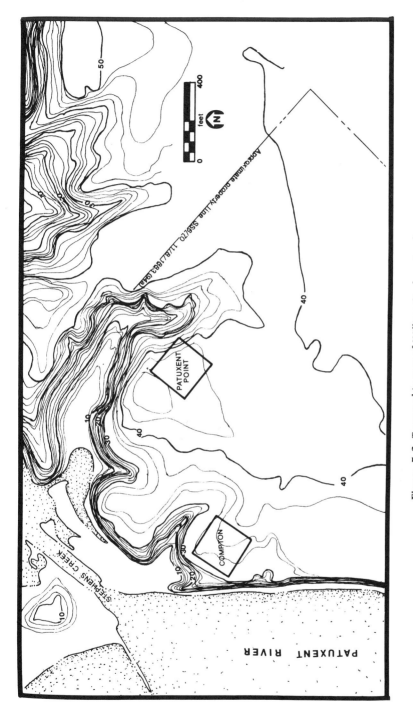

Figure 7-3. Topographic map of William Stephens Land.

plantation" by 1721 (*Wills & Testaments*, 17:41, 1721) and, judging from a 1783 tax list, it remained within the Hungerford family throughout much of the eighteenth century (Carothers, 1977:193; see also *Land Records*, Calvert County Debt Book 1753–1758, f.10). Circumstantial evidence suggests that Edmund Hungerford acquired Stephens Land by 1718 (*Land Records*, Unpatented Survey #14, 27 February 1718), and a Calvert County Debt Book (1753–1758, f.18) clearly identifies Benjamin Hungerford as the owner in the 1750s. Edmund Hungerford may have acquired the tract by 1718, but it was still referred to as Stephens Land in Charles Ashcomb's 1726 resurvey of Compton (*Land Records*, Unpatented Survey #36, 03 July 1726).

Neighboring Hodgkins Neck was in the possession of John Landerkin, about whom little is known, during the first quarter of the eighteenth century. A rent roll entry (*Land Records*, Rent Roll 3:20, 1658–1776) indicates that Landerkin also was in possession of nearby "Timber Neck," until he—along with "Robert Greeves *et Uxor*"—surrendered it to James Roberts and John Greeves on 16 March 1707. The only other entry in the archives pertaining to Landerkin states that he was in debt to English merchant Peregrine Browne to the tune of £53.4.6, a substantial debt (*Provincial & General Court Records*, PL5:139ff, 1719–1723). In sum, the occupational history of Stephens Land, and many adjoining tracts, is unknown for the latter third of the seventeenth century and for as much as a quarter century afterward.

Surviving records from the late seventeenth century could reveal a great deal about kinship relations, household demographics, patterns in the acquisition, and—to a limited extent—use of manufactured goods, agricultural strategies, and homelot organization. Probate inventories and estate accounts are especially informative, particularly when they are detailed, and court cases provide atmosphere and context for the objects enumerated in those inventories and accounts (e.g., Carr et al., 1991). Several such documents exist for the Ashcombs's Point Patience plantation and for the Compton plantation. Unfortunately, documents referring to William Stephens Land and Hodgkins Neck, aside from the original land warrants and patents, appear not to have survived. William and Magdelen Stephens died in Dorchester County, as indicated by a pair of solitary "tablestones" that were moved to the Christ's Church cemetery in Cambridge, Dorchester County, from the Huffington Farm in 1940. The stones are inscribed "Magdelen Stevens, died 1678," and "William Stevens, died 1684" (Marshall, 1965:55, 114).[14] Unfortunately, neither left a will or inventory, so we do not know to whom, if to anybody, they left their Calvert County land. William Stephens Land is not mentioned in any of their descendants' wills or inventories.

John Obder died on the eastern shore in 1667 under dark circumstances. He, and a servant, were alleged to have been murdered by a Wicomico Indian named Anatchcom (a.k.a. Wianamon): "[Anatchcom] Confessed that it was his Wife that was killed at the house of Wm. Hemsley in Talbot County," and, although he was among those present at the murder of Obder and his servant, he claimed to have taken no part in the affair (*Arch. Md.*, II:195 [1669]). Governor Charles Calvert pronounced a sentence of death, which was carried out immediately. Evidence of concern for the death of Anatchcom's wife has not survived.

Precisely who was living at Patuxent Point remains a mystery. If the site was occupied as early as the late 1650s—and archaeological evidence presented in Chapter 9 suggests that is not the case—then either the Stephens family or John Obder built the farmstead and lived there for several years. If the Stephens family lived there, then Compton may have served as a quarter for enslaved or indentured laborers during its later years. Tenants would have succeeded the Stephens family, occupying the site into the 1670s. Had Obder occupied Patuxent Point, then he would have lived there as early as 1657 (when he was appointed commander of much of the lower Patuxent River), leaving for the eastern shore sometime in 1661 or 1662. Tract analysis, including the circumstantial evidence of a property line from an 1883 deed, suggests that both sites are located on Stephens Land, leaving Obder, his predecessors John and Mary Hodges, and one of his successors to Hodgkins Neck, John Landerkin, out of the picture.

SUMMARY

The Chesapeake Bay region was portrayed to prospective immigrants as a land of milk and honey, a place where one could live well with a little effort and capital. There was no "city on a hill," no "light of the world" to be had in the region. It was simply a place for comfortable, secular living. Resources and natural advantages abounded and could be had for a small amount of money or a few years work in the service of others. The ideal was to secure level, fertile land on a neck or peninsula along one of the region's many navigable waterways with a substantial woodlot in which marginally domesticated swine could feed, and in which firewood, barrel staves, and lumber for homelot construction could be procured. Settlement along the brackish waters of the lower tributaries had the advantage of ready access to the rich aquatic resources of the Tidewater.

William and Magdelen Stephens found such a haven on the east side of the Patuxent River, at its confluence with a navigable creek. They built a plantation on this 100-acre. (40 ha) tract, lived there with their children and servants for approximately 10 to 12 years, and then departed for new lands on the eastern shore. Precisely why they left is uncertain. The land may have been worn out, as was common on tobacco plantations, and adjoining coastal lands were unavailable for expansion. Perhaps the political upheaval of the 1650s, followed by the return of proprietary rule, motivated the Stephens family to join with their Protestant neighbors in the exodus to the eastern shore. Unless relevant documents are discovered, the reason or reasons for their departure probably will remain unknown, as will the names and character of the people who occupied the Patuxent Point site. At this point, all that can be said of the occupants of Patuxent Point is that they probably were tenants or squatters, and that they occupied the site at least during the late 1660s and 1670s.

The archival data, sparse though they are, provide details of the Tidewater environment, the religious and ethnic character of its inhabitants, and the years during which the various tracts along the lower Patuxent River were occupied. We now must turn to archaeology, not simply because it fills in missing details, but because it permits a different perspective on colonial life. The focus is on the individual case, the household and the choices made by the household in allocating its resources. The archaeology of the Compton site is presented in the next chapter, followed by that of the Patuxent Point site in Chapter 9.

NOTES

1. John Hammond (1988 [1656]:297) did make reference to the aesthetics of the Virginia countryside, but in a subordinate position to the natural amenities of the region: "The Country is not only plentiful but pleasant and profitable, pleasant in regard of the brightnesse of the weather, the many delightful rivers, on which the inhabitants are settled (every man almost living in sight of a lovely river), the abundance of game, the extraordinary good neighbourhood and loving conversation they have one with the other."
   In a similar vein, van der Donk interrupts his extended description of New Netherlands:

   > We sometimes in travelling imperceptibly find ourselves on high elevated situations, from which we overlook large portions of the country. The neighbouring eminence, the surrounding valleys and the highest trees are overlooked, and again lost in the distant space. Here our attention is arrested in the beautiful landscape around us, here the painter can find rare and beautiful subjects for the employment of his pencil, and here also the huntsman is animated when he views the enchanting prospects presented to the eyes; on the hills, at the brooks and in the valleys, where the game abounds and where the deer are feeding, or gamboling or resting in the shades in full view. (van der Donk, 1968 [1655]:17–18)

   Main's (1982:264) insinuation that abundance was favored over aesthetics by the colonists may hold true, but we must keep in mind the purpose of the writings on which such assessments are made, lest we confuse promotion with appreciation.
2. Luckenbach (1995) describes the early history of Providence, of which the future city of Annapolis was a small part, and reports some preliminary results of excavations at several Providence plantation sites. (See also Miller, 1984.)

3. Fear of attacks by Native Americans continued through the 1680s, but was realistically confined to the eastern shore and the middle Potomac Valley. The Dutch attacked and destroyed a number of vessels in the Chesapeake in the early 1670s during the third Anglo-Dutch war, but made no effort to subjugate the region.

4. Venison, the meat of kings, was not generally available to the people of England, although it may have been relatively abundant in Scotland and Ireland. Alsop (1988 [1666]:345) also notes that venison often was an unwelcome dish, having been served in many places with monotonous regularity.

5. "Lubberland" is a figure from popular English culture that refers to a land of plenty in which one need not work. It appears sporadically in English literature (e.g., Ben Jonson's *Bartholomew Fair* (1614) III.*ii*). Hammond probably is not referring to any particular literary work in this context. He clearly is unfamiliar with More's (1975 [1516]) *Utopia*, a fictional society characterized by its rejection of private property and whose citizens set intellectual pursuits above all others. This is hardly an appropriate metaphor for the Chesapeake colonies of the seventeenth century, even by contrast. See Holifield (1989) on persuasion and assurances of honesty in seventeenth-century writing.

6. An inland tract in lower Calvert County, Maryland, consisting of 1,048 acres, was named by its patentees "the Desart," indicating their assessment of the soil (*Land Patents*, IC#L f.51, 10 May 1682).

7. Today these soils are far clayier and not nearly as deep as a result of erosion and deep plowing. Even in the early seventeenth century, however, such deep soils must have been scarce, occurring only in active flood plains.

8. The right bank of the lower Patuxent River was referred to throughout the seventeenth century as the north side of the river.

9. Ishmael and Ann Wright conveyed Compton to Anthony LeCompte in 1656. They listed fruit trees among the various improvements (*Land Records*, 3:264–265). The earlier of the two sites on William Stephens Land, Compton was incorrectly identified as LeCompte's plantation (Louis Berger & Associates, 1989). It lies squarely within William Stephens Land, hence I attribute the archaeological remains to the Stephens household.

10. LeCompte married Hester Dottando (a.k.a. Doatloan, or Dotlando) in 1661. She was born in Dieppe, Normandy (Virkus, 1972:44). Hester LeCompte, along with her children, applied to the General Assembly for naturalization upon the death of Anthony, in 1674, no doubt in an effort to secure the family patrimony, which might have escheated to the lord proprietor. Only English and Irish people could legally own property in the colony. Hester LeCompte eventually married Mark Cordea, also from Normandy, and a prominent citizen living in St. Mary's City (*Arch. Md.*, V:402–403 [1674]).

11. Variously spelled as "Hogis," "Hoges," and "Hodgkins." Obder used the appellation "Gentleman" and probably remained unmarried.

12. Eldest son Charles stipulated in his will that should his widow or daughters marry a Roman Catholic they would have no part of his estate (*Wills & Testaments*, 11:266, 16 November 1702).

13. Hanson's (1971) formula #3 was calculated on both samples, providing two-standard deviation date ranges of 1629–1677 for Compton, and 1649–1709 for Patuxent Point.
14. I have examined these stones. Both predate the next earliest monuments at Christ's Church by a half century or more. Only Magdelen's inscription is easily read and it mentions only her name and date of death at the east end of the stone. I think it likely that both stones were cut long after William and Magdelen died.

Chapter 8

Compton, 1650s–1660s

INTRODUCTION

The memory of William Stephens Land lingered at least into the late 1720s, if only as the name of a tract in the possession of the Hungerford family. No references to the Stephens family in Calvert County date beyond the second quarter of the nineteenth century. Those few references to "Stephens" surviving from the early nineteenth century pertain to Stephens Creek, soon to be renamed for the Hungerfords. The return of the Stephens family to the collective memory of southern Maryland is due to a minor provision in a county ordinance: a regulation requiring archaeological reconnaissance in advance of multifamily housing projects. The Compton site was found as a result of the mandated survey and determined to be historically significant and worthy of intensive study. Compton is not the oldest site in the region, nor is it exceptional for the quantity or quality of recovered artifacts. Compton was the homelot of a family of modest means. The adjective "unremarkable" perhaps best describes this family and their homelot.

Archaeological investigations at the Compton site (18CV279) are described in this chapter, beginning with field and laboratory methods.[1] Field data are summarized, followed by analyses of several data sets, including architecture, nonstructural feature morphology and content, spatial distributions, and artifacts, specifically tobacco pipes, and ceramic and glass vessels. The data and analyses are presented in such a way as to facilitate comparisons with the Patuxent Point assemblage, presented in Chapter 9, and to provide a basis from which to identify patterns in the use of wealth.

METHODOLOGY

The Compton site was excavated over a period of approximately six weeks in 1988 by the Cultural Resource Group of Louis Berger & Associates, Inc.(LBA), under contract to CRJ Associates, Inc., real estate developers (LBA, 1989). LBA selected three hypotheses for testing:

1. Keeler's (1978) hypothesis that homelot organization became increasingly complex throughout the seventeenth century, observable in terms of the replacement of wattle fences with post-and-rail fences, increases in the number of buildings, and increasing differentiation between work space and formal space.
2. King and Miller's (1987) hypothesis that the organization of homelot space reflects the occupants' ethnicity, as well as site function. Social and functional changes should be reflected in refuse disposal patterns.
3. Miller's (1984) thesis that frontier adaptation and the evolution of colonial culture are evident in changing subsistence practices, as reflected in the shift from "diffuse" food procurement strategies to "focal" strategies (*sensu* Cleland, 1976).

Testing of Keeler's hypothesis entails complete exposure of a homelot's subsurface features and determining the construction sequence of all structures on the site. King and Miller's hypothesis requires identification of sheet middens through plowzone sampling. The contents of the middens are then compared through simple proportional analysis. Testing of Miller's hypothesis involves the recovery of faunal remains from relative dated features, the quantification of those remains by species (particularly in terms of domestic versus nondomestic species), and the identification of temporal patterning in species exploitation. LBA developed a methodology to address each of these hypotheses.

The Compton site was gridded into 10-ft. by 10-ft. (3.05 m by 3.05 m) units over an area of 150 ft. by 150 ft. (45.72 m by 45.72 m), the presumed extent of the seventeenth-century component of the site. Perpendicular transects of 2.5-ft. by 2.5-ft. (7.62 m by 7.62 m) test units, intersecting at the presumed center of the site, were excavated at 10-ft. intervals. Once the limits of the site had been established through field calculations of artifact densities, the remainder of the grid was filled in with units for a total of 162 at regular intervals of 10 ft. or less, a 6.25% sample of the gridded surface (Figure 8–1).[2] All units were excavated to the base of the plowzone, the soils screened through $^1/_4$-in. (6 mm) hardware mesh, and the artifacts collected and bagged by unit. Soil samples were taken from 57 of the units distributed at regular intervals of 15 ft. on the grid. Grid coordinates were

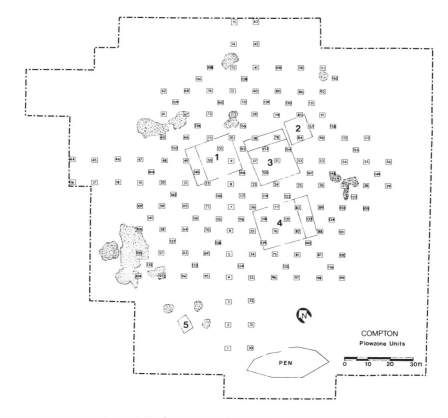

Figure 8–1. Plowzone sample units at the Compton site.

not employed, the plowzone units and features simply having been numbered consecutively.

Upon completion of the plowzone sampling, LBA mechanically stripped the site, reestablished the grid, and scraped and mapped the surface. They stratigraphically excavated the eastern half of each feature and picked the artifacts from each layer. Once the exposed profiles were drawn to scale, the remaining halves were excavated stratigraphically and the soil screened through 1/4-in. mesh. Structural and fence postholes were not excavated because "there were no chronological questions [relating to the sequences of postholes] that needed to be explored" (LBA, 1989:25).

Louis Berger Associates calculated minimum numbers of vessels for the ceramic and glass sherds recovered from select features. Minimum numbers of individuals also were calculated for the faunal material, again from select features only. Pipestem bore diameter frequencies and pipemakers' marks were analyzed for the plowzone and for the features in an attempt to identify changes in artifact patterning. Principal classes of artifacts recovered from the plowzone, including ceramics, bottle glass, European flint, tobacco pipes, and bones, were analyzed for spatial patterning by LBA (1989), and by Gibb and King (1991).

I have reanalyzed most of the materials recovered from Compton. The methodology for examining ceramics and vessel glass was similar to that employed by Meta Janowitz and Mallory Gordon in the initial study of the Compton materials (see LBA, 1989:33–38), although the sample was expanded to include all proveniences. Artifact counts from plowzone units were used in generating artifact distribution maps, as reported in Gibb and King (1991). Ceramic and vessel glass sherds were pulled from the general plowzone unit bags and combined with those recovered from all features (after having been marked with their respective proveniences), and cross-mending was undertaken. Minimum numbers of vessels were calculated on the bases of distinctive rim sherds and pastes, in the manner described by Noel Hume (1975:267), and the results reported (Gibb, 1993a; Gibb and Balla, 1993). Minimum numbers of glass bottles also were calculated based on the numbers of bases with their perimeters or pontil marks more than 50% complete. All vessels, ceramic and glass, have been illustrated and described in detail. All pipestem bores have been measured, and bowl forms and makers' marks illustrated. A variety of small finds (e.g., shoe buckles, door locks, and gunflints) also have been illustrated as part of the permanent record for the site.[3]

Faunal remains from Compton's subplowzone features were analyzed by Marie-Lorraine Pipes (see LBA, 1989:38–39). The analysis focused on bone elements and the distribution of elements for each of the species represented. For reasons not made clear in the report, minimum numbers of individuals were not calculated, a situation that is at odds with the stated research goals of the project. A more complete analysis of the faunal remains has yet to be undertaken.

RESULTS

Mechanical stripping of the Compton site, guided by the results of plowzone testing, revealed a homelot of approximately 140 ft., or 42.7 m (north-south), by 120 ft., or 36.6 m (east-west). Postholes and molds representing five earthfast buildings were exposed. The four largest buildings clustered about the anticipated geographic center of the site (Figure 8–2). Three of the buildings appear to have served as dwellings, the remaining two representing service outbuildings of uncertain function. The investigators state that there is no archaeological evidence of building repair or expansion.

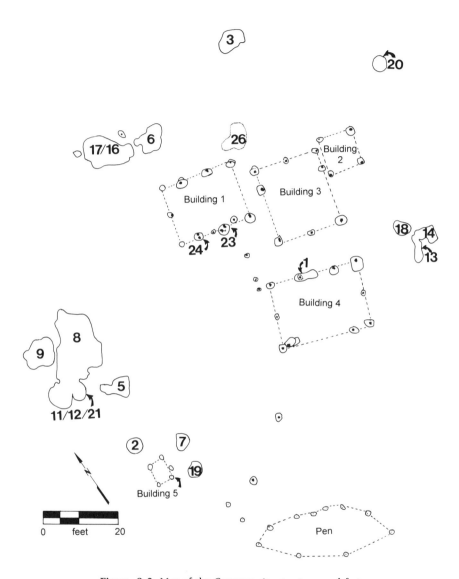

Figure 8–2. Map of the Compton site structures and features.

A lenticular-shaped, fenced enclosure measuring approximately 35 ft., or 10.7 m (east-west), by 12 ft., or 3.7 m (north-south) was uncovered southwest of the core of the site. The investigators also claim to have discovered a much larger enclosure of similar shape overlapping and extending west of Building 1 (LBA, 1989:24, 27). Archaeological evidence for such an enclosure, however, is weak, with tree root molds, building facades, and various pit features included along the hypothetical line of enclosure as fence supports in the absence of conventional postholes and molds. Fence panels of 17 to 18 ft. (5.2 to 5.5 m), the estimated distances between supports, also are improbable. They would require one or more intermediate posts to support the weight of the rails, posts for which there is no archaeological evidence.

A variety of features encompass the homelot on three sides, most of which contain domestic and architectural refuse. In addition to the dozens of postholes and molds, LBA identified what they believed to be an aboriginal grave, two cooking pits, a cluster of three features representing two mortar-mixing pits and a spring, a fire-reddened patch of subsoil, and 10 overlapping refuse-filled pits. Several prehistoric features also were uncovered and excavated, but are not discussed in this work. Historic period features are discussed below and, in some cases, reinterpreted.

FEATURE ANALYSIS

Four types of archaeological data are discussed in this section: architecture, nonstructural feature morphology and contents, spatial distributions, and artifacts. The results are used to re-create the appearance of the site, and to examine consumer decisions in the areas of land and space, labor, and purchases of manufactured goods.

Architecture

Table 8–1 summarizes the attributes of the five Compton buildings. The buildings fall within two groups based on size and morphology (cf. Figures 8–1 and 8–2). Buildings 1, 3, and 4 consist of two or more bays of 16 ft. to 18 ft. in length.[4] Included among these are bays 5-ft. to 6-ft. (1.5 to 1.8 m) wide with central posts on the end walls. These narrow bays probably represent chimneys constructed of wattle and daub. There is no evidence to support the hypothesis that some of these narrow bays represent sheds. Overall building lengths for the first group range from 21 ft. to 25 ft. (6.4 to 7.6 m), chimney bays inclusive. Interrupted sills probably were installed between upright members, providing seats for floor joists and for vertical wall studding.[5]

Building 1 is different from Buildings 3 and 4 in that it has an additional bay, although it is not the largest of this group of buildings. The original investigators implicitly use this attribute to distinguish between the three larger buildings at the site, interpreting Building 1 as a dwelling and Buildings 3 and 4 as outbuild-

**Table 8–1. Architectural Attributes of Structures at the
Compton Site**

Building	Length ft.	m	Width ft.	m	Bays	Chimney
1	21	6.4	16	4.9	3	Yes
2	10	3.0	10	3.0	1	No
3	20	6.1	18	5.5	2	Yes
4	25	7.6	18	5.5	2	Yes
5	6	1.8	5	1.5	1	No

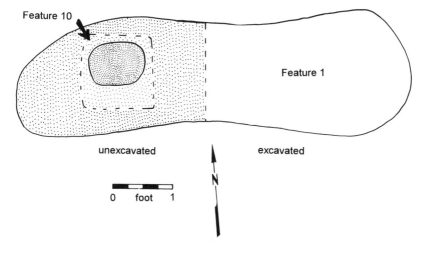

Figure 8–3. Plan and profile of Feature 1.

ings, possibly tobacco barns. This interpretation is difficult to reconcile with the
overall similarity of the structures, including the placement of a 5-ft. to 6-ft. bay
at one end of each structure, the presumed function of which is that of a chimney
frame. Building 4 does have a feature that extends along its north wall (Feature 1;
Figure 8–3). The excavators believed this feature to be an aboriginal burial with
all skeletal material decomposed, leaving little more than a vague soil discolora-
tion and textural anomaly at the "head" end of the feature. The only artifact
recovered was a sherd of unidentified aboriginal pottery. Given the perfect alignment of the feature with the north wall of Building 4, the placement of a posthole

and mold (Feature 10) squarely in the west end of Feature 1, and the lack of skeletal remains, it is far more likely that Feature 1 represents the remains of a door jamb, similar to those used in cross-passage houses (see Neiman [1980] for similar features). Feature 10 probably represents a replacement post. The dark organic material reported at the east end of Feature 1, 1.5 ft. below the graded surface, probably represents the lower end of a removed jamb post, rather than the last surviving remnant of a human skull. Buildings 1, 3, and 4 all appear to be dwellings.

The functions of the two smaller buildings are problematical. Both structures are of light frame, earthfast, single-bay construction. Neither has distinctive structural features that might indicate the uses to which they were put. Building 2 is square (10 ft. by 10 ft., or 3 by 3 m) and it is located at the core of the site, adjacent to the three dwellings. Building 5 is not square, its load-bearing posts are slight (supporting a very light frame), and it is located along the western edge of the site in close proximity to a number of refuse-filled pits. Both structures were identified by LBA as outbuildings of uncertain function, Building 2 possibly representing a meat storage house based on the presence of bone in neighboring features and the plowzone. Gibb and King (1991:124) suggested that Building 2 served as a generalized storage building, but subsequent analysis has neither confirmed nor refuted that hypothesis. The suggestion that Building 5 is a meat house (Gibb and King, 1991:118) is ill-founded, and its function also remains undetermined.

Evidence of building expansion at the site is nonexistent, the occupants apparently preferring to construct additional buildings as they needed them. There is evidence, however, of building maintenance, despite claims to the contrary (LBA, 1989). The northwest posthole of Building 1 intrudes upon, and nearly obliterates, an earlier posthole (Figure 8–4). The southwest posthole of Building 4 is an amalgam of three superimposed postholes. Also, the northeast postholes of Buildings 2 and 4 are considerably larger than the others in their respective structures, suggesting the possibility of posthole enlargement as a by-product of post replacement. Unfortunately, only two structural postholes were excavated (Features 23 and 24 on the south wall of Building 1). Planview and profile drawings of the postholes are lacking, precluding more detailed analysis.

Additional details about the buildings are few. Fragments of common red brick and yellow brick were recovered from the plowzone excavation units and from some of the subplowzone features. Given their relative infrequency, the bricks probably served as firebacks within the hearths. There is no evidence of brick footers or mortar-coated brick fragments to indicate a brick chimney. Several fragments of turned window leads were recovered, indicating that at least one of the buildings had one or more glazed casement windows. None of these leads

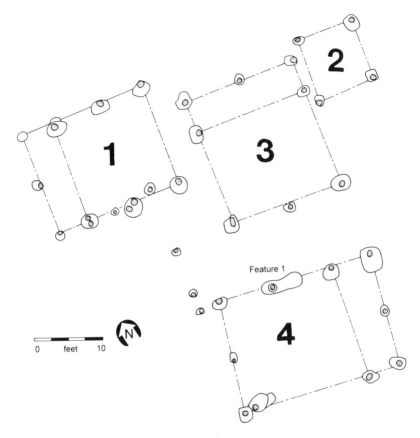

Figure 8–4. Detail of Compton site map.

bear manufacturing dates. Nonglazed windows would have borne either simple shutters or a combination of shutters and oiled cloth.[6] Wall plastering appears to have been absent, indicating simple plank walls. Several locks and bolts have been recovered, although they probably were used on chests or cabinets within the buildings, rather than on doors.

Nonstructural Features

Louis Berger Associates excavated 16 nonstructural features (i.e., features other than postholes and molds). Feature 1, an alleged aboriginal grave that probably represents a structural feature, has been discussed above. The remaining features fall within three functional groups, as defined by the original investigators: cooking pits, "mortar" mixing pits, and borrow pits, all of which served as trash receptacles prior to the abandonment of the site. I base my reinterpretation of these features primarily on their contents, the nature of surrounding features, and evaluation of the original investigators' assumptions.

The cooking pits (Features 2 and 12) measure approximately 4 ft. (1.2 m) in diameter and 2 ft. (0.6 m) in depth. Thin lenses of charcoal separate thin lenses of ash fill, neither containing many artifacts, bone, or oyster shell. Based on the ash and charcoal fill, and the close proximity of pits filled with oyster shell, the original investigators suggested that these pits were used to steam oysters. However, there is no evidence of fire-reddened subsoil along the walls of the pits, a prominent feature of prehistoric cooking pits found on the Stephens Land plantation. Moreover, sintered daub—a by-product of using a prepared hearth—was recovered from Strata 1, 2, and 4, intermixed with ash and charcoal. Sintered daub should not appear in undisturbed layers of ash and charcoal that formed *in situ*, nor should lenses of ash and charcoal have accumulated in pits from which steamed oysters were removed. These two ash-filled pits are very similar to Feature 2 at Patuxent Point (see Chapter 9), and the occurrence of similar pit features at other seventeenth-century sites (e.g., Edwards et al., 1989:83–91) suggests a specific, common function that we have yet to identify. The ash and charcoal, mixed with fragments of sintered daub, probably represent cleanings from a hearth or oven. We do not know why the colonists dug a hole to deposit this sort of material.

A cluster of superimposed features (13, 14, and 18) on the east side of the Compton site was interpreted as a mortar-mixing area. All three features yielded mortar and nails, with Feature 13 also containing layers of sorted gravel. Feature 13 was interpreted as a natural spring. It is uncertain why the occupants of Compton would be mixing mortar in a hole rather than in wooden buckets or tubs, particularly since the small quantity of brick recovered from the site indicates little need for large quantities of mortar. Nor is it clear why nails occur in a mortar mixing feature. Was it in fact mortar, or unburned daub, and was there evidence of lime (i.e., calcified oyster shell) in this material? Unfortunately, the excavation record and technical report are mute on these points. Feature 13, situated on level ground and surrounded by soils identical to those found throughout the site, probably is not a spring. It may represent a tree fall, as several features of similar description, virtually devoid of cultural material, were encountered at the neighboring Patuxent Point site. I cannot interpret any of these features with a high degree of confidence.

The remaining 10 pits (Features 3, 5, 6/16/17, 7, 8, 9, and 11/12/21) have been identified as borrow pits from which loam was quarried for building and repairing the wattle-and-daub chimneys. Once the loam had been quarried, the holes served as refuse pits. This interpretation is widely applied in the region to large, irregular pit features. Such pits were excavated into local silt loams and clay loams, terminating at the sand-loam interface. It should be pointed out, however, that there is no *prima facie* evidence for dismissing the "trash-pit" interpretation; namely, some pits may have been dug specifically to dispose of trash.[7] Most of the pits are irregular to elliptical in shape with inward-sloping walls. Several are superimposed upon one another and, due to the manner in which they were excavated, their contents must be analyzed together; hence, Features 6/16/17 and 11/12/21 (Figure 8–5) are treated as two features or feature clusters. All of the pit features were filled with lenses of silt loam with charcoal, burned daub, artifacts, and oyster shells. Most contained well-defined lenses of oyster shell.

The large number of borrow pits at Compton is consistent with the interpretation of Buildings 1, 3, and 4 as dwellings with wattle-and-daub chimneys. Precisely how much loam would have been needed to construct just one chimney is unknown, but it is certain that the chimneys required periodic replastering—inside and out. The bits of sintered daub appearing amongst the trash (some of which are fairly large and bear the imprints of wattling) indicate a need to replaster the hearth as it was damaged through use. Rain and frost would have taken their toll on the unfired exterior surfaces of the chimneys as well. Superimposed pits suggest episodes of replastering, although why the colonists would have quarried loam so close to abandoned, trash-filled pits is uncertain. Stratigraphy in Feature 11/12/21 (see Figure 8–5), for example, suggests that one pit cut through another pit already filled with trash. If the fill from the later pit was intended for daub, it must have included oyster shells, bones, and artifacts from the fill of the earlier pit. Such inclusions in sintered daub were not reported for the Compton site, but detailed analyses of daub from Compton and Patuxent Point have not been undertaken.

Spatial Distributions

The plowzone at Compton was sampled in an attempt to identify surface middens (Gibb and King, 1991; Keeler, 1978; King, 1988; King and Miller, 1987; Miller, 1986; Neiman, 1980; Pogue, 1988). The method involves computer simulation mapping of various categories of artifacts recovered from regularly placed plowzone units, for example, ceramics (fine and coarse), bottle glass, tobacco pipes, European flint, and bone. The resulting contours, generated with a nearest neighbor algorithm, are overlain on a light table. The analyst defines the middens by drawing lines around all of the overlapping concentrations. Once defined, the midden contents are compared through simple proportional analysis supplemented by chi-square analyses of the frequency distributions. Individual middens are characterized by their contents, reflect the principal function of, and range of activities undertaken in, the nearest structure or room within a building

Feature 8

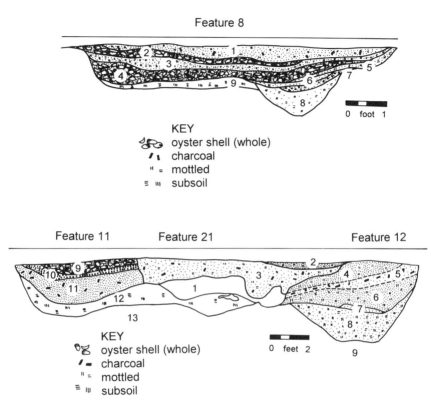

KEY
🐚 oyster shell (whole)
⁄ \ charcoal
" = mottled
≡ �ₘ subsoil

Feature 11   Feature 21   Feature 12

KEY
🐚 oyster shell (whole)   0 feet 2   9
⁄ ▬ charcoal
" = mottled
≡ ₘ subsoil

Figure 8–5. Profiles of Features 8 and 11/12/21. Soil descriptions for Feature 8: 1. Mottled brown silt with ash, charcoal, and sintered daub; 2. Oyster shell; 3. Mottled dark grayish brown silt with ash and charcoal; 4. Oyster shell; 5. Brown silt loam; 6. Mottled dark grayish brown silt and ash; 7. Mottled light olive brown silt loam; 8. Mottled yellowish brown silty clay loam; 9. Subsoil: yellowish brown clayey silt grading into sandy clay. Soil descriptions for Feature 11/12/21: 1. Olive brown clayey silt with strong brown clayey silt and brick fragments [rodent burrow]; 2. Oyster shell in olive brown fine silt; 3. Dark brown silt loam with light olive brown fine silt, reddish yellow silt, and charcoal flecking; 4. White ash and yellowish brown silty clay; 5. White ash and strong brown silty clay and charcoal; 6. Black silt with grayish brown clayey silt and yellowish brown silt; 7. Yellowish red silty clay; 8. Mottled brown silty clay, yellowish brown silty clay, and light olive brown silty clay; 9. Oyster shell with olive brown fine silt; 10. Dark brown fine silt; 11. Very dark grayish brown silt with charcoal flecking; 12. Light olive brown silty clay with yellowish brown clay; 13. Subsoil: Yellowish brown clayey silt grading into sandy clay.

(Gibb and King, 1991; King, 1988; King and Miller, 1987). Soil elements such as calcium, phosphorous, and potash are similarly contour-mapped through computer-assisted simulations.

While King and Miller (1987) and others have successfully reconstructed the organization and use of space on seventeenth-century sites with the SYMAP computer program (Dougenik and Sheehan, 1979), this approach is subject to three limitations:

1. The assumption that sheet midden material represents direct, undifferentiated discard from the locations in which the material was generated.
2. The assumptions that activities were spatially segregated and that those patterns are reflected spatially through the co-occurrence of artifact classes (Simek, 1989).
3. The nature of the univariate analysis that produces nonreplicable results when simulated distributions of individual artifact classes or types are superimposed upon one another in order to identify middens.

The accumulation of cultural material around the doors and windows of eighteenth-century buildings has been noted by South (1977:47ff), leading to his statement of a "lawlike generalization," dubbed the Brunswick Pattern:

> On British-American sites of the eighteenth century a concentrated refuse deposit will be found at the points of entrance and exit in dwellings, shops, and military fortifications.

King and Miller (1987:37; see also Pogue, 1988:43ff) echo and develop this concept: "Refuse disposal at most British colonial sites in North America occurred primarily in surface middens located around structures and only secondarily in so-called trash pits or other features."

South's statement is based on numerous observations, and the generalization appears to hold true for seventeenth-century sites as well, whether they were occupied by English or Dutch settlers. King and Miller's statement, however, is an assertion, and one that might not stand up under scrutiny.

The principal difficulty in characterizing the colonial pattern of refuse disposal as heave-it-out-the-nearest-door-or-window is in reconciling the resulting sheet middens with pits full of trash. Why would people accustomed to casual trash discard carry refuse an additional 50 ft. or more to toss it into an open pit? The chance occurrence of an available open pit does not account for a change in disposal habits, nor is it likely that the gradual filling of an open pit with trash satisfied any safety concerns. Two patterns of trash distribution, existing side by side, suggest that there were at least two kinds of refuse disposal practiced on many colonial sites. Most rubbish and nonrecyclable material was cleaned up and discarded into open pits. Kitchen refuse, consisting primarily of parings and spoiled food, but also odd bits of broken artifacts swept off of the floors of buildings, was tossed out of doors and into the mouths of swine and yard poultry. The latter pattern is a little more complex than the former insofar as it is directly influenced by some primary and secondary discard patterns, as well as by such transformational processes as human and livestock trampling.

Given this model of trash disposal, we might expect poorer preservation of artifacts, and poorer representation of ceramic and glass vessels, in the sheet middens. The highly fragmented nature of plowzone artifacts may be a fairly direct representation of the material as it was deposited, and not simply a product of damage from plowing. The representation of artifacts in sheet middens is skewed because their inclusion into the slop bucket was a matter of chance rather than of regular, systematic practice. Features, on the contrary, yield better-preserved material and a more representative sample of the materials discarded by a household since they contain the bulk of the refuse that was recognized as such and discarded accordingly.[8] This model distinguishes between what the colonists perceived as waste (the contents of pits) and the by-products of what they perceived to be a resource (the odd bits of rubbish included within the slop intended as food for livestock).

A comparative midden analysis should account for the process by which refuse—the data—was deposited in middens—the units of analysis. If midden refuse on seventeenth-century sites is largely the by-product of kitchen cleanup and recycling (as food for livestock), then all middens will be very similar, the differences largely attributable to stochastic events and sampling error. Failure to consider the cultural transformations that underlie midden formation (cf. Schiffer, 1976) undermines much of the earlier analyses of the Compton and Patuxent Point middens (cf. Gibb and King, 1991; LBA, 1989). That is not to say that *intersite* comparisons of midden materials have no value, only that *intrasite* comparisons may reveal few significant differences between the middens of a site, positive chi-square and Fischer exact tests notwithstanding.[9] Midden analysis awaits a theoretical perspective that recognizes and uses the common origins of kitchen middens to advantage.

Along a parallel line of criticism, Simek (1989) suggests that archaeologists devote a great deal of time and energy to the identification of activity areas on archaeological sites without first determining whether or not the structure of the artifact distributions warrants such analyses:

> If [activity] areas are preserved in a distribution, the activity model implies that certain structural characteristics will be present. In general terms, activities comprise local processes; they occur within delimited spaces. Thus, the presence of activity areas will *not* be reflected by patterning in artifact class co-occurrences over the entire site . . . .. When activity areas are reflected in a distribution, there should be clusters of materials at the activity locations, and cluster contents should reflect the activities performed. It follows that clusters reflecting different activities should be composed primarily of the few tools used at that place. Thus, the content of individual activity clusters

Table 8–2. Diversity Analysis for the Compton Middens and General Plowzone

Midden	Tobacco pipes	Fine ceramics	Coarse ceramics	Bone	Bottle glass	Boone's H
A	96	24	102	74	20	0.041
B	64	21	63	65	12	0.070
C	70	24	113	27	11	0.035
D	40	14	42	20	3	0.058
Plowzone	670	126	1,277	239	419	0.006

should have low *diversity* relative to the overall site assemblage composition . . . . At the same time, the presence of activity areas should result in clusters that are *heterogeneous* on a global [i.e., site-wide] scale. (Simek, 1989:59)

We might expect the four middens, previously defined by Gibb and King (1991:118*ff*), to exhibit very low richness and evenness values; namely, the middens, representing activity areas, should yield few artifact classes, and these dominated by one or two classes. The general plowzone should yield a wide range of artifact classes representing many activity sets.[10] Plowzone artifact distributions may be relatively even since the various uneven distributions within activity areas are balanced over the site as a whole. The frequency data in Table 8–2 indicate that this model will not hold for the Compton site: there are but five artifact classes, and these are represented in each midden and across the site.[11]

Boone's *H*, a measure of heterogeneity, has been calculated for each midden (Middens A through D; Figure 8–6) and for the sum of all plowzone units, exclusive of the units assigned to each of the four middens: that is, the general plowzone deposits are regarded, analytically, as a single midden to avoid the apparent circularity of using the same midden data as a baseline against which the computed heterogeneity values for each of the middens would be compared. This technique has an advantage over simple chi–square analysis of middens identified through univariate simulation mapping. Nearest neighbor algorithms compute contour intervals for single variables on a Cartesian grid. The analyst superimposes those contour maps to create a composite map upon which areas of maximum artifact densities—middens—are defined. Boone's *H* addresses the interaction of the variables, treating them together rather than separately. Boone's *H* values also can be replicated, as long as the same algorithm and data format are used. Nearest neighbor analyses require a certain amount of intuition, a "best guess," to tie the various artifact distributions together.

Boone's (1987) analysis of heterogeneity is based on an algorithm consisting of three separate formulae:

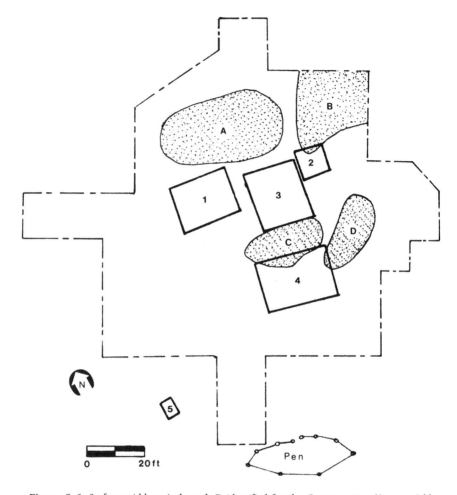

Figure 8–6. Surface middens A through D identified for the Compton site. (Source: Gibb and King, 1991:118)

1.

$$p_{ij} = W_j \frac{y_{ij}}{\sum W_j y_{ij}};$$

where

$$W_j = {}^Y\!/Y_{ij} \; ; \; W_j$$

is a weighting factor that serves as an expression of the site-wide distribution for each class of artifact relative to the most frequently occurring class, in this case, coarse earthenware ceramics. Y is the site-wide total for the most frequently occurring artifact class Y_{ij} and is the frequency of each artifact class for each midden; P_i. is the weighted percentage for each artifact class obtained by dividing the weighted counts by the sum of all weighted counts in the array.

$$2. \qquad\qquad P_j = \frac{W_j Y_i}{\sum W_j Y_j},$$

where P_j is the site-wide expected value for each artifact class, calculated by dividing the product of the weighting factor and the total for each class by the sum of those products for all of the artifact classes. The result is an array of identical values against which the array of observed values are compared. The observed P_{ij} values are measures of deviation from the expected P_j values that would obtain if there were no differences in rates of accumulation by artifact class.

$$3. \qquad\qquad H_i = \sum (p_{ij} - P_j)^2,$$

calculated for each midden at the site. Heterogeneity of any one deposit (H_i) is the sum of the squared deviations of the observed values (weighted to account for differential rates of accumulation by class) from the expected values. Low values for individual middens (i.e., close to zero) indicate heterogeneity or evenness that is consistent with that of the site, in general. Higher values (i.e., close to 1.00) indicate less heterogeneity, namely, less evenness and a more limited range of artifact types than is characteristic for the site as a whole.[12]

The H value for the general plowzone, exclusive of the contents of the individual middens (as defined through nearest neighbor analysis), is very low (0.006; see Table 8–2). This suggests a high degree of heterogeneity, or evenness of distribution, among the five artifact classes, much as Simek (1989) predicts for global or site-wide artifact distributions. Boone's H values for each of the middens are higher (ranging between 0.035 and 0.070), but still are quite low, again suggesting a high degree of heterogeneity and a lack of well-defined activity areas.[13] The limited range of possible artifact classes (5) has some effect on the small deviations of observed from expected values. Each analytic unit (the individual middens) has a richness value of one, since each contains at least one item per class.[14] Boone's H, in this case, is measuring heterogeneity, the representation within each class. A wider range of artifact classes could be identified following South's (1977) classification, for example, but classes other than those indicated in Table 8–2 generally occur in frequencies too low to be statistically meaningful.

Figure 8–7 indicates that the evenness values (H/Hmax) for the Compton site middens, and the general plowzone material, fall within the 90% confidence interval range for the randomized data; that is, there is no evidence of the localized, homogeneous deposits that Simek (1989) hypothesizes for activity areas. Nor does the larger assemblage yield the richness values that we might expect for

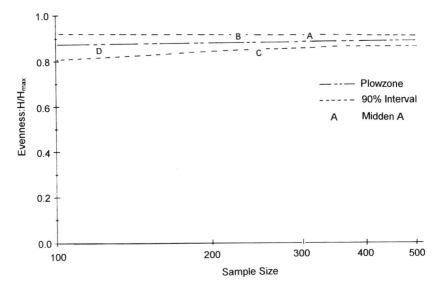

Figure 8–7. Simulations of evenness values for Compton middens.

a site that is composed of a number of different activity areas, each occupying its own space and characterized by its own specialized tool kit and refuse. Again, this lack is attributable to the small number of artifact classes used in the analysis, and by the predominance of ceramics—and to a lesser extent, tobacco pipes—in the assemblage.

The results of the SYMAP nearest neighbor analysis, reported in Gibb and King (1991), also can be evaluated through k-means analysis of the plowzone artifact distributions. As noted in Chapter 6, this nonhierarchical, divisive clustering technique is useful for identifying intuitively plausible, "natural" clusters within multivariate data sets (Kintigh, 1990:185). Observations are assigned to clusters and the resulting cluster solutions are compared to those produced from the randomized sample data.

Five variables were analyzed for the 162 plowzone units at Compton: bottle glass, ceramics, tobacco pipes, European flint, and bone. Locational data (i.e., the grid coordinates of each unit) were omitted. The units were clustered solely on the basis of frequencies for each of the above classes. The three-cluster solution marked the only break in the distribution, and it falls outside of the two-standard-deviation range calculated on 100 runs of the randomized data. Cluster 3 units (n = 21) occur primarily among the structures, while Cluster 2 units (n = 68) more or less define the entirety of the site core (Figure 8–8). Cluster 1 units (n = 73)

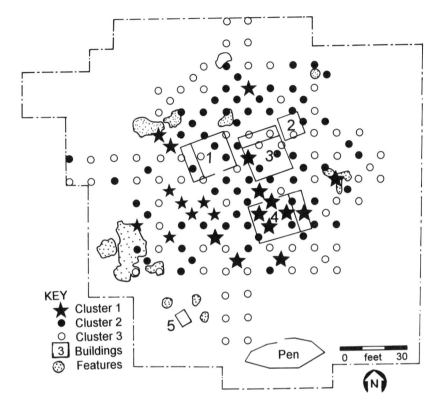

Figure 8–8. Distribution of units at the Compton site, based on k-means clustering analysis.

define the periphery. A few units from each cluster lie within the zones defined for each of the other two. These can be attributed to sampling error.

Those units lying closest to the geographic center of the homelot produced the highest numbers of artifacts in most of the artifact classes; hence, the clustering routine grouped units in a manner that differs little from a clustering, or contouring, on the basis of total artifacts per unit. This problem might be circumvented by converting the data to percentage values. Unfortunately, artifact yields from the Compton units are very low. Converting values that rarely exceed 20 into percentage values seems unwarranted, and potentially misleading.

Discussion

Results from the above analyses are consistent with those achieved by Gibb and King (1991). In that work, we suggested that the general lack of well-defined activity areas was a product of weakly defined gender roles and small, relatively undifferentiated labor forces at the Compton and Patuxent Point sites. Activity areas (and, by extension, gender roles) are only slightly better defined at the St. John's site (18ST1-23), the private dwelling of a succession of wealthy households and a public ordinary in St. Mary's City, Maryland (Gibb and King, 1991). Our inability to identify activity areas at seventeenth-century sites in the Chesapeake Bay region could be a product of the limitations of the data and analytical techniques used in their analysis, and the theoretical constructs in which we interpret those data.

Chi–square analysis, for example, permits direct comparison of midden contents, despite different sample sizes, but it does not account for the reliability of the sample. In other words, any differences between middens may be attributable to inadequate plowzone sampling and stochastic factors in the deposition and transformation of sheet middens, rather than to any meaningful differences in deposition.[15] The problem is particularly pronounced in the analysis of the Compton plowzone units due to their small size and consequent low artifact yields: the lower the artifact yield, the higher the sampling error.

More critical is the assumption that surface middens are direct reflections of activities once-removed from the rooms in which they occurred. The results of the diversity analysis, supported by the cluster analysis of plowzone artifact distributions, suggest that this assumption is ill-founded. The frequency data and Boone's H-values in Table 8–2 indicate little differentiation across the site. Recreation areas, represented by high plowzone concentrations of tobacco pipes and beverage bottles, and task areas, represented by concentrations of European flint and lead sprue or dairy-related vessels do not occur at Compton. Boone's analysis of heterogeneity and Kintigh's k-means analysis cast doubt on the reality of those middens previously defined and analyzed through the SYMAP procedure and chi–square analysis, and illustrated in Figure 8–6.

Reanalysis of the Compton plowzone material suggests that there was little spatial differentiation in the open areas around the structures. The dwellings cluster in the core of the site, with features related to livestock husbandry and trash disposal confined to the perimeter. There is little evidence of functional specialization and segregation. Assertions of a well-defined, gender-based division of labor, deducible from Markham's (1986 [1615]) prescriptions and court documents cited in previous chapters, cannot be confirmed for the Compton site. If discrete, gender-specific tasks such as dairying or food preparation occurred at Compton, they did so amongst numerous other tasks, overlapping in space and, perhaps, in time. Simek's (1989:59) activity area model suggests little, or no, activity structure at Compton.

Table 8–3. Summary of Tobacco Pipe Fragments

Types and bore diameters	Number of fragments
White clay pipe fragments	430
9/64"	59
8/64"	119
7/64"	231
6/64"	20
5/64"	1
Terra-cotta pipe fragments	155
Total tobacco pipes	585
Unit mean	9.4
Unit median	8.0

ARTIFACT ANALYSIS

Artifacts recovered from Compton consist of manufactured goods, some locally made, but most imported from England and the European continent. While their spatial distributions inform on activity patterning on the homelot, the types of artifacts and the places in which they were made betray some of the Stephens family choices. Two classes of artifact are particularly useful insofar as we know something of their place of manufacture, and they occur in relatively large numbers, thereby permitting intersite comparisons: tobacco pipes, and ceramic and glass vessels.

Tobacco Pipes

Plowzone units at Compton yielded 1,095 pipe fragments; 940 are white clay (presumably imported from Europe) and 155 are red or buff-colored terra-cotta of probable local manufacture (Table 8–3). Using Hanson's (1971) multiple regression formula #3 (n = 426 white clay pipestems, mean diameter = 7.4859, standard deviation = 0.7858), I calculate a mean occupation date of 1653 ± 23.57 years (i.e., 1629–1677, using a two-standard-deviation range). The Stephens family patented the tract in 1651 and lived there at least until the ca. 1663. The anomalous mean date is due to the early occupation, which predates the regular, incremental decrease in bore diameters coincident with the increase in pipestem lengths (post–1680). Dutch-made pipes in the assemblage also reduce accuracy: Dutch pipes did not change in the same regular manner as English pipes.

Seventeenth-century English and Dutch tobacco pipe fragments are virtually indistinguishable. Makers' marks, however, can lead us to the identity of the pipemaker and, hence, to a pipe's country of origin. Some decorative motifs also may be useful for identifying country of origin, although I find this approach much less reliable, a point to which I return in a moment.

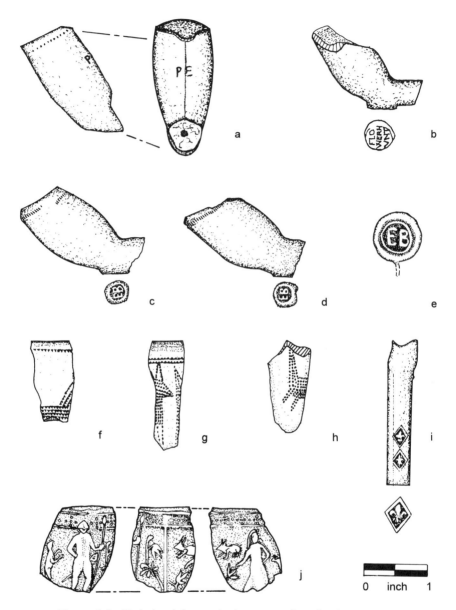

Figure 8–9. Marked and decorated tobacco pipes from the Compton site.

Of the more than 1,000 pipe fragments recovered from Compton, only 44 bear legible makers' marks, of which all but 2 appear on the heels; those 2 appear on the bowls, one marked "LE" (not illustrated), the other "PE" (Figure 8–9a). "LE" is the mark of Llewelyn Evans, a pipemaker in Bristol, England, from 1661 until his death in 1688. His widow, Elizabeth, carried on the business for several years after Llewelyn's death. Bristol pipemaker Philip Edwards, and his son Philip, were active in the export trade from 1649 until the end of the century. Examples of "LE" and "PE" pipes have been found from Maine (Baker, 1985; Faulkner and Faulkner, 1987) to Jamaica (Walker 1977:657–659).

Two makers' marks appear on the 42 marked heels: one "FLOWER HUNT," and 41 "EB" (Figure 8–9b, c-e). Flower Hunt was active between 1651 and ca. 1670. His pipes are among the less common found on American archaeological sites, but their range probably is similar to that of the Evans and Edwards pipes (e.g., Faulkner and Faulkner 1987:173). "EB" probably is the mark of Edward Bird, an English pipemaker active in Amsterdam during the 1630s through 1665. Bird's pipes appear to be rare in Canada and New England, but are common in New Netherland/New York and farther south (e.g., Hall, 1994). De Roever (1987) notes that Bird's pipes, represented by the raised letters "EB" on the heel, encircled by closely spaced or linked triangles, are the most common marked specimens recovered from Fort Orange, New York. She illustrates one specimen (de Roever, 1987:52) that is identical to the more clearly marked Compton pieces (e.g., Figure 8–9d).

Decorative motifs on Compton pipes are of several sorts. Six of the terracotta pipes, probably of Native American manufacture, depict zoomorphic figures (e.g., Figure 8–9f-h). Three ball clay pipestems are decorated with one or more fleur-de-lis, possibly indicating Dutch, Flemish, or French origins (Figure 8–9i), and 87 exhibit rouletting about the rim of the bowl, a decorative technique common on Bristol pipes (see Figure 8–9a).

Eighteen white clay pipes bear a molded design, referred to variously as the pikeman and Minerva, or crusader and huntress, design (e.g., Figure 8–7j). Often attributed to the Dutch, these pipes have been found at Fort Pentagoet (Faulkner and Faulkner, 1987:169–170) and Arrowsic (Baker, 1985:25) in Maine. They also have been reported from the St. John's site in Maryland (Hurry and Keeler, 1991:62–63). Faulkner and Faulkner (1987:169), citing Atkinson and Oswald (1969), state that "pipologists agree that in the 17th century the Dutch had a near monopoly on the production of pipes with molded ornamentation." On the one hand, they suggest, based on this assumption, that the 48 "crusader-and-huntress" pipes in the Pentagoet assemblage derive from Dutch sources, possibly by way of French merchants through the port of La Rochelle (Faulkner and Faulkner, 1987:169). On the other hand, they remark that the crusader-and-huntress pipes have not been recovered from Dutch sites in New Amsterdam/New York City or Fort Orange/Albany, New York (Faulkner and Faulkner, 1987:170). Faulkner and Faulkner (1987:173) recovered only one "EB" pipe, whereas Baker

(1985:23) claims that both of the "EB" pipes from Arrowsic are different from those recovered on seventeenth-century New Netherland sites. Since Edward Bird's career as a pipemaker coincides with the English and French occupations of Pentagoet (1635–1674), it is difficult to relate the absence—or near absence—of the molded relief pipes to the high profile of "EB" pipes. Convincing data linking the crusader-and-huntress pipes to the Dutch has not surfaced.[16]

This brief survey of the Compton tobacco pipes is far from complete, but it reveals certain choices made by the Stephenses. There is little doubt that they purchased items made in Bristol and elsewhere in the west country of England. The large number of "EB" pipes, however, suggests that they purchased some of their goods from Dutch traders. The Dutch connection seems even stronger if we accept the crusader-and-huntress pipes as Dutch in origin. Evidence along those lines, however, is very weak.

One other interesting point is the large number of pipe fragments recovered from the site through plowzone sampling and feature excavation. These people smoked alot. We cannot determine from the pipe fragments precisely who smoked, but the distribution of fragments across the site suggests that smoking was not confined to any one portion of the homelot. Data from the Patuxent Point site (see Chapter 9) will address the questions who smoked and where? Let's turn now to ceramic and glass vessels as evidence of the Stephenses' consumer choices.

Vessels

Computer-aided simulation mapping and cluster analysis may provide means for identifying patterns in the organization and use of space, and, specifically, patterns in the disposal or recycling of kitchen wastes. They tell us little about patterns of food processing, preparation, storage, and presentation because such analyses are based on sherd counts rather than on the types and numbers of vessels represented, and sherd counts may not be representative of what was actually being used by the household. Identifying patterns of vessel use entails the identification and quantification of ceramic and glass vessels used in those food-related activities.

Table 8-4 lists the minimum numbers of ceramic and glass vessels recovered from the various contexts, and combinations of contexts, at the Compton site. A total of 21 possible forms was arrived at by combining the types of vessels present at both the Compton and Patuxent Point sites. Most of the vessel forms are represented at both sites (see the next chapter for the distributions from Patuxent Point), although there are some stylistic differences.

The vessel forms can be grouped into five categories, all of which overlap with one another:[17]

1. Food processing: basins, colanders, jars, milkpans, and pots.

Table 8–4. Vessel Form Distributions at the Compton Site

Vessel form	Plowzone	Feature	Plowzone & feature	Total
Baking plan	0	0	1	1
Basin	1	1	1	3
Bottle	5	23	1	29
Bowl	4	2	2	8
Colander	0	0	0	0
Cooking pot	1	6	0	7
Dish	0	4	0	4
Galley pot	0	0	0	0
Indeterminate[a]	16	10	5	31
Jar	0	0	1	1
Jug	0	0	0	0
Milkpan	0	2	0	2
Table glass[b]	1	2	0	3
Pan	2	2	0	4
Pipkin	0	1	0	1
Pitcher	0	3	0	3
Plate	0	2	1	3
Platter	0	1	1	2
Porringer	0	1	0	1
Pot	0	0	0	0
Skillet	2	4	1	7
Vial	1	1	0	2
Totals:				
21 forms	33	65	14	112

[a]Includes indeterminate and various "or" combinations.
[b]Includes ornate drinking glasses of uncertain form, roemers, snifters, and tumblers.

2. Food preparation: baking pans (Figure 8–10f, from North Devonshire), basins, bowls, colanders, cooking pots (Figure 8–10e, Dutch), pans, pipkins, porringers, pots, and skillets (Figure 8–10a-d, also Dutch).
3. Food presentation:[18] basins, bowls (Figure 8–11d,e), dishes, jugs, table glass, pitchers (Figure 8–11a), cups, plates (Figure 8–11c), and platters or chargers (Figure 8–11b).
4. Food storage: bottles, bowls, jars, jugs, pans, and pots.
5. Health/Hygiene: basins, chamber pots, galley pots, ointment jars, and vials.

The degree of overlap evident in this classification renders a determination of function for any one vessel difficult without reference to archaeological context and, perhaps, use-wear analysis. The former is of little use since all of the vessels

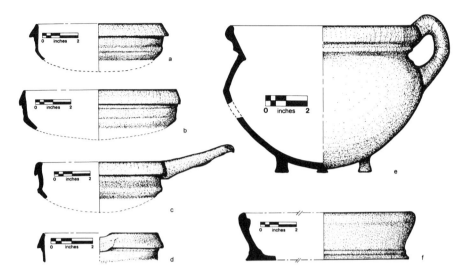

Figure 8–10. Cooking vessels recovered from the Compton site: (a-d) Dutch earthenware skillets; (e) Dutch earthenware cooking pot; and (f) North Devonshire baking pan.

appear to have been recovered from deposits disconnected with their use, namely, secondary refuse consisting of a wide range of material from a number of unrelated activities, discarded in an area other than in which the refuse was produced (Schiffer, 1976). Most of the vessels are too fragmentary to yield reliable results from use-wear analysis.[19]

These difficulties notwithstanding, we can still review the vessel list to determine what kinds of vessels the Stephens family used during their tenure at Compton, the relative frequencies of certain vessel forms, and the range of activities represented—or not represented—by those forms. Of the 112 ceramic and glass vessels recovered from the Compton site, 31 could not be identified as to form, being wholly unidentifiable or indistinguishable between two or more similar forms. More than half of these derive from the plowzone, 10 were recovered from subsurface features, and 5 are composed of sherds that were recovered from both plowzone and feature contexts, that is, sherds from both contexts that could be attributed to a single vessel.

The most common vessel forms at Compton are bottles. Five of these are Rhenish stonewares (both Frechen and Rhenish gray), 2 are glass bottles that are round in section, and the remaining 22 are glass case bottles, square in section and often erroneously referred to as "Dutch gin" bottles.[20] Along with an undetermined number of other, more generalized vessels, these bottles were important

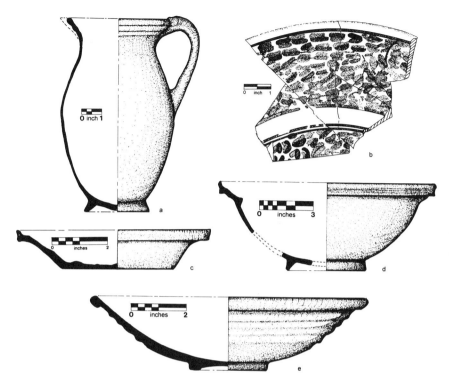

Figure 8–11. Food presentation vessels recovered from the Compton site: (a) probable Dutch white earthenware pitcher; (b) majolica charger of uncertain orgin; (c) small earthenware plate of probable Dutch or Flemish manufacture; (d) North Holland slipware bowl; and (e) North Italian (Pisan?) marbleized slipware bowl.

storage tools. Their status as consumer items should be seen in terms of what was stored in them, and not the bottles themselves.

With the exception of two North Holland slipware bowls and a Pisan marbleized slipware bowl (Figure 8–11d and e, respectively), only three ornate glass vessels, three plates, and two platters can be attributed to the activity set "food presentation." Many of the 29 indeterminate vessels, however, may represent the rims of plates (e.g., Figure 8–11c, a probable Dutch or Flemish plate), platters, cups, and other food presentation vessels. Largely of faience or majolica, they also include a variety of coarse red earthenwares of unknown origin.[21] The highly decorated, fragile, and presumably expensive tin-glazed earthenwares (e.g., Figure 8–11b, a majolica charger) may have lent an air of sophistication and elegant living that would have offered a sharp contrast to the coarsely built earthfast houses and timber furniture. Nonetheless, such vessels appear on most, if not all, seventeenth-century sites identified in the Chesapeake Bay region. Tin-glazed wares recovered from the Compton site (and Patuxent Point), exhibit some use wear, indicating that they were used on the table and were not left hanging on walls or perched upon shelves for decoration.

Vessels that could be attributed to the Health/Hygiene category are limited to two glass vials. Neither tin-glazed galley pots (vessels generally containing ointments or salves) nor chamber pots have been identified for the Compton ceramic assemblage. The vials may have contained medicines or perfumes, representations of a cultural system that valued appearance and health. (The works of Shakespeare, Jonson, Chapman, and others make frequent reference to the desirability of sweetness of breath and clearness of skin, at least for characters of "name" and "note.") Other artifacts related to personal appearance have been recovered from the Compton site, including a bone comb and parts of clothing (clothing hooks, silver-plated copper mesh, glass beads, and a brass spur).

The remaining vessels include pots, bowls, basins, pans, and other vessels of generalized form and probable multiple functions. Even the two North Devonshire milkpans are as likely to have been used as wash basins as for cream separation. Swift's satire on the behavior of English servants provides insight into the misuses to which vessels might have been put:

> When you have broken all your earthen Drinking Vessels below Stairs [in the servants' rooms and workrooms] (which is usually done in a Week) the Copper Pot will do as well; it can boil Milk, heat Porridge, hold Small-Beer, or in Case of Necessity serve for a Jordan [a chamber pot]; therefore apply it indifferently to all of these Uses; but never wash it or scour it, for fear of taking off the Tin (Swift, 1958 [ca. 1725]:499–500).

Facetiousness aside, many vessels probably served multiple functions, particularly if access to replacement vessels was restricted to the annual arrival of the merchant fleet.

The vessel assemblage from the Compton site indicates a degree of elegance that might seem at odds with the rustic character of the site's architecture and the hurly-burly of frontier homelot activities that were unrestrained by segregated spaces. The assemblage is equally divided among the food preparation, storage, and presentation activity sets, assuming that the bulk of the vessels of indeterminate form are food presentation vessels. The bottles are storage vessels of more or less standard size (approximately one quart), whereas the cooking and food presentation vessels betray a high degree of differentiation in form. Whether the vessel assemblage can be viewed as an attempt by the Stephens family to distinguish household members along kin lines remains to be examined. Maintaining harmony while asserting rights to wealth would have been a difficult task for most planters with heterogeneous households, and some planters may have attempted to work out a balance symbolically through the object domains of food and housing.[22]

SUMMARY

Salvage excavations at the Compton site have provided data on the material aspects of life for a seventeenth-century English household in the Chesapeake Bay region. These include homelot siting, construction and maintenance of architectural spaces, trash disposal and the organization of homelot space, and the acquisition and use of tobacco pipes and of vessels connected with the processing, preparation, presentation, and storage of foodstuffs.

The Stephens family selected a plantation tract with direct access to aquatic foods and transportation of the Chesapeake Tidewater. The soils were well suited to the cultivation of tobacco, although they may have had limited value for agricultural diversification. As early arrivals in what would become Calvert County, the Stephens family could choose such an optimal site; however, rapid settlement of prime agricultural lands, and the limitations imposed by Lord Baltimore's "Conditions of Plantation," provided few opportunities for providing sons John and William, Jr., with comparable tracts. The two sons did inherit some land from their uncle, John Hodges. Situated on the "Cliffs," on the bayside of the peninsula, these lands lacked ready access to the water due to the high, eroded cliffs, and their soils were not optimal for tobacco. The senior William's, attempt to acquire additional acreage failed, ending in a lawsuit. Limited coastal lands, fields that were probably robbed of their fertility in a few short years, and the political instability arising from the English civil wars and the Restoration probably provided sufficient motivation for the family to move to the eastern shore. And so they did, along with many of their Quaker and Puritan neighbors.

Behind them, the Stephens family left five structures that they had maintained (chimney replastering, post replacement), but which probably were beginning to show their wear. There appears to have been little or no attempt to improve the dwellings through the construction of additions of specialized function, the construction of cellars, or, for that matter, of simple wooden floors. Two outbuildings were built, but little investment was made in developing them into highly specialized farm outbuildings such as typified many North American farms in the late eighteenth through twentieth centuries. Even the elliptical pen evinces little investment beyond procuring the necessary lumber and the day or two that would have been necessary to build it. The dwellings were small (not much larger than the living rooms of many upper middle class homes in North America in the late twentieth century), leaving little room for spatial segregation of tasks. The coexistence of three separate dwellings provides the best evidence for any kind of spatial segregation of peoples or activities at the site.

Around these buildings, a sheet midden formed. Through computer simulation mapping, Gibb and King (1991) identified four middens. Subsequent analyses using measures of assemblage heterogeneity and artifact clustering, however, failed to detect significant differences among the middens in terms of their contents and, indeed, cast doubt upon their reality. The apparent uniformity in artifact distributions across the site is attributable in part to the gross artifact categories employed in defining and analyzing yard middens. Similarity among the middens may be a product of the similar processes by which they were formed. I have argued that the surface middens represent areas where kitchen refuse, containing some rubbish but consisting largely of organic debris, was tossed out the door and into the mouths of waiting livestock. The results of the k-means analysis support that contention. True rubbish removal is represented in several trash-filled pit features that surround the homelot core. There is little evidence of specialized activity areas beyond the structures themselves, and that lack of evidence may accurately reflect the poorly defined division of labor, and the very limited nature of spatial separation, at Compton.

Analysis of tobacco pipestems reveals a mean occupation range of 1653 ± 24 years. The mean occupation date of 1657, based on the documented Stephens occupation (1651 to ca. 1663), is somewhat later, an expected aberration given the limitations of pipestem dating and the presence of Dutch-made pipes in the assemblage. Those Dutch pipes also suggest direct or indirect trade with the Dutch, an activity forbidden in Lord Baltimore's charter and often legislated against by the English governments.

From the Compton pits and, to a lesser extent, from the sheet middens, 112 individual vessels of glass and ceramic were recovered. Glass and stoneware storage bottles dominate the assemblage. Cooking wares also are prominent and many of these, as well as some of the food presentation vessels, are of Dutch manufacture. The proportion of vessels in the Compton assemblage of non-English manufacture may be as much, or more than, 50%. Vessels were imported from northern Italy, the Iberian peninsula, the Saintonge region of France, and North Devonshire, England. Whether or not the availability of Dutch vessels, or of vessels from other countries, influenced the preparation and presentation of food cannot at this point be determined. It is evident, however, that as many as 9 of the 17 cooking vessels recovered from the site are of small size, scarcely capable of holding more than one pint of liquid. Whether this suggests the preparation of many small dishes for a large household, or a few dishes for a small household, remains to be determined. We know from a 1651 land warrant that William and Magdalen Stephens began their household in Calvert County with two sons and four servants. Subsequent changes to the household's demographics are unknown, and are likely to remain so.

The following chapter presents and evaluates evidence from the neighboring Patuxent Point site. The data are presented in a similar format, with two noteworthy exceptions: (1) even less is known of the inhabitants of Patuxent Point, it very likely having been occupied by at least one or, perhaps, two or more successive tenant households, and (2) data from a family cemetery associated with the Patuxent Point homelot are analyzed. The results are briefly summarized and interpreted within the larger argument of this work.

NOTES

1. Archaeological reconnaissance and data recovery at the Compton site were required under Calvert County's Zoning Ordinance 5–6.04. The reader should consult the technical report (Louis Berger & Associates, 1989) for details of the site excavation. Field notes, as well as the artifacts, are curated by the Maryland Historical Trust at the Jefferson Patterson Park and Museum, St. Leonard, Maryland.

2. The grid was oriented approximately N60°E. Neither the field notes nor the report are clear on how the investigators estimated the geographic center of the site, but subsequent plowzone testing and stripping proved them to be quite accurate in their prediction. The "Virginia" tradition of excavating colonial sites has placed little store in the use of screens or in the sampling of plowzone (e.g., Heite, 1992; Noel Hume, 1975). The use of plowzone units measuring 2.5 ft. on a side represents a compromise between the local convention of 5 ft. units and the "Virginia" convention of no units whatsoever. The debate, "to screen or not to screen," unfortunately, continues (e.g., Heite, 1992; King, 1990, 1992; Pogue, 1992), the combatants appealing to traditions new and old.

3. Drawings for all objects are available from the author and from the Jefferson Patterson Park and Museum. Gibb (1993a) and Gibb and Balla (1993) illustrate some of the more complete vessels.

4. A *bay* is a division of a building as defined by principal horizontal and vertical members. The number of bays in an earthfast house is determined by counting the pairs of principal vertical members (bents) and subtracting one. Typical dimensions for seventeenth-century bays are 20 ft. long (corresponding to the overall width of the building) and 15 ft. wide for buildings of two or more bays. Actual lengths vary considerably, perhaps more so than bay widths. A bay may represent one or more rooms.

5. See Carson et al. (1981) for a detailed discussion of earthfast construction.

6. See Luckenbach and Gibb (1994) for a brief review of the history and manufacture of window leads, and their appearance on sites in Anne Arundel County, Maryland. Some turned window leads bear inscriptions on their interior milled surfaces. These include names or initials of manufacturers, city of manufacture, and/or dates. Harrison (1968 [1587]:310) also reports the use of horn, wicker lattice, and "specular

stone" (mica sheets) for window coverings in England from the Saxon period to the Elizabethan era. Such window coverings have not been documented in the American colonies; however, oiled paper commonly served as glazing in frontier houses of the eighteenth and nineteenth centuries.

7. Gramly (1978) depicts a series of trash-filled pits along the interior walls of Fort Laurens, a Revolutionary War-period fortification. The regular placement of these pits suggests that the soldiers dug them specifically for trash disposal. Purposeful digging of pits for trash disposal contradicts the pitch-it-out-the-nearest-window model (see note 8).

8. Ravines also may have been used as open pits. It should be noted that Netherlandish genre paintings depicting women emptying slop buckets out of windows, usually to the consternation of passersby, should not be taken as evidence of casual discard. While such things no doubt occurred, it also is evident that in portraying such scenes the artists were attempting to convey a moral with humor, equating physical dirtiness with moral depravity (Schaefer, 1994). Also, the contents of those slop buckets consist of kitchen wastes or night soil, but not necessarily large pieces of broken pottery and glass.

9. Implicit recognition that sheet midden materials derive primarily from food preparation is evident in most analyses of midden contents. The types of data invariably include bone, bottle glass, and pottery (the latter may be divided into presumed functional types), and soil chemicals such as calcium and potash (related to the disposal of food waste and ash). Tobacco pipes are an exception, but their role in such analyses is primarily that of a dating tool (e.g., King, 1988).

10. An activity set consists of related actions employing a definable group of tools.

11. The null hypothesis of no significant difference is rejected with a χ^2 value of 349.97 greatly exceeding the critical value of 26.3 ($\alpha = 0.05$, $df = 16$). The differences between the individual middens and the general plowzone, however, are products of the nearest neighbor algorithm used in defining those middens; namely, they are different because we have made them so.

12. Boone's measure of heterogeneity is akin to chi–square analysis in that the analyst calculates expected values, given overall homogeneity, and measures the differences between observed and expected values. That measure will approach zero when the difference between observed and expected values is small, that is, where the artifacts are more or less uniformly distributed, both in terms of number of classes and representation within each class.

13. Again, slightly higher values are expected because the middens are artifacts of the process by which they were identified and defined, and not necessarily of the processes by which they were created; that is, Middens A through D were created as much by the analysts as by the Stephens family.

14. There are only five categories used in the analysis, and they are represented in virtually every sample unit.

15. These somewhat tentatively defined units of analysis (sheet middens) contrast with the architecturally defined midden deposits at Qsar es-Seghir (A.D. 1500–1550), in Morocco, that Boone (1987) used in his analysis of midden catchment.

16. Neither Faulkner and Faulkner (1987) nor Baker (1985) reports Dutch coarse earthenwares from Maine sites. If there was significant trade in household articles, whether direct or indirect, we might expect to find other items of Dutch manufacture.
17. Vessel forms are defined in Beaudry et al. (1983) and Yentsch (1990b).
18. I prefer the term "food presentation, to "serving," both because of the symbolic implications of the former and to avoid the generally negative connotations of the latter.
19. Microscopic inspection of many lead-glazed and tin-glazed earthenware sherds revealed evidence of use in the form of deep, linear scratches and lighter, curvilinear scratches. See Griffiths (1978) for a promising beginning in the analysis of use wear on historic period ceramics.
20. Dutch gin was manufactured for export and shipped in glass case bottles, as were other liquors by other European nations. The appellation 'Dutch gin' bottles may be a survival of seventeenth-and eighteenth-century ethnic slurs by the English against their Dutch competitors (e.g., Schama, 1988:188–193; see also Boxer, 1973:234–235). Of greater import to the issue at hand, such bottles were valuable and were reused to store liquids; probably spirits purchased from local innkeepers and decanted into the cleaned bottles.
21. Faience refers to tin-glazed earthenwares, whereas majolica refers to tin-glazed earthenwares with a lead-tin glaze mix on the reverse side, this usage following Wilcoxen (1987:54).
22. Indentured servants and slaves expressed their discontent through theft, sabotage, and refusal to work. Most conflicts could be condensed into a simple statement of the relationship between reward and investment, labor feeling that they were not adequately rewarded for their efforts and the planters believing that they were not receiving a fair return on their investment.

Chapter *9*

Patuxent Point, 1660s–1670s

INTRODUCTION

On a spring day in 1989, Julia A. King, southern Maryland regional archaeologist, led me and two prospective volunteers to the Patuxent Point site. The plan was to excavate this site with minimal funding and experienced, well-trained volunteers. Julia prepared us well for the planning meeting—crab cakes, the local specialty, and ice tea. Over lunch we discussed scheduling and strategy. We would conduct limited plowzone testing and, it was hoped, some feature excavation. The whole project could be wrapped up in a few months. Fifteen months later, we finished the bulk of the fieldwork, our limited testing having turned into a full-scale excavation with support from the state of Maryland, Calvert County, and the Archeological Society of Maryland.

Archaeological investigations at the Patuxent Point site (18CV271) are described in this chapter.[1] Methods used in the field and in the laboratory are discussed first. The field data are then briefly summarized, followed by analyses of several data sets including architecture, feature morphology and content, spatial distributions, and artifacts. There also is a brief section summarizing and interpreting spatial and forensic data from the associated cemetery.

METHODOLOGY

The site was identified during the course of an archaeological survey, but due to poor collecting conditions and the peripheral location of the site relative to the testing area its significance was not immediately recognized (see Gardner, 1988). The proposed purpose of the project was to study "the evolution of Frontier society and the emergence of rigid status distinctions through an analysis of

171

material culture" (King, 1989:2). The proposed research questions and methodology were substantially the same as those proposed for the Compton site, although in practice the methods differed significantly in several respects.

A preliminary surface reconnaissance revealed prehistoric material representing several periods over the length and breadth of the fields (see Figure 7–3). The seventeenth-century material was highly localized along one edge of the field and extended into adjacent hedgerows. In order to focus efforts on the seventeenth-century homelot, we conducted a controlled surface collection. A local farmer cut, plowed, and disked the field. Moderate rainfall washed the field soon after plowing. Approximately 2 acres (0.81 ha) were gridded into 880 surface units, each measuring 10 ft. by 10 ft. (3 m by 3 m). We intensively collected each unit and quantified the results.

An area of approximately 150 ft. by 150 ft., or 45.72 m by 45.72 m (including a wooded area unsuitable for surface collection), produced virtually all of the colonial material, including: ceramics, bottle glass, clay tobacco pipe sherds, nails, European flint, sintered daub, and brick. The plowzone within this study area was sampled with forty-six 5 ft. by 5 ft. (1.5 m by 1.5 m) test units, excavated to the base of the plowzone, the soil screened through $^1/_4$-in. (6 mm) hardware mesh. These initial units were laid out in a systematic, regular grid pattern at approximately 15 ft. (4.6 m) intervals; sampling approximately 11% of the surface of the study area. Thirteen judgmentally placed units were excavated, four to further expose subsurface features, and nine to verify the limits of the homelot (Figure 9–1). Six more units were dug some distance to the north (not shown on map) in order to examine a thin scatter of brick and nail fragments, with negative results: those units are omitted from further consideration. Excluding those units excavated to further define features, the plowzone sample consists of 59 units covering approximately 13% of the area defined through the analysis of surface materials.

The outermost units in the study area yielded few artifacts, indicating that the limits of the homelot core had been reached. Units on the east side, however, exposed very thin, highly eroded, clayey soils as well as low artifact yields. A pronounced downward slope in this area and the recovery of moderate numbers of artifacts from the surface toward the base of the slope suggest that this area has experienced considerable erosion; hence, the results of the plowzone sampling along the east side of the homelot are equivocal. This is a particularly important qualification, since this area also marks what has turned out to be the east side of the site's principal dwelling, and the low density of domestic material has given rise to speculations about formal yard space (King and Turowski, 1993).

Heavy machinery stripped topsoil from approximately 20,000 ft^2 (1,858 m^2) of the field, revealing a dark yellowish brown silt-loam subsoil in which most cultural and natural features were distinct. The grid system was reestablished

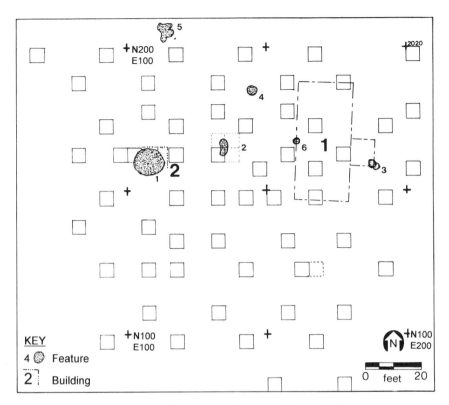

Figure 9–1. Plowzone sample units at Patuxent Point.

(oriented N43.5°W), and each 10 ft. by 10 ft. grid unit was trowel-scraped and mapped at a 1:24 scale. With the exception of the south half of one refuse-filled pit (Feature 1), all features—prehistoric and historic—were excavated stratigraphically. All excavated feature soils were screened through $1/4$-in. (6 mm) mesh, and in many cases sampled for purposes of flotation and chemical analyses. Those analyses have not been undertaken to date. Gibb and King (1991) generated artifact distribution maps of plowzone artifacts with the SYMAP computer graphics program (Dougenik and Sheehan, 1979), the results of which are summarized and reevaluated below.

Ceramic and vessel glass sherds were pulled from the general plowzone unit bags and combined with those recovered from features, and cross-mending was undertaken. Minimum numbers of vessels were calculated on the bases of distinctive rim sherds and pastes, in the manner described by Noel Hume (1975), and the results reported in Gibb (1993a). I used a binocular microscope (30×) and a comparator (6×) to distinguish between similar pastes and to measure and roughly quantify paste inclusions. Minimum numbers of glass bottles also were calculated based on the numbers of bases with their perimeters or pontil marks more than 50% complete. All vessels, ceramic and glass, have been illustrated and described in detail. Pipestem bores have been measured, and bowl forms and makers' marks illustrated. A variety of small finds (e.g., shoe buckles, locks, trade tokens) also have been illustrated.[2]

Faunal remains from Features 1 and 2 were analyzed by Weinand and Reitz (1993). A more complete analysis of the faunal remains has yet to be undertaken. Ubelaker, et al. (1993) analyzed the human remains. Their report provides important details on household demographics and pathologies among the occupants of Patuxent Point and, perhaps, of neighboring sites.

RESULTS

Stripping the plowzone revealed a large number of prehistoric, as well as historic period, features. This chapter deals strictly with the latter.[3] Among the historic period features are structural postholes, fence post holes, postholes of indeterminate function, trash-filled pits, sheet middens, and 18 grave shafts. These features represent a dwelling house measuring 38 ft. by 20 ft. (11.6 m by 6.1 m), a possible building of indeterminate size and function, borrow pits, and a household cemetery (Figure 9–2). Each is discussed below.

FEATURE ANALYSIS

The structure of this chapter closely mirrors that of Chapter 8, thereby facilitating comparisons in Chapter 10. Four types of archaeological data are discussed in this section: architecture, pit features and their contents, spatial distributions, and artifacts, specifically, tobacco pipes, and ceramic and glass vessels.

Architecture

Although there may have been two buildings at Patuxent Point, only one can be defined with certitude. It is rectilinear, and its long axis is oriented northwest-southeast (Figure 9–3).[4] Overall dimensions (measured from postmold centers) are 38 ft. by 20 ft. (11.6 m by 6.1 m), divided into four bays. The northernmost bay measures 6 ft. by 20 ft. (1.8 m by 6.1 m) and probably supported a wattle-and-daub chimney stack and, perhaps, an adjacent closet. Reddened subsoil in the western portion of this bay indicates a hearth, and a shallow, flat-bottomed pit that intrudes into one of the postholes may have served as a small root cellar (Figure 9–4):

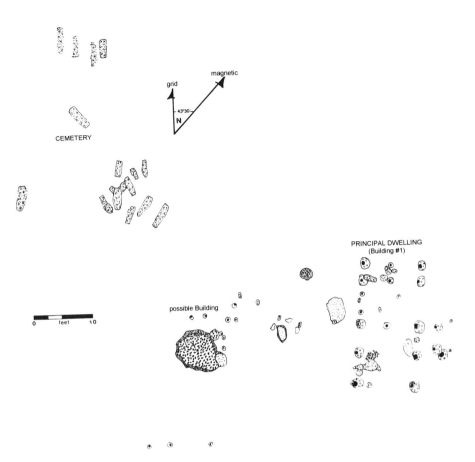

Figure 9–2. Map of Patuxent Point features.

[Potatoes] are so tender, that it is very difficult to preserve them in the Winter; for the least frost coming at them, rots and destroys them; and therefore People bury 'em under Ground, near their Fire-Hearth, all the Winter, until the Time comes, that their seedlings are to be set. (Beverley, 1947 [1705]:145)

Beverley was referring to potatoes that would have served both as food and seed, thereby requiring a cellar of considerable size. The possible cellar in the dwelling is of modest size (4.5 by 2.0 by 0.5 ft., or 1.4 by 0.61 by 0.15 m), and even accounting for truncation due to plowing, it is shallow. The pit may not have served as a store for potatoes, but its placement in front of the hearth suggests that it was meant to store perishables at a constant temperature.[5] Notably, the fill was

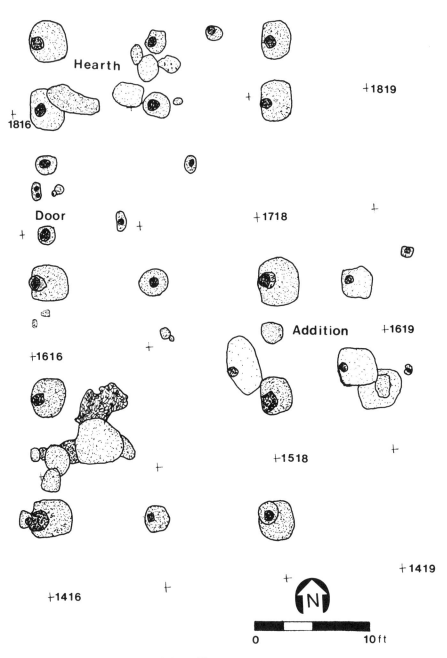

Figure 9–3. Building 1 at Patuxent Point.

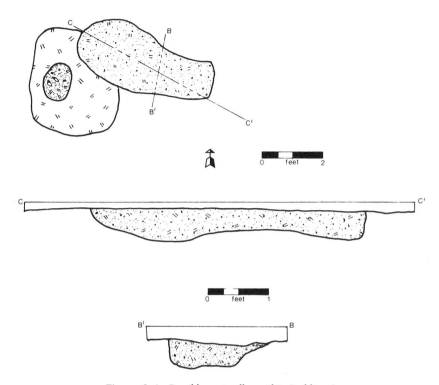

Figure 9–4. Possible root cellar within Building 1.

virtually devoid of artifacts, indicating that the pit remained in use until abandonment of the structure.

The largest bay, that adjoining the chimney bay, is 12.5 ft. by 20 ft. (3.8 m by 6.1 m), with a 6-ft. wide (1.8 m) door centered on the west facade (see Figure 9–3). Two small postholes probably supported the jamb into which the door was set. Another, larger post was set into the center of the floor and may have supported a partition wall between this large bay and the smaller one to the south. The smaller bay measures 9.5 ft. by 20 ft. (2.9 m by 6.1 m), and is joined by an addition on its east facade. The addition measures 7.5 ft., or 2.3 m (north–south), by 6 ft., or 1.8 m (east-west). The fill in both of the east wall postholes for this closet or porch contained little humus, but several artifacts, in contrast to the main load-bearing postholes. Leached humus and numerous artifacts in the fill indicate that the two postholes were dug when the ground around the dwelling had eroded (probably from foot traffic) and some rubbish had been deposited upon the surface.[6] Most of the artifacts in the other postholes are of prehistoric vintage, indicating little or no historic occupation of the site prior to the construction of the building. There also is stratigraphic evidence to suggest that the southeast corner post of the bay had been removed, possibly in anticipation of the construction of the addition. A block of wood may have substituted for the removed post, although why such a modification should have been deemed necessary or desirable is unknown.

The southernmost bay is slightly larger than the last, measuring 10 ft. by 20 ft. (3 m by 6.1 m). There is a shallow posthole in the center of the south wall. Whether this structural member was necessary to support that wall or another chimney stack is uncertain. The posthole pattern is different from that of the north chimney bay. Some scorched subsoil and shallow, overlapping pits in the southwest corner of this bay, however, indicate the presence of a corner chimney hood with an associated hearth and possible storage pits (see Figure 9–3).

The postmolds for all of the load-bearing posts are set against the western edges of their respective postholes, and the holes all appear to have been stepped from the east. These two bits of evidence suggest that the principal walls were constructed as single units and raised into place from the east. Wall units of hewn timber, measuring nearly 40 ft. (12.2 m) in length and of undetermined height, must have required several people to raise, this in contrast to single bent units raised parallel with the main axis of a building (see Carson et al., 1981; see also the buildings at Compton in the previous chapter).

Several of the postholes have a second hole, either entirely within or overlapping a posthole. These "halos" appear in both plan and profile views. I interpret them as replacement postholes (Figure 9–5). The hypothesized process went something like this: the lower portion of a vertical, load-bearing member, set into the ground and subject to decay and termite damage, evinces signs of structural failure. Members of the household fashion a simple lever to raise the affected portion of the building, cut and pry free the decayed portion of the timber, recut the hole sufficiently to insert a wood block, install the block, secure it to the affected vertical member, and backfill the enlarged hole.

The process does seem cumbersome, but it explains the observed facts, particularly when the severe truncation of the features through plowing is considered, the more highly disturbed portions of the postholes having been destroyed. The alternative explanation that the halos encapsulating smaller, darker, postmolds represent stages of timber decay is not tenable since some of the halos clearly extended beyond the limits of the postholes. The post replacement hypothesis being the most tenable, it appears that people maintained the principal dwelling at Patuxent Point. The addition also represents expansion, albeit on a diminutive scale.

The second possible structure at Patuxent Point may have been a lightly constructed frame building with ground-laid sills and a wattle-and-daub chim-

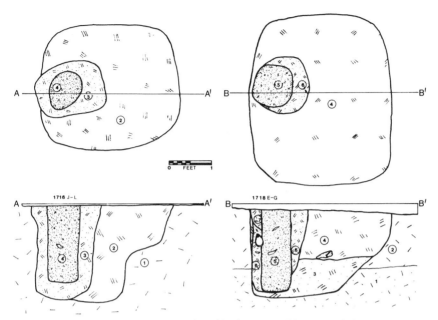

Figure 9–5. Planviews and profiles for two Building 1 postholes.

ney (Figures 9–6 and 9–7). All that remains of this structure are several small postholes and molds, some scorched earth, and a thick layer of burned daub suggestive of chimney collapse. The postholes encompass approximately 25% of the perimeter of Feature 1. Measuring approximately 12 ft. in diameter, Feature 1 was filled with layers of soil and oyster shell, all intermixed with domestic refuse. Below the layer of shell in the east half of the pit—the side around which the postholes occur—was a layer of burned daub that appeared to have collapsed into the open pit (see Figure 9–7).

Feature 1 has a maximum depth of about 3 ft. below the graded surface, terminating at a natural layer of sand that underlies the silt loam of the B-horizon. The pit may have been excavated as a source of daub from which the chimney or chimneys of the principal dwelling were constructed, and then served as a cellar for a service outbuilding until the destruction of that building. Feature 1 served as a trash receptacle for some time, the domestic refuse overlying the burned daub. Two identical trade tokens were recovered from Feature 1. The better-preserved token was found in the upper stratum of oyster shell and loam. Its obverse side (Figure 9–8) bears the name and initials of Alice Row. The reverse depicts St. George slaying the dragon and the name Ilemester, a small town in Somerset in the west country of England. The motif suggests an ordinary called the George

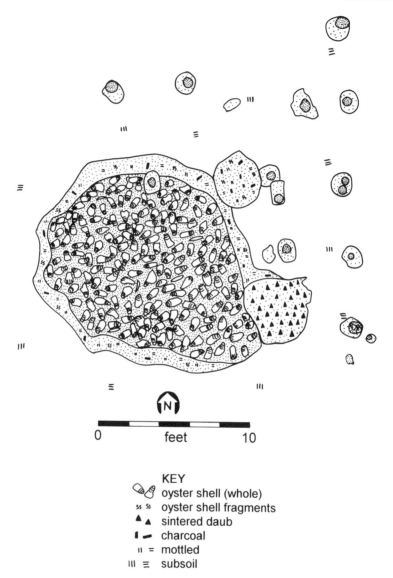

Figure 9–6. Planview of Feature 1 and the Building 2 postholes.

and Dragon, a common name for English inns and one which appears on numerous tokens illustrated in Boyne (1970 [1857]). Among the tokens described in Boyne's catalogue is one for Alice Row of Ilemester (Boyne 1970 [1857]:982)

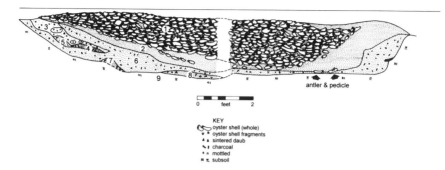

antler & pedicle

KEY
- oyster shell (whole)
- oyster shell fragments
- sintered daub
- charcoal
- mottled
- subsoil

Figure 9–7. East–west profile of Feature 1. Soil descriptions for Feature 1: 1. Oyster shell and dark brown silt loam, artifacts, and bone; 2. Dark brown silt loam with some whole and crushed shell, and many artifacts; 3. Brown to yellowish brown silt loam and some whole and crushed shell, sintered daub, and artifacts; 4. Dark brown silt loam and sintered daub, yellowish brown clay loam, some charcoal, bone, and artifacts; 5. Dark brown silt loam with some shell, charcoal, and artifacts; 6. Brown silt loam, yellowish brown clay loam, and some yellowish brown silt loam, scattered shell, charcoal, and artifacts; some shell, charcoal, and sintered daub; 8. Dark yellowish brown silt loam, some shell, charcoal, sintered daub, bone and artifacts, including poorly preserved token; 9. Subsoil.

dated 1664. Of the two tokens recovered, the better-preserved specimen bears the date 166[?], providing a *terminus post quem* of the mid-1660s for the filling of Feature 1.[7] The function of this possible building is not readily apparent, although it may have been a dwelling, the cellar providing considerable storage space.

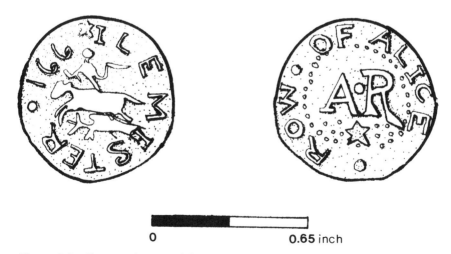

0   0.65 inch

Figure 9–8. Obverse and reverse of the better preserved of two trade tokens from Feature 1.

Few construction details survive, archaeologically, at Patuxent Point. Fragments of common red brick and yellow brick in the plowzone suggest firebacks within the hearths. There is no evidence of brick chimneys at the site, but framing posts (represented by small postholes and molds along the north gable end of Building 1 and, possibly, the postholes of Building 2), and large quantities of sintered daub indicate that chimneys were constructed of wattle and daub. Turned window leads indicate at least one glazed casement window. None of these leads appears to bear an embossed inscription. There is no evidence of wall plastering, indicating simple plank walls. Several locks and bolts have been recovered, although it is uncertain whether they were used on the doors or on large chests or cabinets within the buildings.

Nonstructural Features

Aside from Feature 1, there were three other pit features uncovered at Patuxent Point. (The remaining pits are either prehistoric or are related to a tobacco barn of late nineteenth- early twentieth-century vintage.) Feature 2 lies between Feature 1 and Building 1. It is small, measuring approximately 4.5 ft. by 3.2 ft. (1.4 m by 0.98 m), steep sided, and approximately 17 in. (0.43 m) in depth (Figure 9–9). Removal of the south half of the feature in one level revealed 15 strata of ash and silt, some appearing to be little more than pockets of debris, and most producing large numbers of fish and mammal bone, bottle glass, and ceramics, including large conjoinable sherds representing one glass case bottle and a coarse red earthenware bowl (Figure 9–10). Two largely intact terra-cotta pipe bowls, and fragments of several others, also were recovered (Figure 9–11).[8]

Feature 2 is similar to Features 2 and 12 at the Compton site, the fill of each consisting of alternating strata of ash and silt. All of the ash-filled pits differ from the larger, shell- and refuse-filled pits present at both sites. The intended functions of these ash-filled pits have not been determined, although it is possible that they represent cesspits, the ash from kitchen hearths being used to reduce odors. Small postholes around Feature 2 and the lack of fire-reddened soil (which might suggest a smokehouse) support this hypothesis.

Feature 3 is a pit feature of uncertain function that was intruded by the southeast posthole of the Building 1 addition. At least four fragmentary glass case bottles were recovered from this feature. King (1993) has suggested that the presence of four upturned bottles in the pit could be attributed to occult practices, although it is difficult to reconcile that interpretation with the recovery of only three bottle necks to match the four bottle bases: truncation through plowing should have resulted in fewer bases than necks, if the bottles were in fact upturned. Moreover, the "witch bottles" reported by Becker (1978) are intact.[9] Feature 3 probably represents a posthole that was reexcavated in the course of repairing or modifying the ell.

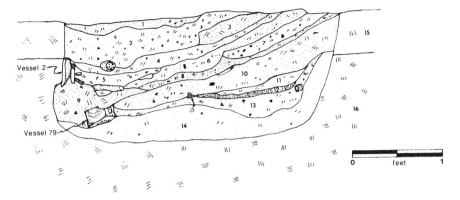

Figure 9–9. Profile view of Feature 2. Soil descriptions for Feature 2: 1 & 2. Yellowish brown silt loam with some dark brown silty clay, pale brown silt loam and ash, charcoal, and sintered daub; 3. Yellowish brown sandy clay and dark brown silt loam, with some yellowish brown silt loam and charcoal. No artifacts; 4 & 5. Pale brown silt loam, yellowish brown silt loam, and yellowish brown silt clay and charcoal; some sintered daub, bone, and artifacts; 6. Dark yellowish brown loam with dark yellowish brown sandy loam and yellowish brown sandy clay, some sintered daub, bone, and artifacts; 7. Brownish yellow sandy loam with pale brown silt and ash, some dark brown sandy loam and charcoal, bone, sintered daub, bottle glass, and shell; 8. Dark yellowsh brown silt clay with dark yellowish brown silt loam and strong brown clay, charcoal, shell, and sintered daub; 9. Dark yellowish brown silt clay with some ceramics, charcoal, shell, and sintered daub; 10. Yellowish brown silt clay with yellowish brown sandy clay and dark yellowish brown silt loam, and lots of charcoal; 11. Light yellowish brown silt loam and ash, with some white silt and ash, charcoal, daub, and bone; 12. Dark yellowish brown silt loam with some yellowish brown sandy clay, bone, ceramics, and charcoal; 13. Yellowish brown silt clay and pale brown silt loam and ash, charcoal, egg shell, bone, and glass; 14. Yellowish brown clay loam.

Feature 4 is a circular, shallow, dish-shaped pit measuring approximately 4 ft. (1.2 m) in diameter and 0.9 ft. (0.27 m) in depth (Figure 9–12). There are six strata within the feature, three of which consist largely of oyster shells. Large quantities of fish and mammal bone, including a deer antler, occur in the fill. A few ceramic sherds, and the remains of at least one case bottle were recovered. There was no evidence of *in situ* burning. The function of this pit has not been determined.

Spatial Distributions

We sampled the plowzone at Patuxent Point to determine the extent of the homelot, to guide subsequent mechanical stripping and feature mapping, and to attempt the identification of surface middens. Unlike the investigation of the Compton site, conditions for surface collecting at Patuxent Point ranged from

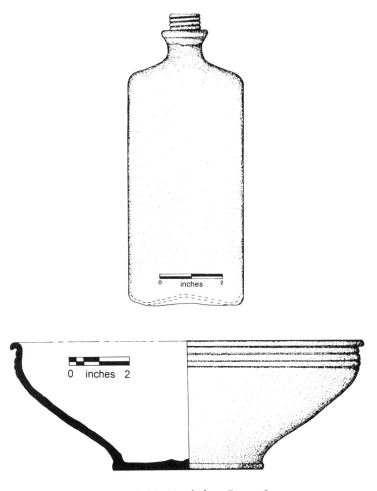

Figure 9–10. Vessels from Feature 2.

good to excellent, facilitating identification of the homelot bounds. Plowzone sampling enhanced boundary definition while providing a large sample for sheet midden definition. Gibb and King (1991) used SYMAP, a computer graphics package, to simulate the distributions of various artifact categories, and to define middens. Four middens (A through D; Figure 9–13) were identified, their contents compared, and the significance of the frequency distributions assessed through chi-square analysis. As with the Compton middens, few significant differences among the four middens could be identified, and those that were noted could be products of sampling error. Although the chi-square analyses under-

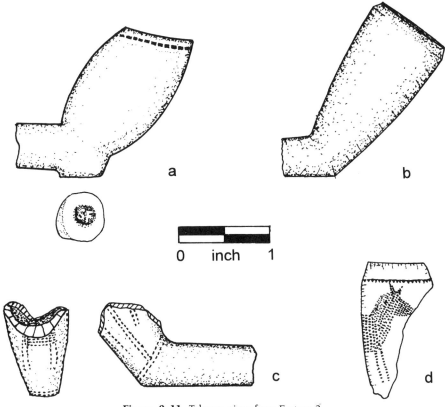

Figure 9–11. Tobacco pipes from Feature 2.

taken in that study were useful for identifying statistically significant differences among the middens within predefined confidence intervals, they did not account for the nature of the samples, namely, the small numbers of plowzone units upon which each of the middens were identified.[10]

The hypothesis advanced in the previous chapter regarding the formation of sheet middens can be tested with the Patuxent Point data. Again, Boone's H is a useful measure for determining whether or not the middens, defined through computer simulation mapping, are more homogeneous than the general plowzone materials. As with the Compton analysis, the contents of those plowzone units not otherwise assigned to one of the four middens have been lumped together to form a fifth midden. The resulting H values are presented in Table 9–1.

The results of the analysis are similar to those obtained from the analysis of the Compton site materials. The H-values are consistently low (ranging from

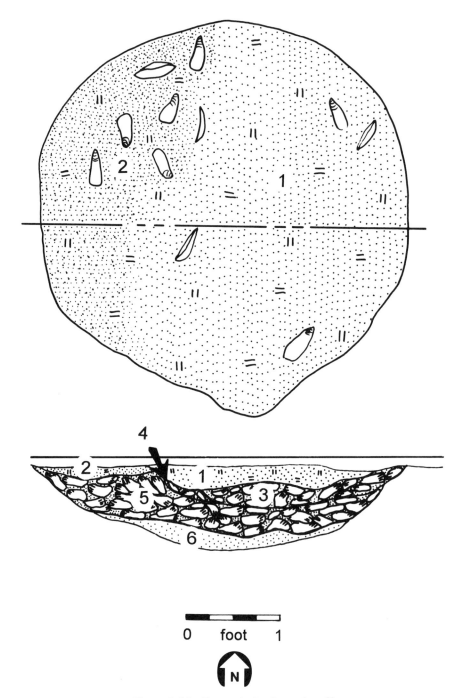

Figure 9–12. Feature 4 planview and profile.

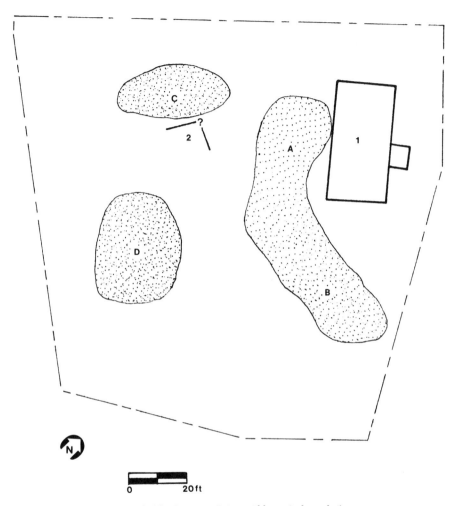

Figure 9–13. Patuxent Point middens, A through D.

0.012 to 0.032). The value for the general plowzone is particularly low (0.002), but in assessing such differences it is important to keep in mind the manner in which the middens were defined. Slight differences in H-values could be artifacts of the analysis. Again, the results do not differ from those of the original analysis presented in Gibb and King (1991); namely, there is little evidence of activity areas at the Patuxent Point site. The midden formations at the site are consistent with the model of refuse discard proposed in the previous chapter.

Table 9–1. Diversity Analysis for the Patuxent Point Middens and General Plowzone

Midden	Tobacco pipes	Fine ceramics	Coarse ceramics	Bone	Bottle glass	Boone's H
A	201	55	174	192	11	0.032
B	171	61	190	186	31	0.004
C	46	31	80	95	8	0.013
D	107	24	136	104	25	0.012
Plowzone	551	269	933	1240	181	0.002

The results of the SYMAP analysis also can be evaluated through k-means cluster analysis of the plowzone artifact distributions. The analysis was conducted in the same way that it had been for the Compton site materials (see Chapter 8). Five variables were analyzed for 59 plowzone units: bottle glass, ceramics, tobacco pipes, European flint, and bone. Locational data (i.e., the grid coordinates of each unit) were omitted: units were clustered solely on the basis of frequencies for each of the above classes. Significant breaks occurred at the three- and six-cluster solutions. Plotting of the six unit clusters on the site map revealed dispersed, overlapping clusters, a pattern inconsistent with the discrete middens defined through the SYMAP analysis. On the other hand, the three-cluster solution produced a spatial pattern similar to that produced for the Compton units: Cluster 3 units ($n = 12$) concentrate in the yard west of the dwelling, with Clusters 2 ($n = 23$) and 1 ($n = 24$) forming successively larger, more dispersed distributions enveloping the homelot core (Figure 9–14). The pattern, like that produced for the Compton site, is reminiscent of a density contour map, with the concentration of artifacts recovered from plowzone units decreasing toward the periphery of the site's core.

Unlike the Compton site, Patuxent Point was sampled with relatively large units that yielded large numbers of artifacts for one or more of the five principal artifact classes. These frequencies were transformed into percentages; for examples, Unit 1809D yielded five artifact classes in the following proportions: vessel glass (4%), ceramic sherds (40%), tobacco pipe fragments (10%), European flint (3%), and bone (43%). Ten cluster solutions were calculated with the transformed data and compared against the mean and standard deviation trend lines for 100 simulations of the randomized percentage data.

Reanalysis based on percentage distributions of each of the five variables (locational data excluded) yielded weak breaks in the trend line at three and four clusters. The solutions were very similar when examined for spatial distribution and constituent units. The three-cluster solution is described first and the distribution of units illustrated in Figure 9–15.

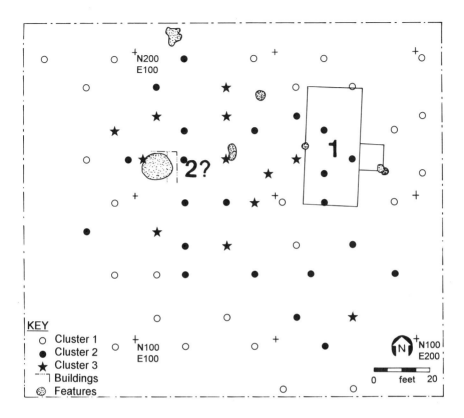

Figure 9-14. Clusters defined through k-means analysis, three-cluster solution.

Cluster 1 units ($n = 35$) are spread over the entire site, providing, perhaps, a baseline against which the other units can be compared. With the exception of ceramics, all of the Cluster 1 means are intermediate between those of the other two clusters, the ceramics being somewhat higher. Cluster 2 units ($n = 11$) also are widespread, but cling to the northeast and southwest corners of the study area. They are characterized by glass, pipe, and flint means that are higher than those of the other two clusters. Cluster 3 units ($n = 13$) are the only ones that are spatially clustered. They are concentrated within the yard directly west of the house (with isolated units occurring within the house and 50-ft. south of the house). This is the same area in which the three principal trash-filled pits are located (Features 1, 2, and 4). Cluster 3 units are characterized by high percentages of bone (mean of 52.5 and a standard deviation of 7.5).

The four-cluster solution consists of three clusters that are very similar in terms of constituent units and spatial distribution to those described above. The

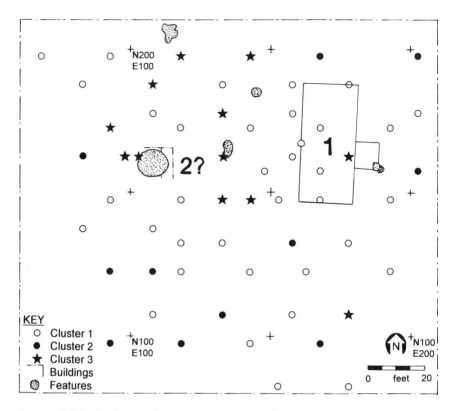

Figure 9-15. Distribution of units at Patuxent Point, based on k-means clustering of the percentage data, three-cluster solution.

fourth cluster (*n* = 8) was created with units from Clusters 1 and 2 of the three-cluster solution on the basis of high percentage yields of ceramics. Most of the Cluster 4 units occur east of the house, in an area that had been highly eroded.

The results of the clustered percentage data suggest that there is some spatial structure to the distribution of artifacts at Patuxent Point. That structure appears to be the result of plowing. Bones and other artifacts were torn out of features by the plow, creating the high concentrations of artifacts in the core of the site (see Figure 9–15). Of the five artifact classes analyzed, only bone deteriorates rapidly from weathering and soil acids. Bones deposited in sheet middens during the seventeenth century probably have disappeared. Those recovered from the plow-zone excavation units may be largely products of plowing; hence, the concentration of bone is highest closest to its sources, the features that are rich in bone. Again, the resulting distribution is reminiscent of a density contour map, with the

Table 9–2. Summary of Tobacco Pipe
Fragments

Types and bore diameters	Numbers of fragments
White clay pipe fragments	552
10/64 inches	2
9/64 inches	19
8/64 inches	69
7/64 inches	193
6/64 inches	198
5/64 inches	71
Terra-cotta pipe fragments	118
Total tobacco pipes	670
Unit mean	9.7
Unit median	9.5

concentration of artifacts recovered from plowzone units decreasing toward the periphery of the site's core, and with increased distance from the subsurface features.

ARTIFACT ANALYSIS

As is the case for Compton, European manufactured goods dominate the Patuxent Point assemblage. The unidentified tenants chose among a limited variety of goods transported to the colony by merchants and newly arrived immigrants. New immigrants brought manufactured goods to the colony with the intention of selling those items to established colonists, taking advantage of the price differences between Old World and New. The two categories of material discussed below—tobacco pipes, and ceramic and glass vessels—probably were exported from the same ports, regardless of who actually paid for the shipping.

Tobacco Pipes

Plowzone units at Patuxent Point yielded 552 measurable pipe stem fragments and 118 red or buff-colored terra-cotta pipe fragments (Table 9–2). Using Hanson's (1971) multiple regression formula 3 (mean diameter = 6.5887, standard deviation = 1.001), I calculate a mean occupation date of 1679 ± 30.03 years (i.e., 1649–1706, using a two-standard deviation range). Applied to the Compton pipestem data, Hanson's formula 3 produced a mean occupation date of 1653 ± 23.57 years (i.e., 1629–1677, using a two-standard-deviation range). Although it should be clear from these calculations that Compton is the earlier of the two sites, the wide date ranges may be misleading. Hanson's formula defines a range in

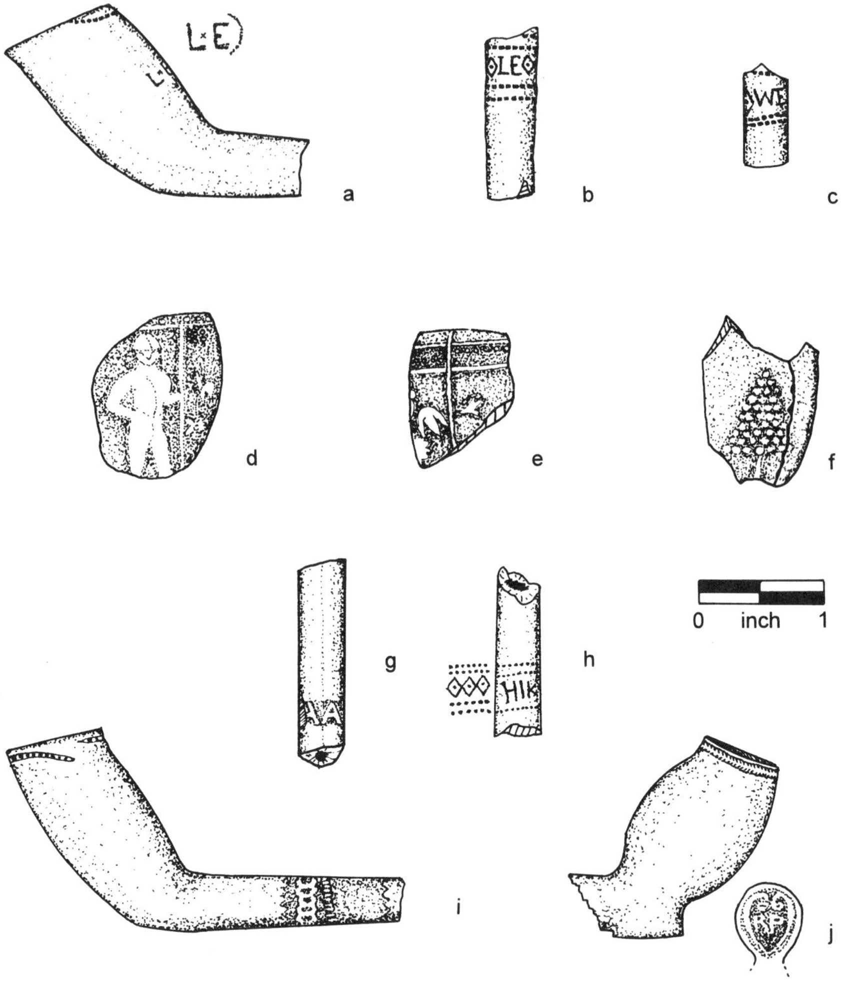

Figure 9–16. Tobacco pipes from the Patuxent Point site.

which 95% of the sample means occur. The range is a statistical formulation and should not be taken to represent that actual period of occupation. That said, a one-standard-deviation range provides a more realistic measure of where the respective mean occupation dates fall: Compton (1641–1665) and Patuxent Point (1664–1694).

Patuxent Point's mean pipestem date may be the more accurate of the two, lacking, as it does, clear evidence of Dutch pipes in the assemblage. The "EB" maker's mark, so prevalent in the Compton assemblage, is absent from the Patuxent Point assemblage. In part, Patuxent Point was occupied at the end of

Table 9–3. Vessel Form Distributions at the Patuxent Point
Site

Vessel form	Plowzone	Feature	Plowzone & feature	Total
Baking pan	0	0	0	0
Basin	0	0	1	1
Bottle	4	25	2	31
Bowl	7	2	1	10
Colander	1	0	0	1
Cooking pot	0	0	0	0
Dish	2	2	0	4
Galley pot	0	2	0	2
Indeterminate[a]	20	5	1	26
Jar	1	0	0	1
Jug	0	1	1	2
Milkpan	0	3	1	4
Table glass[b]	0	3	0	3
Pan	1	1	0	2
Pipkin	1	0	1	2
Pitcher	0	1	0	1
Plate	0	0	0	0
Platter	3	2	0	5
Porringer	0	0	0	0
Pot	0	2	0	2
Skillet	0	0	0	0
Vial	0	0	0	0
Totals:				
21 forms	40	49	8	97

[a]Includes indeterminate and various "or" combinations.
[b]Includes ornate drinking glasses of uncertain form, roemers, snifters, and tumblers.

Edward Bird's career (1665), but it also was occupied after stringent enforcement of the English Navigation Act (1651) effectively curbed Dutch trade in the North American colonies. In contrast, "LE," the mark of Llewelyn Evans (1661–1684+), is the most common maker's mark in the Patuxent Point assemblage, with 16 examples (Figure 9–16a,b). Archaeologists find his products, and those of other probable Bristol pipemakers, throughout English North America (Walker, 1977:657–658). One pipe marked "WE," or William Evans (ca. 1660–1700), nine pikeman and Minerva, or crusader-and-huntress, pipe fragments, and other molded and marked pipes also were recovered (Figure 9–16c-j; see also Figure 9–11a). Again, the molded relief pipes do not occur in association with "EB" pipes

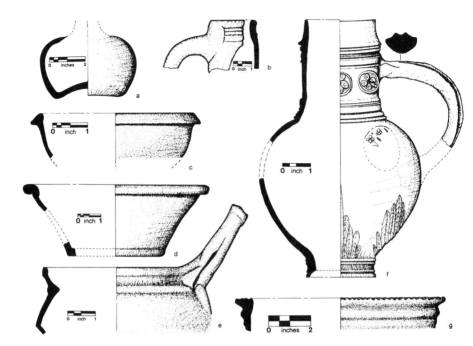

Figure 9–17. Vessel forms from the Patuxent Point site: (a) glass bottle; (b) Rhenish stoneware bottle; (c) earthenware bowl; (d) North Devon earthenware pan; (e) earthenware pipkin, possibly North Devon, (f) Rhenish stoneware jug or mug; (g) earthenware pot, possibly English.

or Dutch coarse earthenwares (see below), supporting the hypothesis that they are not Dutch in origin.

Vessels

Vessel identifications and the calculation of minimum numbers of vessels were undertaken in a manner identical to that used in evaluating the Compton assemblage. The results are reproduced in Table 9–3. The vessels from Patuxent Point are grouped into four categories: Food Preparation, food presentation, food storage and health/hygiene. There is a great deal of functional overlap as noted in the previous chapter; therefore, some vessel forms cannot be attributed to any one category with confidence. Bowls, for example, may have been used in all four of these activity domains, and a single bowl could have been used to collect milk or fruit in the morning, mix cornbread dough at noon, clean a wound in the afternoon, and store food in the evening.

Of those vessels that can be attributed to a particular activity, bottles stand out most clearly (Figure 9–17a,b). Along with a single earthenware jar, the 31

Table 9–4. Vessel Form Distributions for the
Compton and Patuxent Point Sites

Vessel form	Compton	Patuxent Point
Baking pan	1	0
Basin	3	1
Bottle	29	31
Bowl	8	10
Colander	0	1
Cooking pot	7	0
Dish	4	4
Galley pot	0	2
Indeterminate[a]	31	26
Jar	1	1
Jug	0	2
Milkpan	2	4
Table glass[b]	3	3
Pan	4	2
Pipkin	1	2
Pitcher	3	1
Plate	3	0
Platter	2	5
Porringer	1	0
Pot	0	2
Skillet	7	0
Vial	2	0
Totals:		
21 forms	112	97

[a]Includes indeterminate and various "or" combinations.
[b]Includes ornate drinking glasses of uncertain form, roemers, snifters, and tumblers.

glass and stoneware bottles form the largest group of vessels, comprising 32 of the 97 vessels (32%) at Patuxent Point, or 45% (32 of 71) of the vessels that could be identified as to form. Vessels that were used in food presentation, including dishes (4), platters (5), a pitcher, two jugs, and three table glass vessels, comprise 15 of the 71 identifiable forms, or 21%. Four milkpans, two pots, two pipkins, and two pans compose 10 vessels (approximately 14% of the 71 identifiable vessels) that probably were used in food processing and preparation. The proportion of cooking vessels recovered from Patuxent Point is considerably less than that recovered from Compton. The Patuxent Point cooking vessels also appear to be larger than those used by the Stephens family at the Compton site. Unfortunately, few of the vessels from either site are sufficiently complete to permit calculation of their respective volumes and a more objective evaluation of possible differences in size.

Two tin-glazed galley pots, a form that does not occur at the Compton site, also were recovered from Patuxent Point.

The range of ceramic vessels is similar in some respects to that recovered from the Compton site (Table 9–4). Many of the same wares, and certain styles, are present at both sites. Rhenish stonewares—both blue and gray, and brown-for instance, occur at both sites, as do North Devonshire coarse earthenwares and North Italian slipwares. Dutch coarse earthenwares, common in the Compton assemblage, are all but absent in the Patuxent Point assemblage, represented by only one pinched handle from a vessel of indeterminate form, and a few nondiagnostic sherds that may have been from Dutch vessels.

Differences between the Patuxent Point and Compton assemblages, for the most part, appear to be in terms of presence-absence of infrequently occurring vessel forms; again, the Dutch-made skillets and cooking pots stand out as important exceptions. Whether these differences represent alternative food preparation practices, or simply reflect changes in the availability of vessel types as a result of changing international trade patterns, is uncertain. Given what is currently known about Dutch trade in the Chesapeake Bay region during the 1640s and 1650s, the latter hypothesis is more tenable. The occupation of Patuxent Point (1660s–1670s) postdates the apogee of Dutch commercial activity in the region.[11]

Boone's *H* values calculated for Compton (0.02) and Patuxent Point (0.03) are low. Both assemblages exhibit a great deal of heterogeneity, although bottles dominate the assemblages. Vessels of indeterminate form (excluded from the above calculations) could lower those values further if the various vessels could be identified as to form: the majority probably represent dishes, plates, platters, and cups, namely, food presentation vessels. Dutch origins aside, the Compton assemblage is comparable to that of Patuxent Point. Only a more detailed analysis that involves finer categories and the results of use–wear analysis is likely to further differentiate between the two vessel assemblages.

PATUXENT POINT CEMETERY

The cemetery at Patuxent Point lacks a parallel at Compton. Deceased family members and servants at Compton conceivably could have been buried at Patuxent Point. Nonetheless, the spatial layout and pathology data from the Patuxent Point cemetery provide valuable insight into the households occupying the homelot in terms of the treatment accorded each burial and its location relative to other interments. Those same data contribute to our understanding of how the occupants of Patuxent Point "consumed," or allocated, space, and how the household defined itself in terms of membership and rights to wealth.

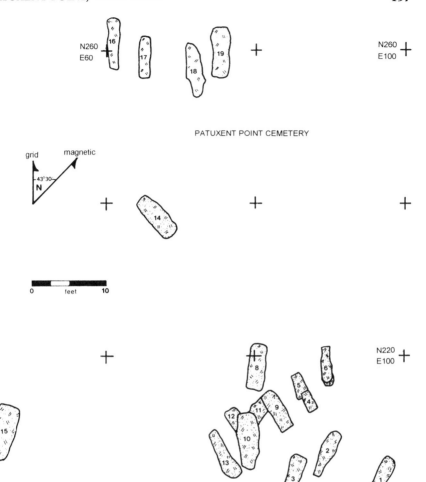

Figure 9–18. Patuxent Point cemetery.

Some of the most important information to come out of the cemetery became available as the 18 graveshafts were troweled and mapped (Figure 9–18). (Grave 7 turned out to be a natural feature of unknown origin. It is very similar to Feature 13 at Compton in terms of its size and poorly sorted, compact sand and gravel fill. Both probably are natural features.) Some of the shafts were quite small, indicating that they were the graves of children. While this may not be a particularly illuminating discovery on later colonial sites, it was considered to be a find of considerable import on a rural seventeenth-century Chesapeake site. The reader will recall from the earlier background chapters that women represented only 20% to 25% of the colony's population into the early eighteenth century. Some plantation households consisted only of men. In short, we cannot assume that there were women in residence on any particular plantation. There is archival evidence of women at Compton: Magdelen Stephens and Margaret Aylin. But the names of those who lived at Patuxent Point are unknown, and are likely to remain so. The presence of children at the site leaves little doubt, and the physical evidence of the skeletons discussed below removes all doubt, that there were women living and working at Patuxent Point.

Demographics were not the only patterns evident from the graveshafts. Some of the shafts were shaped like shouldered coffins, and others were more or less rectangular, indicating possible variability in burial patterns. Moreover, there were patterns evident in the distribution of graveshafts betraying a degree of social segregation. Tables 9–5 and 9–6 provides summary data on the 18 inhumations.[12]

Seven children (including two infants), five women (including one who died with a near-term fetus), and six men were exhumed at Patuxent Point. This group should not be regarded as representative of the population at large, nor even directly representative of the household. As discussed in earlier chapters, mortality rates varied across the population, with as many as 50% of all children born during the seventeenth century in Maryland dying before attaining the age of majority. Women also suffered higher mortality rates than men, in part due to the hazards of childbirth. With the exception of one young man who appears to have been African, the decedents are of European extraction.

All of the 18 graves occur within an area of approximately 60 ft. by 60 ft. (18.3 m by 18 m). Rather than identifying a single pattern of inhumation, it is clear from a visual inspection of the cemetery map that there are several clusters. The group of four at the north end of the cemetery constitutes one cluster, while Graves 14 and 15 are outliers. Two-thirds of the graves, however, are clustered within a 20 ft. by 30 ft. (6.1 m by 9.1 m) area, in some cases overlapping one another and oriented to different cardinal points. A k-means clustering procedure has been used to tease apart the graves into different groups based upon the northing and easting values of the 10 ft. by 10 ft. (3 m by 3 m) grid square in which each is located, and the orientation of the body.

The analysis (Tables 9–7 and 9–8, and Figure 9–19) suggests cluster solutions of five and eight, based on the logarithmic transformation of the percentage difference in squared summed errors for the original and randomized data. Given a population of 18, an eight-cluster solution is excessive, obscuring rather than illuminating patterns. The five-cluster solution is more satisfying, dividing the group along lines that we might have recognized through a simple visual inspection of the cemetery map. It is flawed in that Graves 15 and 19 are lumped together in Cluster 5 due to their similar orientations. Removing Grave 19 from Cluster 3 seems counterintuitive, and there is no other evidence to justify this allocation. Clearly, the orientation of the body relative to the head exerts far more influence in the analysis than can be justified.

Selecting the orientation of the body relative to the head as a variable was based on the understanding that Christian burials are generally oriented to the east (e.g., Gittings, 1984:139; Noel Hume, 1992:39). Upon Judgment Day, the dead would rise facing in the direction of the rising sun (a metaphor for the return of Jesus Christ, the Son of God). A reexamination of the burial orientations, however, indicates that seven of the burials do not face east, and an eighth faces due south. In order to account for incomplete knowledge on the part of those directly involved in burying the deceased, and for an unjustified imposition of Christian cosmology on the occupants of Patuxent Point, the orientation of the bodies was recalculated without reference to the head; only the orientation of the long axis of the graveshaft relative to magnetic north was measured. The results appear in Tables 9–9 and 9–10, and in Figure 9–20.

Again, the solutions are five and eight. The five-cluster solution appears to be satisfactory in that it conforms to a visual inspection and analysis of grave clustering. Grave 10 intrudes through individual members of Clusters 1 and 3, and therefore is treated as an outlier. Grave 15, the pregnant woman, also appears as an outlier, a result that is consistent with her relatively isolated location and her condition at death, one that may have had overtones of ritual impurity, regardless of her marital status at time of death. Grave 14, curiously, is assigned to Cluster 3, an indication of the weight of the orientation variable in the analysis. Correcting for that undue weighting through standardization of the data probably would result in a solution of six clusters without any significant change in cluster membership, other than assigning Grave 14 to a cluster of one.

Based on the k-means analysis of the graveshafts, it is possible to define three clusters and three outliers (Figure 9–21). Cluster 1 consists of five individuals: three women, one man, and one child. Only the man was not interred in a coffin. The intrusion of Grave 9, and possibly Grave 12, through Grave 11 suggests that Cluster 1 was succeeded by Cluster 3. The latter consists of one man interred in a coffin and five children, two of whom were infants. Two of the children (Graves 5 and 6) were interred in coffins. Grave 10 postdates both clusters, since it intrudes through graves from both. Outlying Graves 14 and 15 cannot be dated. The relative dating of Cluster 4 is equally uncertain.

Consisting of two women, one man and one subadult, Cluster 4 may represent the portion of the burial yard devoted to servants. None of them were buried in coffins and one of them (Grave 18) appears to be an African, the only one identified among the 18 graves. Notably, he was the only one buried with artifacts other than brass shroud pins or iron coffin nails: a white clay tobacco pipe and a

Table 9-5. Forensic Data Part I, Patuxent Point Cemetery

Burial	Age	Sex	Stature	Ancestry	Coffin	Shroud	Orientation
1	24	Female	5'5	European	Yes	Yes	S13°E
2	55–60	Female	5'4½	European	Yes	Yes	S16.5°E
3	37–43	Female	5'3	European	Yes	Yes	S28°E
4	0.8	?	?	?	No	Yes	N67.5°W
5	1.2–1.4	?	?	?	Yes	Yes	S62°E
6	8–9	?	?	?	Yes	Yes	N46.5°W
8	28–33	Male	5'7	European	No	?	S34.5°E
8	28–11	Male	5'7	European	No	?	S34.5°E
9	10–11	?	?	?	No	?	N77°W
10	30–35	Probable male	5'7–5'9	European	No	Yes	S43.5°W
11	5	?	?	?	Yes	Yes	S7°E
12	27–32	Male	5'3–5'5	European	Yes	Yes	S77°E
13	13	?	?	?	No	Yes	N72.5°W
14	33-38	Probable male	5'6–5'8	European	Yes	?	N87°W
15	26–33	Female	5'4–5'6	Probable European	No	Yes	N29.5°W
16	13–14	?	?	?	No	?	S43.5°E
17	25–30	Female	4'9–5'2	European	No	Yes	S43.5°E
18	15–17	Male	5'7–5'11	Probable African	No	?	S46.5°E
19	38–45	Male	5'3–5'5	European	No	?	N43°W

Table 9-6. Forensic Data, Part II, Patuxent Point Cemetery

Burial	Caries	Abscesses	Pipeware	Harris lines[a]	Other pathology
1	4	2	Yes	None	Spina bifida, sacral and cervical
2	3	None	Yes	None	Osteoporosis, osteoarthritis; extensive tooth loss; spondylolisthesis
3	32	5	None	None	Minor osteoarthritis
4	N/A	N/A	N/A	N/A	No evidence
5	N/A	N/A	N/A	N/A	Slight anterior bowing of leg bones
6	10	None	N/A	3	Possible minor cribra orbitalia, left and right orbits
8	9	1	Yes	None	Generalized osteoporosis; grooved incisors
9	1	None	N/A	None	Possible minor cribra orbitalia O.S/O.D; extreme porosity of vertebral centra
10	2	2	Yes	1	Slight generalized osteoporosis; minor periostitis, lower left leg
11	3	None	N/A	None	Exceptional porosity and pitting of vertebral centra
12	13	2	No	None	Slight osteophytosis; fractured metacarpal
13	None	None	Yes	6	Slight cribra orbitalia O.S/O.D.
14	4	3	Yes	1	Osteoarthritis upper bones of limbs; periosteal deposits lower lombs
15	None	None	No	1	Slight arthritis, near-term fetus
16	3	None	No	?	Moderate cribra orbitalia O.S/O.D; healed left femoral fracture
17	8	0	No	1	None
18	0	0	No	1	Evidence of exceptional use of upper body
19	5	1	Yes	None	Remodeled periosteal lesion; healed navicular fracture

[a]Periods of nutritional stress in children arrest longbone growth and are manifested in fine transverse lines (known as Harris lines) on the longbone shafts.

Table 9-7. Cluster Analysis of the Patuxent Point
Graveshafts

Cluster solutions	Original SSE	Mean random SSE	Log(%SSE) Random-Original
1	122277	122277	0.00
2	16292	15811	–0.01
3	10475	10892	0.02
4	7169	7823	0.04
5	4548	5548	0.09
6	3214	3927	0.09
7	2219	2804	0.10
8	1433	2012	0.15
9	922	1461	0.20
10	734	1074	0.17

Table 9-8. Cluster Membership for
the Five-Cluster Solution

Cluster	Members				
1	1	2	3	8	11
2	4	6	9	13	14
3	16	17	18		
4	5	10	12		
5	15	19			

glass button in a copper alloy setting were found among his carpal bones. The absence of children also supports the servant interpretation, since servants were prohibited from procreation during the terms of their indentures. Outlying Graves 14 and 15 also might be those of servants, and Grave 10 may postdate the occupation of the homelot altogether. Based on this analysis, we can infer two successive households whose members were interred in orderly clusters at one end of the burial yard. Servants were similarly clustered, albeit at the other end of the yard, farthest from the homelot core. The outliers cannot be associated with either of the family clusters, or with the servants' cluster.

SUMMARY

There were at least 18 people who died at Patuxent Point. We can assume that there were many more who lived there at one time, dying elsewhere in the

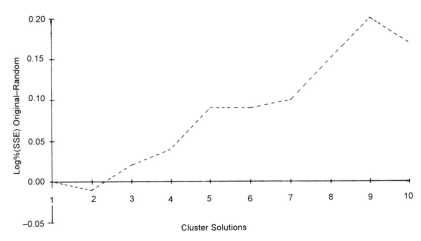

Figure 9–19. Graph of possible cluster solutions based on the location and orientation of the body, relative to the head.

Table 9–9. Cluster Analysis of the Patuxent Point Graveshafts, Based on Shaft Orientation

Cluster solutions	Original SSE	Mean random SSE	Log(%SSE) Random-Original
1	87821	87821	0
2	18391	18251	–0.00
3	10994	10593	–0.02
4	4208	5799	0.14
5	2677	4075	0.18
6	1779	2860	0.21

Table 9–10. Cluster Membership for the Five-Cluster Solution, Based on Grave Location and Orientation

Cluster	Members					
1	1	2	3	6	8	11
2	10					
3	4	5	9	12	13	14
4	16	17	18	19		
5	15					

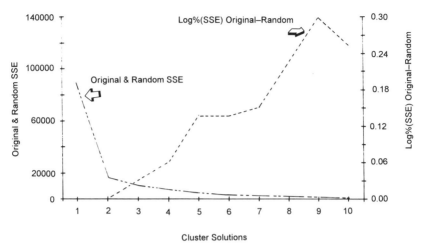

Figure 9–20. Grave cluster solutions based on location and recomputed orientations.

colony or abroad. Unlike the occupants of Compton, we have no idea who these people were or whence they came. They settled a tract with the same soil qualities as did the Stephens household, although by the 1660s the soils may have been depleted somewhat by the Stephenses. Natural resources also may have been somewhat depleted, although there is little indication of that in the large quantities of oyster shell and fish remains recovered from Features 1 and 2.

By the time of their arrival in Calvert County, the occupants of Patuxent Point could not share in the opportunities for land acquisition that had existed only 10 years earlier. Indeed, they probably were tenants, holding short-term leases that enjoined them to make certain improvements on the plantation, but provided neither long-term security nor a future for their children. Eventually, they departed, to where we do not know, and it was not until the second decade of the eighteenth century that a family once again laid claim to this land. Behind them, the people of Patuxent Point left a dwelling that had been expanded upon with the addition of an ell, and that had been maintained (e.g., chimney replastering, post replacement). They may have built a second structure with a large cellar and chimney stack, but that structure was apparently destroyed and the open cellar used as a trash receptacle. No other outbuildings appear to have been built, and there is little architectural evidence of separation and segregation of activities.

Around the homelot, a sheet midden formed. Through the use of a computer simulation mapping procedure employing a nearest neighbor algorithm, four discrete middens were identified. Subsequent analysis using measures of assemblage heterogeneity, however, failed to detect significant differences between the

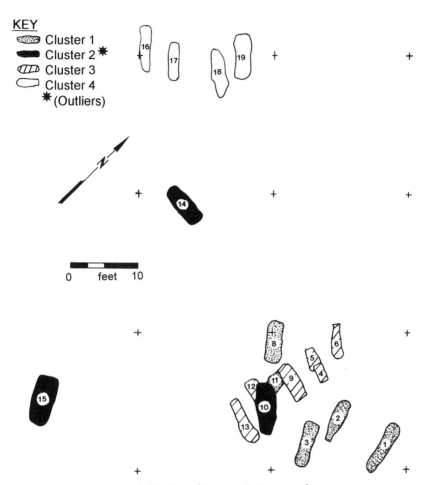

Figure 9–21. Map of Patuxent Point grave clusters.

middens and the contents of the general plowzone. The k-means cluster analysis casts doubt on the reality of those four middens. The apparent uniformity in artifact distributions is attributable in part to the gross artifact categories used in defining and analyzing yard middens. The hypothesis advanced in the previous chapter is supported by the analysis of the Patuxent Point plowzone material: the similarity between the middens is a product of the similar processes by which they were formed. They probably represent areas where kitchen refuse, containing some rubbish but consisting largely of organic debris, was tossed out the doors of the dwellings and into the mouths of waiting livestock in an open yard. That pattern was then modified by plowing, which truncated features and scattered their contents throughout the west yard. Differences between the four SYMAP-defined middens, and perhaps the middens themselves, may be artifacts of the methodology. True rubbish removal is represented in the several trash-filled pits that lay to the west of the principal dwelling.

There is little evidence of specialized activity areas beyond the structures themselves, and that lack of evidence may accurately reflect the poorly defined division of labor, and the very limited nature of spatial separation and segregation of tasks, practiced at the Patuxent Point site. The household, or households, occupying Patuxent Point did not rigidly define and apportion homelot space.

From the trash-filled pits and, to a lesser extent, from the sheet midden, 97 individual vessels of glass and ceramic were recovered. Storage vessels in the form of glass and stoneware bottles dominate the assemblage. A variety of food presentation vessels were identified, as well as vessels of a nonspecialized nature (e.g., bowls). Unlike the vessel assemblage from Compton, food preparation vessels were few, and no vessel identifiable as to form could be attributed to Dutch manufacture, although some of the tin-glazed wares eventually may be attributed to one of several Netherlandish towns involved in the "delft" trade. Non-English vessels have been identified, including wares made in the Rhine Valley and northern Italy, but coarse red earthenwares of probable English or colonial manufacture dominate the assemblage. Whether this represents the establishment of British hegemony in the colonial trade (a hypothesis supported by the tobacco pipe data) or chance events surrounding the acquisition of ceramics has not been determined.

The burial data from Patuxent Point have been cause for enthusiasm and disappointment. A thorough analysis of the skeletal remains has yielded potentially valuable data on colonial household demographics and pathologies that could have been useful in assessing current interpretations advanced by historians. An analysis of the locations and orientations of the graves, however, suggests that we are looking at a minimum of two households divided among three clusters with as many outliers.[13] Indeed, it is possible that one or more of the clusters or outliers is associated with an early to middle eighteenth-century occupation of the site, evidence of which was found by Gardner (1988) a short distance to the southeast of the seventeenth-century homelot site. Dividing this already small sample into several parts, including two household cores (representing five and six individuals each), a group of four servants, and three outliers, casts doubt on the utility of forensic analysis in this case. The numbers simply are too small to generalize about household demographics or health.[14] Even interment rituals, most clearly manifested in the presence or absence of a coffin, are unclear due to the small sizes of the individual clusters.[15] The cemetery data, however, provide unequivocal evidence of households composed of both sexes, exhibiting occasional bouts with malnutrition and poor dental health. Grave 18 is the first physical evidence of a seventeenth-century African presence in Maryland. Unfortunately, whether or not that young man was a servant or slave cannot be determined from the physical evidence.

Expectations for examining symbolism in burial rituals also have been frustrated, at least in regard to Christian cosmology. We had anticipated that at the sounding of some celestial gong, all of the bodies would sit bolt upright facing the rising sun. In fact, only Grave 12 is oriented within 15° of east, and only 6 of the 18 graveshafts are oriented within 30° of east.[16] While each cluster exhibits a common alignment, those alignments probably relate to one or more cultural features rather than to any liturgical prescripts. Indeed, the long axis of the principal dwelling is oriented approximately N37°W (323°) and the orientation of the presumed short axis of Building 2 is N60°W (300°). With a mean orientation of N52°W (308°; median = 316°) and a standard deviation of 30°, 13 graveshafts fall within the general alignment of the two structures. Neiman (1980) encountered a similar pattern at the Clifts Plantation site (44WM33) in Westmoreland County, Virginia (ca. 1670s–1730).[17] The 16 graveshafts at Clifts are all aligned approximately 15° to 20° south of east, but parallel to the traces of fence lines and the overall configurations of the principal dwelling and quarter.

The presence of two successive households at Patuxent Point also complicates interpretations of the architectural and artifact data. It is possible, for instance, that the elusive Building 2 was an early structure on the site, occupied by the first household and razed sometime during the occupation of the first or second household. The Alice Row trade token provides a *terminus post quem* date of 1664 for the filling of Feature 1.

The presence of what probably are servants among the burials raises an important question: whose servants were they? Were they from a single household or do they represent two to four households? In short, the occupants of Patuxent Point, although both households were tenants, may have pursued different strategies, making different choices. The short-term occupation of the site (probably under 20 years) precludes reliable segregation of the deposits based on temporally diagnostic artifacts, and the attribution of any one consumer strategy to one household or the other.

These problems aside, a few generalizations can be made about the occupants of Patuxent Point. Most clearly, reinvestment in the homelot infrastructure was minimal, with few or no buildings or features of specialized function, fence lines that are poorly defined if they exist at all, and no specialized activity areas. Building 1 was maintained with minimal expansion and expedient cellar construction (e.g., the 'root' cellar), and Building 2—if it existed at all—was ephemeral and apparently not worth the effort entailed in rebuilding. Indeed, Building 1 may have been intended as a replacement for, rather than a supplement to, Building 2.

Furnishings beyond the barest of necessities are in evidence. Imported glass and ceramic vessels were available for storing foods, and the presentation of food on tin-glazed earthenwares and other imported vessels suggests a quality of material life at odds with the image of the medieval peasant fingering food in wooden trenchers. There is no evidence of intensive dairying. The limited array of vessel forms—some of them quite fine—and the lack of specialized structures and activity areas suggest a fairly limited range of domestic activities, but not poverty. The archaeological evidence suggests that the majority of household members—women, men, and children—spent much of their labor time in household maintenance, and in the cultivation and processing of tobacco. Household maintenance included homelot construction and maintenance, livestock raising (represented by cow and pig bones in several pits), hunting and fishing (represented by the bones of wild mammals, birds, and fishes, and oyster shells in various features), and gunflint knapping and shot casting. Most consumer choices probably revolved around the demands of an essentially cash crop economy.

Finally, the distribution of graves in the burial yard suggests that kinship was an important structuring principle, particularly when contrasted with the wider household that contained individuals who were unrelated to the planter family and who held no legal claim over the profits and assets of the plantation. Indeed, kinship appears to have had a more prominent organizational role in this rural household than did gender. The distinction between planter and laborer is manifest in the layout of graves (a pattern also evident at Clifts Plantation, cited above), whereas that between men and women is not clear in the cemetery or in terms of space around the homelot. If there was a spatial expression of gender relations, it was in terms of the dichotomy of homelot/nonhomelot rather than in segregated homelot spaces (see Chapter 4; see also Gibb and King, 1991).

With these data we can examine efforts by the households of Compton and Patuxent Point to express themselves through material culture. The following chapter undertakes such an analysis, focusing on these two sites, but where appropriate—and where possible—bringing in data from contemporary sites in the region and elsewhere in North America. Comparisons with other sites should lead to the identification of widely held beliefs and general practices, as well as those that are more household specific.

NOTES

1. Further details on the work at Patuxent Point are available through an extensive collection of field notes, forms, photographs, and artifacts curated by the Maryland Historical Trust.

2. Drawings are available from the author. Renderings of some of the more complete vessels are reproduced in Gibb (1993a) and Gibb and Balla (1993).

3. Stuart A. Reeve analyzed some of the prehistoric material. His data sheets and a preliminary interpretive note are available at the J. Patterson Park and Museum, St. Leonard, Maryland.

4. For clarity of presentation, references are to grid north, which lies 43.5° west of magnetic north.

5. Kimmel (1993) provides a very brief, and somewhat unsatisfying, review of the cultural origins and functions of historic period subfloor pits.

6. The southeast posthole, which contains a good deal of trash, intruded upon another feature that contained the remains of four case bottles, possibly accounting for the debris found within.

7. See Gibb (1993b) for a discussion of the role of trade tokens in the seventeenth-century economy.

8. Pollen and flotation samples were collected from each level, but as of this writing have not been analyzed.

9. Becker (1978) reports a tightly plugged, intact wine bottle containing six brass pins from Governor Printz State Park, Essington, Pennsylvania. The bottle was found buried outside of an addition to the stone foundation of "Printzhoff," believed to be the 1643 home of John Printz.

10. Chi-square analysis of the midden frequency distributions for pipestems, fine earthenwares, coarse earthenwares, bone, and bottle glass against those from the remainder of the plowzone produced a χ^2 value of 136.79, greatly exceeding the critical value of 26.3 ($df=16$, $\alpha = 0.05$). While this value indicates a statistically significant difference, the difference probably is an artifact of the nearest neighbor analysis by which the individual middens were defined.

11. This issue is addressed in greater detail in Gibb (1994).

12. Data on the skeletal analyses have been drawn from Ubelaker et al. (1993). The reader is directed to their report for details on methods and minor pathologies. The author is particularly indebted to Abigail Turowski, University of Maryland-College Park, for helpful discussions about nutrition, illness, and death in seventeenth-century England, and possible implications for the Patuxent Point sample.

13. See Brown (1993) for a similar analysis of graveshaft distributions for an eighteenth-and early nineteenth-century cemetery in Massachusetts.

14. A large number of seventeenth-century burials have been documented for the Chapel Field site, the location of the Jesuit chapel and homelot at St. Mary's City, Maryland. Few of the burials have been excavated as of this writing.

15. Availability of suitable wood planks may have determined whether or not a decedent was interred in a coffin. The absence of coffins in the north cluster is suggestive of social differentiation only in conjunction with the distance from the geographic center of the cemetery, the lack of children, and the presence of an African among the four individuals.

16. If we take into account the unlikely error of the pallbearers switching the body around, some of the graves could be oriented N90°W, that is, facing west. If we further speculate that east and west were determined by reference to the rising and setting

sun, a maximum error factor of 23.5° at this latitude—depending on the season—can be used to define two ranges in which graves ought to have been oriented: 66° to 114° and 246° to 294°.

17. See also Aufderheide et al. (1981).

Chapter **10**

Material Variability along the Shores of the Chesapeake

INTRODUCTION

In Chapter 3, I proposed a consumer choice model for interpreting archaeological and archival data. The model consists of three propositions:

1. All material culture is wealth, or potential wealth, until discarded.
2. Wealth is situated in the household.
3. Households express their identities, and their aspirations, through their uses of wealth, namely, through consumer choices.

The model recognizes the importance of relationships between household members and the pivotal role played by wealth and consumer choice in creating and maintaining those relationships. Such issues as ethnicity, class, and race are extensions, rather than determinants, of decisions made within the household: they are expressions of household relationships and aspirations, and the perceived—or sought after—relationship between a household and the larger community of which it is a part. Applied to seventeenth-century homelot sites, the model enjoins researchers to regard all material culture—from homelot spaces, tracts of land, and architectural forms to vessel sherds and carpentry nails—as the material remains of wealth. Although legally controlled by the male head of household or his designee in England and English America, wealth was available to, and used by, the entire household. It is through wealth, and more particularly through the use of wealth, that the household projected itself to itself, as well as to its neighbors. In using this model, the object is to interpret how households articulated

211

their views of themselves through choices made in the acquisition, use, and discard of material culture.

A variety of literary, judicial, and political tract data was analyzed in Chapters 4 through 6 to identify those values and objectives that appear to have been particularly important to the English. Most of our subjects probably did not give a great deal of thought to such anthropological and sociological issues as the nature of wealth and its function in cultural and social systems; however, they were concerned with values and goals. More important, they tell us—although not always in as frank and unambiguous a manner as we might wish—what those goals were and what they conceived to be legitimate means of achieving them. By no means an exhaustive list, the following six concerns are prominent in the archival record:

1. Perpetuating patrilineal groups, both in terms of progeny and honor.
2. Expressing the personal power, honor, and social position of the male head of household, and the virtue of the women under his care.
3. Providing for the financial future of sons and daughters alike, albeit in different ways.
4. Perpetuating ideal family relations in a manner modeled upon that of the English monarchy, although in an idealized form similar, but not identical, to the Stuart governments.
5. Achieving self-sufficiency and control over the land.
6. Cash-cropping as a means of achieving security, honor, and wealth.

The following analyses and interpretations focus on these objectives in terms of five object domains: plantation siting, architecture, spatial organization of the homelot, vessels, and family cemeteries.

PLANTATION SITING

Both Compton and Patuxent Point occupy prime tobacco lands at strategic locations along the shores of the Patuxent River and a small tributary. As long as the soils survived the effects of intensive cultivation and erosion, they produced high yields of tobacco within easy reach of transatlantic and coastal shipping. Such locations were preferred stopovers for merchants and their local agents, since the holds of their ships could be filled quickly and easily for the race back to European ports. Those returning first received the best prices. Colonists like the Stephens family benefited not only from high yields and good prices, but also from the first pick of those manufactured goods brought from Europe and the Caribbean in trade.

Access to navigable water was critical to the Stephens family and to the households that occupied Patuxent Point if they were to succeed in shipping the bulky, fragile tobacco leaf. It would not have been as important for those households raising grains and livestock, but few seventeenth-century colonists appear to have been interested in mixed agriculture. Livestock, grains, and vegetables were raised by households for their own use, and for small-scale local exchange and a very limited coastal trade. But tobacco was the cash crop and it was with the intention of growing tobacco that many emigrated to the Chesapeake Bay region.

In choosing the Stephens Land tract as the site for their plantations, the occupants of Compton and Patuxent Point tell us something of themselves. More important, they were telling themselves something. They committed to a cash crop economy in which they raised most of their own subsistence and a crop for sale. Their wealth, if not necessarily their survival, was tied to a succession of successful harvests and strong markets. Good returns promised material comfort, economic security, and—if we accept at face value Volpone's observation, quoted in Chapter 4—a degree of honor and prestige in the community. Consistent success meant the ability to acquire more slaves or servants, thereby increasing returns and providing for a more secure future. A poor crop, plummeting tobacco prices, or disruptions of international trade through warfare or plague were sufficient to postpone, if not outright destroy, those prospects.

Fair weather, rising prices, and unrestricted trade, however, did not guarantee success. Poor farming practices ravaged the land, undermining the ability of households to produce tobacco. Also, as sons came of age and pursued their own futures, new lands were needed for them to establish plantations. William Stephens's choice of lands proved salutary at first, but it constrained his ability to expand and to provide lands for his sons. Most of the coastal lands around the Stephens plantation (see Figure 7–1) were soon taken up by other adventurers with similar ambitions. The only lands available for patenting in Calvert County by the late 1650s or early 1660s were the less desirable interior lands and those situated along the precipitous cliffs of the bay coast. Neither the Stephens family, nor their successors, could expand the plantation without encroaching on the lands of their equally pressed neighbors.

The interior and bay coast lands were not valueless, and indeed most were farmed from the late eighteenth-century through the middle of the twentieth century. But they were not what colonists were looking for during the seventeenth century. As the analysis of settlement patterning in Chapter 6 demonstrates, most sought lands within a few thousand feet of navigable water. Those plantation sites that lie much further inland, or that lack direct access to a landing site, are very exceptional cases—so exceptional, in fact, that they warrant our particular interest in future survey and excavation plans. As for the occupants of William Stephens Land, they resemble most of their fellow colonists in their choice of lands. In this respect and, of course, in their decision to leave family, friends, and homeland behind, the Stephens family had a great deal in common with their fellow colonists.

By the early 1660s, the Stephens family removed themselves and their household to the eastern shore counties of Dorchester and Talbot. Available evidence suggests that William Stephens Land was subsequently occupied by tenants, possibly two successive households, there being no evidence of conveyance. It is also possible that the first occupants of Patuxent Point were elements of the Stephens household, still in residence at Compton around the very early years of the 1660s. The tenants also moved away and the land was abandoned for several decades. The lack of available land for expansion, and particularly land for new generations of Stephenses and tenants, may have compelled them to abandon the site. The land policies of the lords Baltimore and local political turmoil provided additional incentives.

In short, the Stephens and Patuxent Point households sought new opportunities. The Stephens family did achieve a high degree of economic security and prestige on the eastern shore of the Chesapeake Bay, becoming substantial landowners (something they attempted and failed to do in Calvert County).[1] George Fox (b. 1624–d. 1691), the individual credited with having founded the Society of Friends in ca. 1650, honored William and Magdelen Stephens with two visits, and the home of Mary and William Stevens, Jr., with one visit, in 1673.[2] Both of the Stephens men also served in local political and judicial positions. The later histories of the Patuxent Point households, unfortunately, are unknown.

Architectural Form and Space

Considered by themselves, the architectural forms at Compton and Patuxent Point are puzzling. The buildings at Compton form a small cluster, with little evidence of differentiation of space and few added amenities beyond chimneys and glazed windows. None of the buildings were expanded, although the dwellings were maintained and repaired periodically. Limited repairs and the lack of additions suggest rapid construction and short-term occupation, an interpretation supported by the narrow range of temporally diagnostic ceramics recovered from the site (see Chapter 8). Alternatively, the clustering of structures and lack of additions may represent a cultural tradition from the southern and western counties of England (Durand, 1934 [1687]:119; Fischer, 1989:271). If the latter is true, this homelot arrangement suggests a certain attachment to the home country that may have been expressed in other object domains as well.[3]

The erection of three dwelling houses also segregated household members, a separation that may have given material expression to the allocation of resources and surpluses within the household. It cannot be proven with the data at hand, but we can speculate that one of the dwellings housed William, Sr., Magdelen, and their sons John and William, Jr., and the second and third dwellings accommodated their indentured servants and/or slaves. The ages of William, Jr., and John are unknown, but neither appears to have married prior to the early 1660s; hence, a second dwelling was not needed for a separate nuclear family. On the other hand, William Stephens transported his kinswomen Catherine Ware to Maryland in 1653 (*Land Records*, AB&H:336, 26 July 1653), and a separate dwelling may have been constructed for her.[4] Did such a division of residences represent a hierarchy of needs and claims on household resources? This is a question that has been touched on by some (e.g., Deetz, 1988; Neiman, 1990), and that warrants future archaeological and archival analysis.

The architecture at Patuxent Point stands in marked contrast to that of Compton. A single dwelling, large and complex relative to those at Compton, dominates the homelot site. There is evidence of shallow cellars or storage pits, and a small addition that may have served as a pantry or closet off of the parlor/principal bedroom.[5] Such an arrangement suggests an attempt to store and control access to—and perhaps to hide—household surpluses or wealth.[6] A second structure, possibly predating Building 1, but certainly abandoned while Building #1 was occupied, was simpler in design than the structures at Compton. It must have been erected upon ground-laid sills, since only small postholes sufficient to support chimney frame posts survive. The extensive fire reddening around the east side of the shell-filled pit or cellar, and the sintered daub layer descending along the east slope of the cellar suggest that the structure burned and collapsed.[7] If the pit was indeed a cellar, it provided a large storage area for household wealth, and it did so out of view of visitors and perhaps with very limited access for the household.

There are at least two qualities that the architectural forms of both sites share: simple, earthfast construction, and periodic maintenance and repair. Similar construction has been documented on seventeenth-century domestic sites throughout Virginia (Carson et al., 1981; Edwards, 1987; Edwards et al., 1989; Kelso, 1984; Muraca, 1989; Neiman, 1980, 1990; Outlaw, 1990) and is markedly different from the large masonry and partial masonry dwellings that were built in and around St. Mary's City as early as the 1630s (see Keeler, 1978; King and Miller, Miller, 1984; 1987; Stone, 1982).

Repair work on seventeenth-century structures is not well documented. Some researchers have accepted the observation of a seventeenth-century writer that earthfast buildings could not survive above five years without repair, and have postulated short-term occupations tied into the exhaustion of agricultural land (e.g., Carson et al., 1981; Louis Berger & Associates, 1989:41; Outlaw, 1990), high mortality, and the imperative to invest in labor rather than in household amenities (Carson and Walsh, 1981). Close attention to the excavation and documentation of holes and molds from load-bearing posts, however, revealed

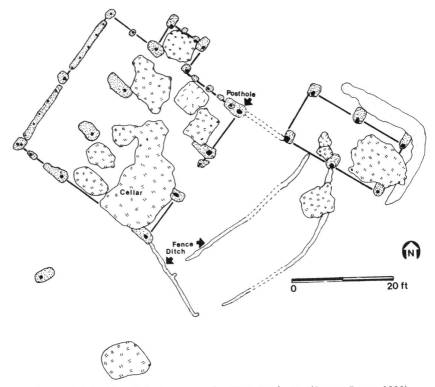

Figure 10–1. Map of the features at the King's Reach site. (Source: Pogue, 1990)

evidence of repair at Patuxent Point. The reevaluation of the Compton architectural data (See Chapter 8) also points to building maintenance as seen in chimney replastering and post replacement. Evidence of building maintenance points out the importance of distinguishing between permanence and durability when describing architecture, the former evoking presentist biases and the latter referring to complex maintenance relationships (St. George, 1983).

An equally important observation for the Compton and Patuxent Point sites is the general lack of expansion in architecture. Pogue (1990) has noted multiple cellars and a pantry or buttery addition to the principal dwelling at the Kings Reach site (18CV83), as well as the replacement of a forecourt fence (Figure 10–1). This site lies just a few miles upriver from the Stephens Land plantation, and dates to ca. 1690–1715. Neiman (1980) uncovered extensive evidence of rebuilding and expansion at the Clifts Plantation site in Westmoreland County, Virginia (ca. 1690–1730; 44WM33), as did Edwards et al. (1989) at the Hampton University historic site (44HT55). Reconstruction and expansion also have been documented for the St. John's (Keeler, 1978; 18ST1–23) and van Sweringen (King and Miller, 1987; 18ST1–19) sites in St. Mary's City, and for the principal dwelling at the Addison Plantation site (18PR175) in Prince George's County, Maryland (Snyder and Roulette, 1990; see also McCarthy, Snyder, and Roulette, 1991).

A concern for maintaining, rather than expanding, plantation buildings, and creating new specialized spaces, may characterize the majority of rural seventeenth-century households. Rather than reinvest the proceeds of tobacco and other commodity sales into new buildings, the households of Compton and Patuxent Point devoted their wealth to the acquisition of new lands; replacing those lands that had been exhausted through poor agricultural practices, and providing for future generations.

Maintenance without expansion need not indicate stasis; it simply marks a different strategy in the use of wealth—a consumer choice. St. George (1983) addressed the issue of maintenance relations in colonial English America and the use of material culture—and particularly architecture—to create and sustain community relations of mutual dependence. That same argument can be applied to household relations (particularly given the paucity of craft specialists in the Chesapeake region), since cooperation was needed among household members to literally maintain roofs over their heads. The "permanent" architecture alluded to by Carson et al. (1981) can be described as an assertion of independence from maintenance relations and, by extension, from the community (St. George, 1988).

Improving and expanding an existing plantation, and appropriating new lands for settlement, represent different choices on the parts of households. Each had different repercussions for the redistribution of wealth in the household, and for the relationship of the household to the community. Expansion of the existing facilities may have provided additional comfort for all household members (Wilk, 1991), while limiting access to surpluses through the creation of separate rooms protected by symbolic "liminal spaces" (e.g., Donley, 1982), or by locks. Lock parts have been recovered from both sites, although they may have been used for such smaller, free-standing storage facilities as chests and wardrobes (Figure 10–2). Evidence for liminal spaces is weak, the footprints of the small, rural dwellings usually consisting of only two or three ground-floor rooms without connecting corridors or self-contained, formal entrances. Floor plans of the rural dwellings of wealthier households illustrated in Neiman (1980) and Kelso (1984), however, indicate more complex arrangements of rooms segregating people and activities, and imposing greater control over movement with formal entrances and corridors.

Investing in land and livestock to provide for one's offspring removed wealth from the homelot and made it inaccessible to nonfamily members of the house-

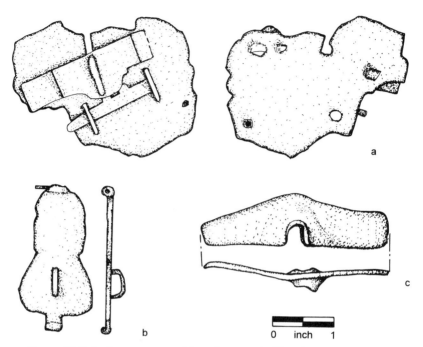

Figure 10-2. Lock parts recovered from Compton (a, b) and Patuxent Point (c).

hold. Such wealth essentially was held in trust for the future of the planter family. Nonkin members of the household held no legal claim on these lands, nor could they benefit in the short term from exceptional harvests and profits. Surpluses, in effect, were exported from the plantation.

Both strategies served to perpetuate the family name and honor, but the reinvestment of surpluses into land may have been of greater long-term benefit for one's offspring, to the disadvantage of the servants and slaves who helped produce the wealth. Growing tobacco was difficult without new lands, and the investment of wealth in the homelot and its furnishings could mark a shift in strategy toward mixed agriculture or such service-oriented activities as operating an ordinary (e.g., Carson et al., 1981:171). Those colonists arriving on the frontier with sizable fortunes could purchase very large tracts in favorable locations. Through proper management, they were able to develop those sites and eventually purchase neighboring tracts. Such plantations are likely to have supported large households and homelots with complex architectural forms, as some wealth could be reinvested into the homelot rather than exported in the purchase of new and distant lands.

HOMELOT SPATIAL ORGANIZATION

Most studies of seventeenth-century sites in Maryland have addressed the issue of spatial organization using plowzone sampling of artifact distributions and computer simulation mapping techniques. As discussed in Chapters 8 and 9, attempts at identifying activity areas have met with only modest success, due in part to the methods and assumptions underlying such analyses. Gibb and King (1991) argue that the middens from the Compton and Patuxent Point sites betray little evidence for a sexual division of labor due to the small sizes of their respective households; that is, the households lacked sufficiently large labor forces to realize or justify strongly drawn lines between men's and women's tasks. Evidence for a sexual division of labor is stronger for the St. John's and Clifts Plantation sites, both of which, for example, had separate dairying areas and a variety of other special-use buildings (Chaney and Miller, 1989, 1990; Keeler, 1978; Neiman, 1980).[8] These two sites, and the van Sweringen Ordinary (King and Miller, 1987), also have yielded evidence of specialized structures and, in the case of two ordinaries in St. Mary's City—St. John's and van Sweringen—formal dining and entertainment areas.

Compton and Patuxent Point, not surprisingly, lack formal dining and entertainment areas. Neither was an ordinary. The middens produced generalized kitchen assemblages of coarse and fine earthenwares, vessel glass, and bone, along with large numbers of tobacco pipe fragments and some flint. There is no area on either site in which coarse earthenwares are particularly prominent: only two milkpans were recovered from Compton, and a minimum of four from Patuxent Point. If dairying occurred at either site, it was on a small, irregular scale, requiring little or nothing in the way of specialized structures or equipment. Indeed, the six vessels identified as milkpans may well have been used for purposes other than dairying.

Task differentiation appears not to have figured prominently in the organization of households on William Stephens Land. Given the nature of tobacco cultivation, with its periodic need for intensive labor followed by lengthy periods of relative inactivity, small rural households could not sustain a rigorous sexual division of labor. The claims of pamphleteers notwithstanding, many women probably spent some time in the tobacco fields. Male heads of household likewise were hard pressed to play the role of monarch when they, too, spent their time in the fields planting, cultivating, and harvesting tobacco alongside of family members, slaves, and servants. During lulls in the season, particularly during the winter months, men probably worked around the homelot, perhaps even sharing in general household chores.

Committed to self-sufficiency and tobacco cash-cropping, most Chesapeake colonists could ill afford the inflexibility of a rigid division of labor. Nor could male and female heads of households afford to divorce themselves from the daily routines of cash-cropping and household production (e.g., Beverley, 1947 [1705]:271–272; but cf. Durand, 1934 [1687]:111–112). To do so required large households with enough able-bodied women and men to undertake and manage the daily affairs of the plantation. Only the wealthiest of planters could afford such an arrangement, like those who occupied the St. John's and Clifts Plantation sites. Perhaps by the time the Stephens family established themselves on the eastern shore, they too could afford to take a less active role in the workings of the plantation, with indentured servants or slaves doing all of the work under the supervision of contracted overseers, or "lieutenants." The activities of the Stephens family on the eastern shore have not been studied; hence we cannot make such a determination.

In a gross sense, there were at least two patterns of homelot organization and architectural investment on the Chesapeake frontier. The majority of the colonists probably concentrated on the maintenance of existing structures and the household relations that built and occupied those structures. These households used much of their resources to procure additional lands, both for immediate use and for the future of their male offspring. Other planters, of considerably greater wealth, also invested resources in expanding their homelots. They could afford to recruit additional labor and to apportion that labor among a variety of tasks in a manner that Adam Smith would speak of in glowing terms a century later. In this way, wealthier households could increase their wealth more rapidly, although it is unlikely that such increases led to a more equitable distribution of wealth within the household. On the contrary, more complex floor plans and yard divisions represent not only reinvestment of wealth in the homelot, but attempts at exercising greater control over that wealth.

FOOD PRODUCTION, PREPARATION, STORAGE, AND PRESENTATION

One of the remarkable findings at Compton and Patuxent Point is the large number of vessels (112 and 97, respectively) found throughout their respective plowzones and features. These minimum numbers of vessels (MNVs) are less surprising if we keep in mind that a large percentage of vessels were used for cooking and food storage, functions provided for in the twentieth century by more durable vessels. Yentsch (1990b, 1991a,b) has analyzed the distributions of vessel forms from a number of seventeenth-century sites in English America, including those reported by Louis Berger & Associates (1989) for the Compton site, providing a baseline against which the Compton and Patuxent Point finds can be compared.

Table 10–1. Distribution of Vessel Forms by Functional Category

Cluster/Site	Process/Prepare		Prepare/Store		Presentation		Total
	n	%	n	%	n	%	
Cluster 1							
Compton	2	2	51	56	38	41	91
The Maine	2	3	39	44	47	53	88
Patuxent Point	5	7	39	51	32	42	76
Pettus	30	9	151	45	154	46	335
Utopia	8	14	23	42	24	44	55
Pasbehay	3	16	8	42	8	42	19
Cluster 2							
Kingsmill	12	15	25	32	41	53	78
Van Sweringen	5	8	21	33	38	59	64
Drummond	9	9	29	28	64	63	102
Cluster 3							
Clifts 1	14	41	5	15	15	44	34
Clifts 2	11	34	6	19	15	47	32

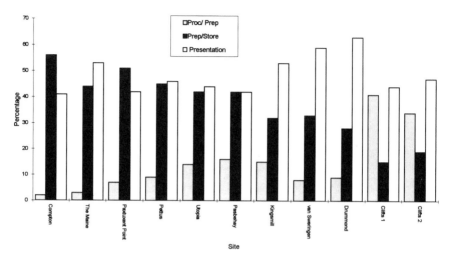

Figure 10-3. Distribution of vessels among three functional categories. (Source: Yentsch, 1990b)

Yentsch's (1990b) intentions were twofold:

1. To reveal patterns of women's behavior obscured by twentieth-century concerns for acquisition rather than use.
2. To trace the development and expansion of courtly culinary traditions through various segments of Anglo-American society.

One of the principal difficulties in Yentsch's (1990b) methodology is the variety of sources from which the data have been collected. Few, if any, of those vessel analyses have been fully reported: the contexts from which the vessels were recovered are unknown, as are the methods for calculating MNVs. Unfortunately, these are the best comparative data available.[9]

Minimum numbers of vessels, representing 8 of the 14 sites and 9 of the 17 components in Yentsch's analysis (1990b:34–35), are analyzed below, along with the data from Compton and Patuxent Point (the remaining sites and components date to the eighteenth century). Yentsch's (1990b) functional groups are redefined to include food processing/preparation, food preparation/storage, and food presentation. Overlap in functional categories is necessary because some vessel forms probably were used in more than one activity. Bowls, for example, could have been used in food processing (e.g., dairying) or food preparation (e.g., cooking). Individual forms are assigned to each category on the basis of their presumed primary function; hence, each vessel for each of the sample sites is

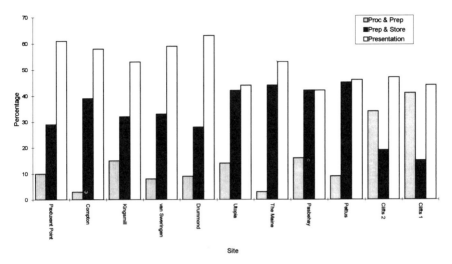

Figure 10–4. Distributions of vessels among three functional categories, recalculated.

assigned to only one category. Only vessels from the food domain are included, and vessels of indeterminate form or function have been eliminated entirely. The resulting frequency distributions and percentage values are presented in Table 10–1 and illustrated in Figure 10–3.

Disregarding, for the moment, the fact that the various vessel analyses used by Yentsch were conducted by different analysts using different methods, it is clear that there is considerable variation in the distribution of vessels among the three functional categories. A k-means analysis of the percentage distributions (circumventing the problem of different sample sizes) yields a three-cluster solution, and facilitates the graphical seriation of the distributions (see Figure 10–3).

Each cluster is set off from the others by an arrow along the abscissa. Cluster 1 is the largest of the three, consisting of six assemblages. These are characterized by more or less equal percentages of preparation/storage and presentation vessels, and with very low percentages of processing/preparing vessels. Cluster 2, consisting of three sites, has markedly higher percentages of Presentation vessels. As in Cluster 1, the percentages of processing/preparing and presentation vessels are low. Cluster 3 consists of two components of the Clifts Plantation site. The distributions appear to be very similar for these two assemblages, with processing/preparing and presentation vessels constituting a large percentage of the identified vessels. The existence of a dairy at the Clifts Plantation may account for these distributions, with earthen milkpans prominent in the two small assemblages.

Vessel glass was included in the analysis of the Compton and Patuxent Point assemblages, whereas it appears to have been excluded from the sites in Yentsch's analysis. The percentages have been recalculated for the William Stephens Land sites, removing glass bottles and drinking glasses, and the modified distributions illustrated (Figure 10–4). Again, a k-means cluster analysis of the percentage data facilitates the graphical seriation. The procedure defines three clusters on the basis of vessel distributions among the three functional categories. The resulting clusters are virtually identical to those achieved with the first analysis, with one important exception: the recalculated Patuxent Point and Compton assemblages have been reassigned to the cluster containing Kingsmill, van Sweringen and Drummond (now Cluster 1).

The above charts illustrate variability among the 9 assemblages, with some correspondences or clustering evident. Several problems, however, preclude meaningful comparisons:

1. Since the various methods for identifying and recording vessel forms and minimal numbers of vessels have not been documented for most of the above sites, we cannot be certain that comparable data sets are being used. For example, it is not clear whether glass vessels are included in any of the above MNV counts other than those reported for Compton and Patuxent Point. There is no analytic reason for excluding them from a study of vessel acquisition and use, but significant differences occur in creating taxa and classifying the assemblages when glass vessels are excluded.

2. Ideally, all of the assemblages should be analyzed by a single individual to mitigate the effects of differential ability and conservatism. Many of the indeterminate vessels from Compton and Patuxent Point might have been identified as to form by an analyst with greater experience or a less conservative approach. Those attributions would increase representation in the Food Presentation category since many of the indeterminate forms probably are plates, cups, and small bowls.

3. The three analytical categories overlap with one another, precluding meaningful statistical evaluation of the distributions. A more definitive identification of vessel use through the study of use-wear patterns may eliminate some overlap.

Although an intensive pattern analysis of the vessel form distributions is inappropriate, it is important to note that the 11 assemblages display some variability. It remains to be seen whether or not the differences are statistically significant. A comparison of the assemblages from Compton and Patuxent Point suggests that the differences evident in the above charts are significant. A chi-square analysis of the frequency distributions for the above three functional categories demonstrates that the two assemblages are essentially the same, regardless of whether glass bottles and drinking vessels are included.[10] Assuming that the functional categories correspond to the emic categories of the occupants of Compton and Patuxent Point, similar choices were made in vessel purchases. Moreover, the similarity should apply to all of the assemblages in any one cluster.

To a certain extent, the similarity between Compton and Patuxent Point is reflected in the comparable ranges of vessels recovered from the two sites and the prominence of glass bottles in both vessel assemblages. As noted in Chapters 8 and 9, there are differences in the styles of vessels, and the representation of vessel forms is by no means identical for the two sites, although the ranges of vessel forms are similar. Whether these distributions represent consumer choices, market availability, or sampling error, or whether significant differences exist among the 11 assemblages, cannot be determined without a larger comparative database, accompanied by details of field and laboratory methods.

Comparisons with vessel assemblages elsewhere in English North America present greater difficulties. In many cases, homelot sites have been reoccupied, obscuring earlier patterning in vessel acquisition and use (e.g., Cranmer, 1990; Thomas and Schiek, 1988).[11] Moreover, many of the sites excavated and reported for New England and Canada are trading posts or forts (Baker, 1985; Camp, 1975; Cranmer, 1990; Faulkner and Faulkner, 1987; Kenyon, 1986). Such sites are best characterized as specialized activity areas, the temporary residences of some households and quarters of itinerant trappers, traders, soldiers, and explorers.

Trading posts and forts could provide some interesting contrasts with the plantation households of the Chesapeake once comparable data are available. The kinds of wares that appear on those sites, for example, are similar in many respects to those recovered from sites in Maryland and Virginia. Baker (1985) reports a number of ware types for the Clarke and Lake Company trading post on the Kennebec drainage of southwestern Maine, all of which are familiar to those working in the Middle Atlantic region: North Devonshire earthenwares, Iberian jar fragments, Rhenish stonewares (both blue and gray, and brown), North Italian slipware, a French or Dutch cooking pot, bottle glass, and, of course, lots of red paste earthenwares of uncertain origin.

Unfortunately, complete MNV lists are unavailable for most of the reported New England and Canadian assemblages. Kenyon (1986), for example, provides us with the following inventory for the Hudson's Bay Company trading post at Fort Albany: wine bottles (47), case bottles (18), pharmaceutical bottles (16), tin-glazed galley pots [and cups?] (13), pitchers (2), one tin-glazed mug or tankard, a large French earthenware jug, and an unspecified number of tin-glazed earthenwares, lead-glazed earthenwares, and stoneware "bowls of some sort" (Kenyon, 1986:55). He also notes that there are no plates in the assemblage, although we cannot assess the validity of that statement without full reporting of the uninventoried portion of the ceramic assemblage. The number of galley pots

Table 10–2. Minimum Numbers of Vessels
from Pentagoet and Cushnoc

Vessel form	Pentagoet	Cushnoc
Bottle	20	3
Bowl	2	2
Bowl/cup	1	1
Bowl/pan	0	6
Chafing dish	3	0
Costrel	1	0
Cup	2	0
Galley pot	5	0
Galley pot/preserves jar	10	0
Glassware	6	0
Jar	6	8
Jar/pot	3	0
Jug	7	3
Jug/mug	0	2
Mug	2	0
Pharmaceutical bottle	6	0
Pitcher	4	0
Plate	4	0
Pot	31	1
Sauce boat	2	0
Saucer/porringer	2	0
Soup plate	1	0
Tankard	1	0
Tureen lid	1	0
Indeterminate	21	19
Total vessels	121	45

and pharmaceutical bottles at Fort Albany also appears to be very high, relative to the Chesapeake sites analyzed by Yentsch (1990b), but the significance of the distribution cannot be assessed without full reporting of the vessel assemblage.

Cranmer's (1990) inventory for the Plymouth Company's trading post at Cushnoc, and Faulkner and Faulkner's (1987:184–185, 232, 237) list of vessels for the various occupations of Fort Pentagoet, are more detailed and complete (Table 10–2). Both assemblages date to the second and third quarters of the seventeenth century and contain many of the same wares, but the similarities end there. The Cushnoc assemblage is smaller and less well preserved than that of Pentagoet. Of the Cushnoc vessels, 42% cannot be identified as to form as opposed to 17% for Pentagoet. Perhaps because of the larger number of identifiable vessels from Pentagoet, Faulkner and Faulkner (1987) identified nearly three times as many forms (22, as opposed to 8 from Cushnoc). Bottles figure prominently in the assemblage (20 vessels, or 17%), but may be underrepresented since some of the glass specimens may have been assigned to later deposits.

Many of the Pentagoet forms are similar to those recovered in the Chesapeake region, although French-made vessels substitute for the English West Country and Dutch forms found at such sites as Compton and Patuxent Point. Since Pentagoet remained under French control for 25 of its 45 years, this should come as no surprise. Because of the succession of occupations at Pentagoet, more detailed analyses will have to wait until individual vessels can be assigned to deposits for each of the three periods of occupation. Lumping the consumer choices of officers, enlisted men, traders and their families, and visitors would have little value for the problem at hand; however, Cranmer and the Faulkners have made an excellent beginning in calculating and reporting MNVs for their respective sites.

In sum, ceramic data may be used at some future point to distinguish between one or more household strategies for processing, preparing, storing, and presenting food. Different social units—planter households, company settlements, and military garrisons—should have expressed themselves differently through choices in imported goods. Differences between the Compton and Patuxent Point assemblages—the only two that can be compared with confidence—appear to be negligible. At this level of analysis, and with the available vessel data, it is not possible to determine whether or not these households were pursuing similar strategies. It is possible that vessel assemblages are not the best means for divining household strategies, a conclusion at which Friedlander (1991) arrived in looking at one component of household strategies—competitive social status display. Perhaps we should withhold judgment until additional data are available and a broader theoretical approach is adopted.

DISPOSAL OF THE DEAD

Family cemeteries potentially provide the clearest evidence attainable through archaeological research of familial and household relationships. Where markers survive, the relationships are literally carved into stone (e.g., Brown, 1993). Unmarked cemeteries, such as characterize the Chesapeake Bay region of the seventeenth and early eighteenth centuries, also provide high quality data. The names of the deceased and their specific relationships to one another are not directly accessible; however, it is possible to discern larger household relations and details of mortality and morbidity from both the physical remains and the distribution and treatment of those remains.

Few family cemeteries associated with seventeenth/early eighteenth-century sites have been excavated in the Chesapeake region.[12] Patuxent Point and

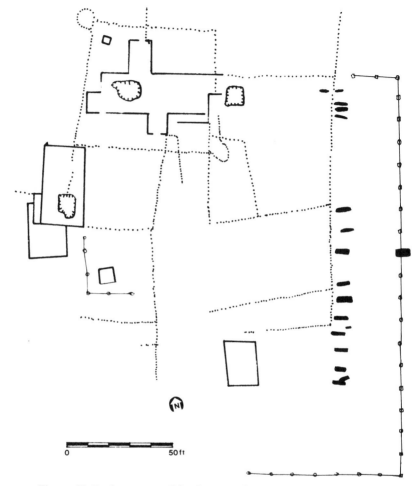

Figure 10–5. Cemetery at Clifts Plantation. (Source: Aufderheide et al., 1981)

Clifts Plantation cemeteries are discussed in Chapter 9. Additional data are available from two sites in Virginia: the College Landing site #7 (Edwards, 1987) in Williamsburg, and Site A at Martin's Hundred (Noel Hume, 1992).[13] Although small, this sample of family cemeteries should serve to point out interesting patterns and to draw the Patuxent Point cemetery into clearer focus.

All four cemeteries reveal one particularly important pattern: the graves occur in clusters, and—at least in two instances—those clusters can be attributed to components of the household. Anatomical and spatial analyses of the interments at Patuxent Point indicate that there were at least three distinct clusters of

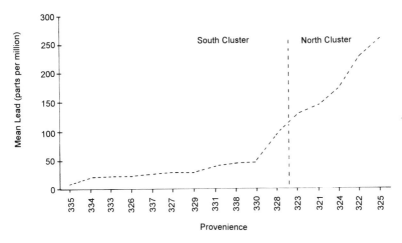

Figure 10–6. Distribution of Clifts Plantation skeletons based on lead levels. (Source: Aufderheide et al., 1981:289)

burials and as many isolates. Ubelaker et al. (1993) state with some confidence that one of the individuals in the north cluster was an African. Taking this as evidence of a separate plot for nonkin burials (notably, the cluster farthest from the homelot and the one devoid of coffins and children), I have hypothesized that the two overlapping clusters to the south represent the principal families of the household, separated temporally and, possibly, genetically from one another.

Anatomical and spatial data from the Clifts Plantation suggest a similar pattern, although there is no evidence in the family cluster for a succession of tenant families. The north cluster consists of five individuals (two children and three adults), closely spaced and parallel. All are European (Aufderheide et al., 1981:285). The second cluster consists of 11 individuals located 40 ft. and more to the south. This cluster consists of one child and ten adults, only one of the latter being of European ancestry. The rest of the individuals exhibit skeletal traits that indicate African origins (Figure 10–5). Graveshafts for both clusters are distributed along a fence line that runs parallel to the principal dwelling, with the planter-family remains closest to the principal dwelling.

Aufderheide et al. (1981), examined the lead content of each skeleton and found significantly higher levels among those in the north cluster (Figure 10–6). The different levels of lead are attributed to differential ingestion, the planter-family members eating food cooked and served in lead-glazed earthenware pots; nonfamily members presumably ate out of wooden trenchers. Precisely how the higher lead levels were achieved among those in the north cluster is not as important as the differences themselves. The single adult European in the south cluster

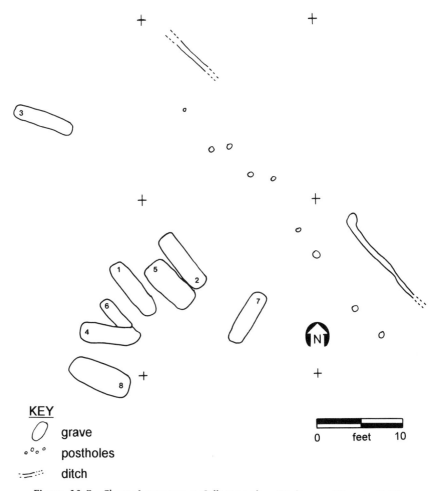

KEY

∅ grave
₀°₀° postholes
:⁓: ditch

0   feet   10

Figure 10-7. Cluster 1 cemetery at College Landing #7. (Source: Edwards, 1987)

(#328) has a lead level that is intermediate between those of the Africans in the south cluster and those of the European adults and children in the north cluster. These results, in connection with the spatial and racial distributions of human remains, clearly differentiate between two groups of people at Clifts Plantation, groups defined in terms of kinship rather than age, sex, or race.

Cemeteries at College Landing #7 and Site A at Martin's Hundred also exhibit clustering into two or more groups (Figures 10-7 and 10-8). Preservation of human remains was poor at the former site, precluding reliable age, sex, and race determinations. Preservation at Martin's Hundred ranged from good to poor, per-

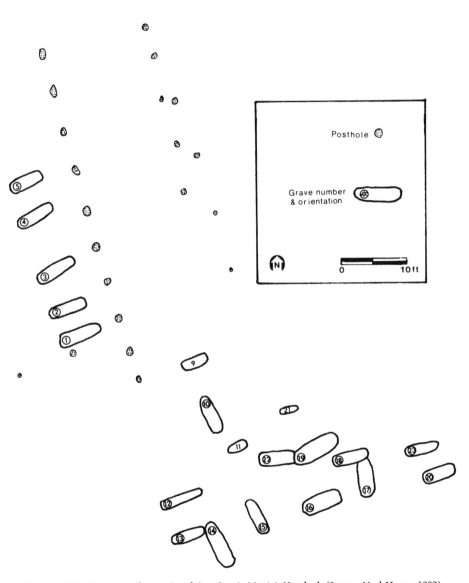

Figure 10–8. Cemetery Clusters 1 and 2 at Site A, Martin's Hundred. (Source: Noel Hume, 1992)

mitting determinations only of age and sex, but not race. Cluster 1 at College Landing #7 consisted of eight graveshafts, one of which was somewhat removed from the others, but still within 20 ft. of the center of the cluster. Five were oriented east to east-southeast, two west to northwest, and one south–southwest. Cluster 2 (not shown) consists of two graves 70 ft. to the northeast and oriented northeast and southwest. The second cluster was within approximately 60 ft. of the homelot core; that is, was closer to the principal dwelling than was the larger group in Cluster 1.

Three grave clusters, comprising 19 individuals, were uncovered at Site A at Martin's Hundred. Cluster 1 consists of five individuals, all oriented to the east, and aligned perpendicular to a north–south fence line. Two of the individuals were females, and all were adults. Cluster 2 is a hodgepodge of 15 burials, 5 of which are poorly preserved or completely decayed. Age and sex determinations were possible for 8 of the 15, revealing 4 men and 4 women. The remaining 7 individuals were probably subadults. Eight of the graves were oriented to the east, two to the north, two to the south, and three cannot be determined.

Cluster 3 at Site A (not shown on the map) lies approximately 150 ft. west of Clusters 1 and 2. It consists of an adult male oriented to the east, an adult female immediately to the north and oriented west, and a third individual, the location, orientation, and physical characteristics of which have not been reported. Cluster 3 is situated on the opposite side of the homelot from Clusters 1 and 2.

Noel Hume (1992:36; Figure 3.1) has suggested that based solely on their alignment the five individuals in Cluster 1 represent a single event in which all five died and were interred. If this argument was used to explain the patterns at Patuxent Point, Clifts Plantation, or College Landing #7, we would have to appeal to particularistic arguments of catastrophic events in each case. A more plausible explanation is careful burial of the dead in a consistent manner, with variations attributable to successions of new occupants, or to changes in the participation of various groups within the household in burial rituals. The lack of clear patterning in body orientation suggests that concerns other than Christian cosmology are represented in graveshaft orientation. In some cases, graves may have been consciously oriented relative to then extant cultural features (e.g., buildings, fences, and tree lines).[14] Cluster orientation may represent statements about the relationships between decedents, their surviving kin, and rights to the wealth of the plantation. Based on the findings from Patuxent Point and Clifts Plantation, and the analyses in Chapters 4 through 6, kinship was the dimension along which such determinations were made and, perhaps, contested.

SUMMARY

High-quality data on seventeenth- and early eighteenth century sites in the Chesapeake region are not generally available, and much of what are available exist only in limited distribution technical reports. Sufficient comparative data, however, have been assembled and analyzed to place the Compton and Patuxent Point sites into a larger archaeological context. Patterns in plantation siting (dealt with at length in Chapter 6), architectural expansion and maintenance, homelot spatial organization, and grave placement are evident among the sites examined. Patterns in vessel purchases are less evident, but then the quality of available ceramic data is particularly poor.

The distribution of seventeenth-century archaeological sites in the Chesapeake region indicates a strong preference for coastal lands with soils well suited for tobacco culture. This preference suggests a common purpose among the majority of colonists in Maryland: to establish plantations upon which a cash crop could be raised, and surpluses generated, to afford security for the heads of household, and to provide plantations for sons and substantial dowries for daughters. Some atypical domestic sites, particularly those situated among poor soils or in the interior, may indicate alternative strategies; for example, operation of ferries, public landings, or ranches for the raising of livestock. The Turner site (18CH209) in Charles County, Maryland, is sufficiently distinct in terms of its location and the large numbers of terra-cotta tobacco pipe fragments recovered from its surface to suggest that it was an aboriginal or creole site, or a place in which interethnic contacts were particularly intensive or frequent, and where household interests and priorities were different from those of the majority of English colonists.

Even a cursory examination of architectural data from seventeenth- and early eighteenth-century homelot sites suggests two distinct patterns: short-term occupations consisting of one or a few dwellings with little evidence of repair or expansion, and complex sites with several buildings—some of specialized function—fence lines, and considerable evidence of building repair, replacement, and expansion. I have hypothesized that these two patterns represent different household choices in the allocation of surpluses. Some households, those of Compton and Patuxent Point among them, invested little in the homelot. Much of their surpluses probably went into the acquisition of new lands for the household, and for the future of the planters' offspring.[15] Other households, possibly the wealthier ones as evidenced by the St. John's and Clifts Plantation sites, invested in large numbers of servants and slaves. These large labor forces could work with increased efficiency through specialization, thereby further increasing the wealth of the planters and insuring higher standards of living for the moment and for the future. These households already had access to ample lands.

Specialization of labor also can be seen, to a limited extent, in the definition of activity areas at some sites. Both St. John's and Clifts Plantation have yielded evidence of dairies, indicating special resources and skills devoted to home production. Identifying activity areas on seventeenth- and early eighteenth-century sites, however, has not been without difficulties. The gross categories used in analyzing the spatial distributions of artifacts, the techniques used in such analyses, and the lack of adequate linking arguments necessary to justify and interpret spatial patterns all limit our ability to use plowzone samples in a meaningful way. Nonetheless, some sites betray a greater degree of spatial separation of activities. The co-occurrence of complex architectural spaces and activity areas at some sites, and simple architectural spaces and generalized middens at others, indicates two distinct strategies.

Vessel analysis has been of limited utility. The difficulty, however, is in the lack of adequately reported data; specifically, detailed site reports describing methods, defining vessel forms (e.g., Beaudry et al., 1983), and providing complete vessel lists. Yentsch (1990b) has published aggregate data from some 14 sites in New England and the Chesapeake region, and she has detected shifts in the acquisition of vessels within certain functional categories. Insofar as those shifts reflect known patterns of ceramic production in Europe, they conform to expectations. However, the quality of that data is inadequate for examining household practices: there simply is no way of determining whether these data are comparable and suitable for statistical analysis.

Cemetery data provide some of the best insights into household strategies. Family graveyards stand as clear reminders to the living as to how household members related to one another, and to the plantation and its products. The small sample of cemetery data indicates the importance of the distinction between kin and nonkin in organizing the household. This basic dichotomy may have pervaded early colonial Chesapeake society, assuming greater importance than distinctions made on the bases of age, sex, or even race. Kin relations, and to a certain extent property relations, are deducible from forensic data and from the spatial arrangements of graves. The two grave clusters that could be attributed to planter families on the basis of forensic data (Patuxent Point and Clifts Plantation) lie closer to the homelot core (i.e., the principal dwelling and other structures) than do those of servants or slaves. Bone lead level analysis also may provide a rigorous technique for distinguishing between two segments of colonial households: the owner family, and the servants and slaves with minimal claims on the estate.

Each of these data sets—plantation location, architecture, artifact spatial patterning, vessel patterning, and cemetery organization—informs on the choices made by households in perpetuating themselves. Each data set represents choices as to how household wealth was used, and there may be incidences where choices in two or more domains are discordant. For example, architecture and spatial organization may have been employed in asserting the planter-family's claims to the products of the plantation. At the same time, cognizant of the servants' displeasure over such an arrangement, the planter family may have used food vessel purchases to assure all members of the household that they would have a reasonable share in the products of the plantation, at least on a daily basis. Cooking and eating as a household, and the indiscriminate use of tablewares—particularly fine earthenwares in food presentation—may have asserted the common goals and rights of household members. Widespread distributions of fine tablewares and faunal remains at domestic sites could reflect just such a strategy.

Archaeological evidence indicates that the households of Compton and Patuxent Point were relatively small and undifferentiated. They came to Maryland to establish families, to achieve security and honor, and to provide for their children. Resources were used to meet immediate needs, but surpluses probably were invested in new lands in which they hoped to find security and a future. Wealthier neighbors, already land-rich, could afford larger households in which tasks could be spatially and temporally segregated and assigned to specialists: but the paramount interests of the Stephens family and their successors at Patuxent Point centered on the future; a future that would take them away from their first home in the new land and to a place with greater promise.

NOTES

1. The land records of Dorchester, Talbot, and other Eastern Shore counties note many land patents for William, William, Jr., and John Stephens. Twelve tracts in Dorchester County were patented between 1668 and 1683 by William Stephens, totaling 874 acres.
2. William and Magdelen's children, and their descendants, preferred the spelling "Stevens." Mary and William Stevens, Jr., settled across the Choptank River from William and Magdelen Stephens's Horne Point plantation. The fact that they opted for this separation at a time when they probably could have settled next to one another suggests that they had other plans; perhaps the establishment of a ferry?
3. See also Anderson (1971:21ff) regarding the relationship between architectural complexity and wealth, particularly in East Anglia. Fischer (1989) catalogs a number of traditional "ways" among the Chesapeake colonists, although he lacks an explicit theory for the retention of Old World traditions on the New World frontier.
4. "Stephens Plains," a 50-acre (20 ha) tract some distance north of William Stephens Land, was patented by Katharine Stephens in 1668; whether or not she was the same 'kinswoman' has not been determined (*Land Records*, 11:464, 12:124, 06 May 1668).
5. The north end of the dwelling probably represents the hall/kitchen, or public end, of the ground floor on the bases of the large open hearth, the possible root cellar, and the positioning of the doorway on the west facade.
6. See DeBoer (1988) for a discussion of the potential household strategies represented

by below-ground versus above-ground storage in prehistoric communities on the Normandy Plateau, Tennessee.

7. Shaffer (1993), citing his own experimental work in Calabria, Italy, suggests that burned wattle-and-daub structures leave little trace in the soil. See also Noel Hume (1992:249–250) and Bankoff and Winter (1979).

8. Household dairying, historically women's work in English society, is a labor- and skill-intensive activity intended to meet household needs directly, or through limited local exchange. St. John's served as an elite residence and governmental meeting place and, beginning in the late 1660s, served as a public ordinary, or inn. The quasi-public function of the site may account for some of the segregation of space and separation of activities. Public usage, however, does not account for the construction of a nursery or a dairy.

9. For example, are those values based strictly on vessels recovered from features, or do they represent those recovered from the plowzone as well? Are glass vessels included and, if not, why not?

10. With glass: $\chi = 2.08$, $df = 2$, $\alpha = .05$, $c.v. = 5.991$. Without glass: $\chi = 3.11$, $df = 2$, $\alpha = .05$, $c.v. = 5.991$. The null hypothesis of no significant difference is accepted in both instances. The use of the chi-square statistic presupposes mutually exclusive categories. None of the vessels is assigned to more than one category, although functionally some may have been used in more than one of the three activity sets.

11. Yentsch (1990b) used only two New England sites in her analysis of English culinary traditions, both of which date to the first half of the eighteenth century: Wellfleet (1690–1740) and John Howland (1710–1730).

12. A handful of interments from the Chapel Field cemetery in St. Mary's City and scattered graves from a number of sites along the James River in Virginia have been excavated. A family cemetery at the Smith site (18CV93) also has been partially documented, but remains unexcavated and unreported. The results of professionally excavated household cemeteries from elsewhere in the region lurk within the "gray" literature of the field, while others remain unreported.

13. Virginia state inventory numbers are not available.

14. See Gibb and Turowski (1994) for a study of graveshaft orientation and coffin use in seventeenth-century Maryland and Virginia.

15. An alternative explanation, not previously broached for lack of data, is that surpluses were siphoned off by other households and overseas merchants through debt relations. The important topic of debt in the development of patron-client relations, political tension, and consumer choice remains to be studied.

Chapter 11

Consumer Behavior in Seventeenth-Century English America

INTRODUCTION

The introduction of consumer behavior modeling to historical archaeology may have been inevitable. As a contemporary social issue, pervading much of our public discourse, consumer behavior has been incorporated into academic discourse, much as ecology was in the 1960s and 1970s. But this new interest is not simply an academic fashion. Consumer behavior theory fills a critical need in historical archaeology: it links objects with social behavior, and with choice. Centered in the household, consumer behavior also draws attention to variability at the level of the domestic site, the principal sampling domain for much of historical archaeology.

But consumer behavior theory is not without shortcomings. Much of consumer behavior research in historical archaeology has relied on an implicit, static concept of material culture where objects and groups of objects "reflect" equally static social relations or "statuses." The term "consumer behavior" also has been defined in only the vaguest terms, but implicitly is contrasted with producer behavior. The dichotomy of production versus consumption is artificial and betrays twentieth-century biases more than it illuminates past perceptions and values. Finally, while much of consumer behavior research in archaeology has focused on Euro-American society of the late eighteenth through early twentieth centuries, a period characterized by industrial and capitalist expansion, it is not clear whether this approach is also suitable for noncapitalist societies. If consumer behavior is inappropriate for analyzing and interpreting noncapitalist societies, it may prove inappropriate for capitalist societies as well.

Theoretical points addressed in Chapters 2 and 3 are briefly reviewed in the following section. Whether or not consumer behavior theory can be applied successfully to seventeenth-century archaeological assemblages is then addressed, using the contexts developed in Chapters 4, 5, 7 and 9, and the results of the analyses in Chapters 5, 8, 9, and 10. In the conclusion, I propose that by examining the choices made at the level of the household we can see how households create themselves and their communities. Those decisions extend beyond choices between specific goods, and relate to the full range of productive and consumptive activities that occur within households. Consumer behavior is best defined as the patterned decisions that people as individuals and as groups make in the use of wealth. It is an effective concept for analyzing household assemblages, both those from noncapitalist and capitalist societies, because it addresses the locus of practice and change, and it circumvents the arbitrary consumption-production dichotomy.

CONSUMER BEHAVIOR THEORY IN HISTORICAL ARCHAEOLOGY

The principal difficulty in applying consumer behavior theory in archaeology is that it is not, properly speaking, a theory— at least not in the way that it has been used in historical archaeology. It is axiomatic in the field that relationships exist between objects and the social characteristics of their users. Those relationships, and the manner in which social qualities are projected onto material objects, have not been adequately explored: consumer theory has not developed in concert with a theory of material culture.

Miller (1987), McCracken (1988), Mukerji (1983), and Kopytoff (1986), among others, have made some advances in this area, contributing to a theory of material culture in general, and a theory of consumption in particular. They have moved away from the information and social interaction theories of Wobst (1977), Conkey (1980), and Weissner (1983), rejecting the simple metaphor of material culture is like language (see also Barthes, 1972 [1957]). McCracken (1988), paralleling Weissner's (1983) concept of assertive style, looks at how individuals create their identities through what they consume. Miller (1987) emphasizes the interpretive aspects of acquisition and use. Both differ from Wobst, Conkey, and Weissner in several respects:

1. The focus is on variability in the distributions of identical forms among households, rather than on formal variations within single artifact

classes, that is, acquisition and use rather than style (see Weissner, 1983:256).

2. Emphasis is placed on the strategizing, rather than on the functionalist and integrative, aspect of behavior.

3. Expressions of goals, values, and aspirations are privileged over the transmission of status information.

4. Emphasis is placed on dialogue and reinterpretation, rather than on the simple projection of status.

5. The concern is for the use of wealth, rather than its exchange.[1]

Miller, in particular, is concerned with the use of wealth at the level of the household, rather than that of the individual or community.

We are still on uncertain ground when dealing with household consumption, because the processes by which compromises are sought and reached by members of a household have not been adequately addressed.[2] Consumer behavior refers to decisions made by individuals in the allocation of resources—the use of wealth. Those decisions can be compromises, or they can be acts of defiance: they seldom are made in isolation. Wilk (1990) explored this point briefly in his essay on Kekchi Maya domestic architecture. Investment of household surpluses in Westernizing houses and acquiring appliances was a strategy for mollifying household conflicts over the allocation of surpluses. For archaeologists, it is still necessary to integrate a theory of household into a theory of consumption, or vice versa. Perhaps the two are inseparable.

The above-cited works also contribute to the concept of the object as a mutable entity, its meaning defined and redefined in social discourse. Here the emphasis shifts from the context of acquisition, which represents a brief moment in the "life" of an artifact (Kopytoff, 1986; Yentsch, 1991a), to the varied contexts of use, where actors, relationships, and meanings constantly change. In order to appreciate their full meaning, artifacts must be read—to revert to a linguistic metaphor—within the context of other objects and actions. That, of course, creates difficulties for archaeologists recovering artifacts that are no longer active in a cultural context.[3]

A second, less-pressing concern in using consumer behavior theory is the implicit distinction drawn between consumption and production. As noted above, such a distinction may be inappropriate for early modern Europe and its colonies. Nor is it necessary: preindustrial European households often were the centers of both production and consumption. The distinction is arbitrary, and it puts unnecessary constraints on our analyses and interpretations. In archaeological studies of women's activities, for example, there is a tendency to assign private sphere (i.e., homelot) tasks to women and public sphere tasks to men. Moving off of that singular point and into the fundamental question of gender as a structuring principle has been very difficult, partly due to the implicit division of household activities into production and consumption.

Emphasizing meaningful contexts and historical development, consumer behavior theory focuses analytical attention on culturally defined goals, values, and means; variability in those definitions; and the changes arising from variability. Identifying the contexts in which objects were interpreted, however, can be an intimidating prospect. It is one thing to elicit varied meanings of objects from live informants, and quite another when our informants are long dead. Fortunately, our informants are not quite dead.

Historical archaeology derives its greatest analytic power from the innovative use of documents (e.g., Beaudry, 1988; Little, 1992b). Documents provide analysts with access to the people under study. It is possible, in effect, to ask people long dead how they felt about certain issues, what a particular object or event meant to them, and what they thought was important in life, even though the process is not as interactive as one might experience in conducting an interview with a living informant. One must develop questions and then seek the answers in a variety of archival materials that, by fluke or design, have survived. Answers can be confirmed through multiple sources or by seeking answers to parallel questions and examining them for contradictions. Extensive and intelligent use of archival sources also represents something of a courtesy, insofar as we give our subjects the opportunity to speak for themselves. Their comments, of course, are still filtered through the researcher.[4]

Once meaningful contexts for a range of activities and objects have been identified through archival research and analysis, it is possible to look at those contexts archaeologically. Here archaeological methods can be used to their fullest potential as certain types of behavior are examined at a broad range of sites representing many and varied segments of society—more varied than are likely to be represented in the documentary record. Where only a limited, nonrepresentative sample of a community may be interrogated through archival materials, archaeological methods can be used to "interview" many individual households (and, perhaps one day, individuals) about certain beliefs, practices, and strategies. The end result is a richer view of behavioral variability, the logic behind that variability, and its effect on the course of cultural-historical development in the community under study.

In sum, the emphasis of consumer behavior theory is on past meanings. Historical archaeology is in an enviable position in the social sciences in that meanings are accessible from archaeological patterning at the levels of the domestic site and regional settlement patterning, and from the answers awaiting our questions in the various sources preserved in public and private archives. By focusing on the household, within a contextualist framework developed from archival and archaeological sources, it is possible to identify strategies among seventeenth-century households as they sought to define themselves for themselves, and for their neighbors. Some of the strategies identified in this study are summarized in the following section.

CONSUMER BEHAVIOR IN ENGLISH AMERICA

Consumer behavior provides an interpretive framework around which methods are organized. Finer structures within this framework are necessary to more efficiently organize the data, and to allow us to discriminate, analytically, between meaningful seventeenth-century contexts. The concept of "object domains" has been used in the foregoing analyses as such a structure. It refers to classes of related objects that are likely to have had meaningful associations for the people who used them.

The object domains used in this study are plantation siting, architecture, homelot organization, ceramic and glass vessels, and family cemeteries. These have been selected on the bases of three criteria: they represent types of data that typically are recovered from seventeenth-century colonial sites; the archival record informs, to greater and lesser extents, on their contexts; and they may represent distinct phenomena that the colonists recognized—if only obliquely. For example, there are numerous observations by visitors to the Chesapeake colonies regarding plantation siting, and the criteria considered by their contemporaries in selecting certain sites over others. Most of these comments point to the organization of tobacco production and the nature of the market and transportation systems to explain the criteria; however, some also make reference to strategies of resistance, as planters refused to settle in towns, and to aesthetic considerations. Choices made in the acquisition and use of ceramic and glass vessels, on the other hand, are not as accessible, most of what is known having been based on twentieth-century interpretations of probate inventories (e.g., Main, 1982), archaeological assemblages (e.g., Pogue, 1993), and genre paintings (e.g., Janowitz, 1993).

Two models also have been proposed to further develop the interpretive framework, one general, as regards households, and the other specific, as regards seventeenth-century Anglo-American households. The general, or theoretical, model includes all material culture within the category of wealth, actual or prospective. Wealth, as material culture, is situated in the household, which is to say, the household accumulates goods and stores them at the homelot; exceptions being overseas holdings or credit and investments. Households use this wealth cum material culture to express their identities to themselves and, secondarily, to their neighbors.

The specific, or descriptive, model proposes at least six motivations underlying choices made in the household, based on the historical contexts derived in
the earlier chapters. These include the perpetuation of the patrilineal group, and
its honor and prestige, through the investment of resources in the organization of
the household, and in the future households of both sons and daughters. Economic strategies were designed to meet these objectives, which is not to say that
they had in fact succeeded. Indeed, Grettler and Seidel (1993) suggest that indebtedness may have been pervasive in Delaware during the late seventeenth and
early eighteenth centuries, depriving householders of their independence, and
their offspring of their inheritance.

Self-sufficiency and control over resources were important issues in the developing ideology of mercantilism, and they appear to have been a part of the
colonial householder ethos, despite the land-granting policies of the lords Baltimore that imposed dependence, and that removed control not just from the
household, but from the community. The lack of complete accord on such issues
as land ownership and the legal status of labor provided greater latitude for strategic thinking and resource allocation than would have been possible with more
rigidly defined, and generally accepted, concepts.

Analysis of the archaeological remains from Compton and Patuxent Point,
and from a few contemporary sites, suggests that at least two overlapping strategies were practiced in the Chesapeake colonies, and that these strategies are more
readily observed through some object domains than through others. One strategy
entailed investment in the homelot, the other in new lands. Both involved distinguishing between the rights of family and nonfamily members to the resources
and surpluses of the household.[5] Plantation siting, patterns in the creation and
maintenance of architectural spaces, and the disposal of the dead in family cemeteries speak most clearly to issues of household organization, the allocation of
resources, and rights to resources and surpluses. Due in part to the quality and
limited extent of data reporting for seventeenth-century colonial sites, and due to
the limited development of appropriate methods, homelot organization and the
distribution of vessel forms among sites have been less useful for examining
household practices.

The analysis of plantation siting is particularly useful for identifying both
variability and commonalties among Chesapeake region planters. All plantations
were not created equal. Limited availability of prime locations along navigable
waterways, land engrossment by a relatively small but politically powerful group
of planters, and the irregular distribution of soils well suited to tobacco culture
contributed to this variability. Early settlement usually meant first choice and
selection of the best locations. But those choice tracts were encompassed rapidly
by other settlers seeking similar sites, greatly constraining the ability of individual planters to expand their plantations or to acquire adjoining lands for their

sons. Those early settlers arriving with large households and substantial resources acquired larger tracts, enabling them to expand their operations within their own plantations and, subsequently, to purchase those of their neighbors. The Ashcomb family, neighbors of the Stephens family of Compton, is an example of one such household that eventually acquired neighboring lands from those who could no longer achieve their individual ends with locally available resources.

Competition for a limited resource—prime plantation sites as defined by high-yield soils and proximity to navigable water—is not the only behavior that can be inferred from the distribution of archaeological sites. The preference for premium plantation sites evident in that distribution, and the comments of period observers regarding site selection, suggests a high degree of uniformity, or common purpose, among the seventeenth-century Chesapeake colonists. They were intent on participating directly in the market economy of the circum-Atlantic region through cash-cropping. There were those who were involved to varying degrees in the fur trade, the coastal trade in provisions, and even in the raising of silkworms and prospecting for precious minerals. But virtually everyone with the means—and little was required—raised tobacco.

To what extent this common interest set the English colonists apart from their compatriots in the various parts of England, Wales, Ireland, and other English colonies is uncertain. Defoe (1971 [1724–1726]) tells us that regional specialization in the raising of cash crops was well developed in England by the end of the first quarter of the eighteenth century, and probably much earlier. Were the seventeenth-century colonists creating a new economy and social order, or were they simply bringing with them a system of agricultural economy that already was well developed? The analysis of settlement patterning in Maryland and the analysis of available archival material suggest that the latter is true: these were not peasants practicing subsistence farming in their homeland, inventing an advanced economic form in a new land. They brought with them practices and strategies in commercial agriculture with the expressed purpose of acquiring wealth. How they used that wealth is the subject of the analyses of architecture, and to a lesser extent of homelot organization, and of patterning in family cemeteries.

In previous chapters, I examined the extent to which we can determine the wealth of a household on the basis of archaeologically recovered ceramics and glass. Even a superficial comparison between the architecture of the St. John's and Clifts Plantation sites, and that of Compton, Patuxent Point, and King's Reach, should make it clear that such determinations are unnecessary. The wealthier St. John's and Clifts Plantation households created larger, more complex, more durable architectural spaces than is seen on most seventeenth-century sites. Structures were expanded and replaced, and yards were defined and redefined by

wealthier households intent on creating specialized spaces for a variety of different tasks.

Only the wealthier planters could afford to practice intensive agriculture,
and if the presence of special-use buildings is any indication, they did; for example:

> The Private Buildings are of late very much improved; several Gentlemen
> there [in Virginia], having built themselves large Brick Houses of many
> Rooms on a Floor. . . . All their Drudgeries of Cookery, Washing, Da[i]ries,
> etc. are performed in offices detached from the Dwelling-Houses. (Beverley,
> 1947 [1705]:289–290)

William Fitzhugh, a wealthy planter, describes his plantation in Virginia to a
prospective buyer in Bristol, England, as follows:

> Upon it there is three quarters well-furnished, with all necessary houses,
> ground, and fencing, . . . Upon the same land is my own dwelling house,
> furnished with all accommodations for a comfortable and genteel living, such
> as a very good dwelling house, with 13 rooms in it, . . . and all houses for use
> well furnished with brick chimneys; four good cellars, a dairy, a dovecoat,
> stable, barn, henhouse, kitchen and all other conveniences. (Fitzhugh, 1972
> [1686]:124)

Complex, segregated floor plans and special-use buildings were not the only
tools used by the colonists in generating wealth. Nonarchitectural space also was
used, particularly homelot space. Again, St. John's and Clifts Plantation both
exhibit some differentiation in sheet midden deposits, suggesting activity areas.
Specifically, a gunflint-knapping area appears to have been located near a side
door at St. John's, and dairying areas have been identified for both sites. Results of
the spatial analyses in Chapters 8 and 9 indicate that these activity areas should be
reevaluated. Nonetheless, both St. John's and Clifts Plantation exhibit changing
patterns of yard definition through the remains of fences. The fence lines represent activity areas, although what those activities may have been remains a subject for further study. Activity area definition at Compton, Patuxent Point, and
King's Reach, on the other hand, has met with little success. With little evidence
of fence lines, efforts at defining activity areas at these sites have relied on the
spatial analysis of artifact distributions, and those efforts have been poorly
rewarded.[6]

Our inability to identify activity areas at plantation sites (even at the larger
sites the patterning is weak) can be attributed to the use of inadequate analytical
techniques and gross artifact categories that mask variation. It is likely, however,
that the degree of task specialization, particularly along gender lines, was too
weak to have required task-specific areas; hence, few of those areas have been
identified archaeologically. Households of lesser wealth built and maintained

generalized structures, but did little else to develop their homelots. Taking the Stephens family at Compton as an example, it appears that those of lesser wealth channeled their surplus resources into the purchase of new lands, both for the heads of households and for their children.

The relationships between complex spaces, large, diversified households, and the ability to increase wealth production through specialization are more easily justified than any link between the objects that a household acquires and the social standing of the household. Moreover, an analysis of architecture is an analysis of how wealth is used, not simply of what is acquired and accumulated. Consumer behavior studies in which assemblages are regarded as reflections of status, whatever "status" means, necessarily deal with acquisition. Precisely how wealth is converted into different forms, and how those forms are used on a daily basis, promises to be a more complex and interesting phenomenon, one likely to illuminate the attitudes and ambitions of the seventeenth-century colonists.

Household strategies are detectable not only from the creation of complex spaces within buildings and around homelots, but from the spaces created between homelots, and between homelots and towns. The diffuse nature of seventeenth-century settlement in the Chesapeake region is axiomatic and usually attributed to the demands of tobacco, the cultivation of which requires large quantities of land . . .or does it? Many of the colonists were not strangers to cash-cropping and it seems unlikely that they could not have managed more intensive agricultural practices, for example, manuring and crop rotation. Such practices were common in the drained fens of England, and in New England and the Netherlands. Swidden agriculture was a choice; it was not a physical necessity. The Stephens family, and many of their neighbors, accepted the conditions of the tobacco market and cash-cropping when they adopted swidden agriculture.

Analyses of the concepts of land ownership and town formation suggest two reasons why the colonists adopted a diffuse form of settlement. First, all planters were renters, beholden to the lords Baltimore, their lands subject to escheatment under several conditions. The sense that one did not own what one had created from "the wilderness" may have affected the ways in which many planters viewed their relationship to the land. The Chesapeake region was colonized at a time when notions of who owned the land—the lord of the manor or those who worked on the manor—were at issue. New property relations were emerging, partly from the process of enclosure, that led to the eviction of thousands of English farmers by their landlords. Were those new property relations exported to the American colonies? Analysis of the political and legislative history of the colony suggests that the answer is yes: planters viewed the land in a way that was different from the traditions of England, and that different perspective was expressed in their choices of agricultural strategies and resource allocation. At the same time, the lords Baltimore were trying to institute a system of land tenure and jurisprudence that is best described as feudal and retrogressive.

Many planters, particularly those seeking opportunities to expand their plantations and acquire new tracts for their sons, probably saw little point in improving their plantations: they were destined to leave within a decade or so of their arrival, in search of greater opportunities. Given the generally volatile prices of tobacco, and the clear trend toward lower prices, intensive agricultural practices within a monocropping system would not fulfill the needs of those who still had not acquired a sufficient amount of land to provide for both their security and the future of their children.

Avoidance of clustered settlement also is evident in the distribution of seventeenth-century colonial sites, and it is confirmed by seventeenth-century observers. It is no coincidence that attempts at legislating the creation of towns were accompanied by stipulations that tobacco warehouses be established in those towns. While such structures were intended to serve as places in which tobacco could be stored safely while awaiting shipment, that was neither their only nor principal use. They were called tobacco inspection warehouses, and it was at such points that planters would be required to bring their crops for inspection. Tobacco leaf adjudged substandard would be burned to maintain the reputation of the colony's principal commodity and to reduce supply in anticipation of higher prices.

Most planters, and particularly the smaller planters, were not anxious to submit their tobacco for inspection and to see the product of their labor burned before their eyes. Nor were they keen on conducting all of their commercial activities in front of the proprietor's agents, where all exchanges could be taxed. The vast majority of planters refused to support legislated towns and inspection warehouses: they did not buy town lots, and they continued to conduct trade from private wharves. Town lots, however, were purchased by some planters, and patterns in town lot purchasing await study.

Diffuse settlement could be interpreted, in part, as an attempt by planters to assert their rights to both the land and its products. But rights to resources and the products of labor were directed not only from the household out, but within the household as well. Every able-bodied person contributed to the creation of wealth, either through home production (production for use within the household) or commodity production (production for exchange). Most were involved in both. The questions as to who could claim a part of that wealth and how the wealth was to be distributed must have been difficult to resolve. The planter's family asserted its right by virtue of the land patent or lease that they held, and by virtue of the debt and property relationships that existed between them and their indentured servants and slaves. (The reader will recall from Chapter 4 that Cecil, Lord Baltimore, made a similar argument in his defense of the Calvert family's claim to Maryland and their right to issue land patents and govern the colony.) But, of course, the slaves and servants produced wealth, and that point would have been very difficult to deny or mask. Slaves, as property, were wealth, and could not legally claim anything. Indentured servants occupied a more ambiguous status, being neither property nor free agent, further complicating the issue of rights to surplus.

Within the family—namely, the biological unit in residence on the homelot holding legal claim to its assets—we can expect there to have been additional claims on household wealth. Male heads-of-household held legal rights to all that was produced and to virtually all of the household's assets. As a rule, they signed all contracts and established debt relations. Women, however, frequently brought wealth to the marriage, including household furnishings, livestock, money, occasionally slaves, and sometimes land. They produced, processed, prepared, presented, and stored much of the food. Often, particularly in the smaller households, they worked in the fields. Upon the death of her husband, however, a woman could claim only her widow's third part of the estate. Any property that her husband might have left her usually was held only for the duration of her life, or in trust for her husband's children. The remainder belonged to her deceased husband, to be disposed of in whatever way suited him. Did men and women within the family clash over wealth?

Family cemeteries provide one means of looking at the organization of households and rights to household assets. Graves have been identified at Patuxent Point, College Landing #7, Clifts Plantation, and Site A at Martin's Hundred, and in each case they were distributed among two or more clusters. Clusters of individuals whom we can infer to have been slaves or servants were found at Patuxent Point and Clifts Plantation. In both cases, the laborers' grave cluster is situated furthermost from the principal dwelling. The remaining cluster at Clifts Plantation and the two overlapping clusters at Patuxent Point probably represent the planter families. Clustering at Site A of Martin's Hundred and at College Landing #7 may represent a similar pattern, with the orderly graves closest to the principal dwellings being those of the planter family. Poor preservation precludes determinations of race and patterned pathologies that might confirm this hypothesis.

Separation, in death, of the planters from the servants and slaves does not necessarily state to the respective groups that one had full claim to the wealth of the household and the other did not. It does indicate, however, that the division between the planter family and nonfamily members of the household was more important than a division on the basis of age, sex, or race. No patterning was observed in the placement of men and women, nor of children, and interracial mixing was observed at both Patuxent Point and Clifts Plantation. One's relationship, legal and moral, to the plantation was being expressed, not for the benefit of the decedent, of course, but for the survivors on both sides of the graveyard. The planter's kin were placed near the principal dwelling, the heart of the plantation, alongside his or her kin. Nonkin were remanded to the more distant part of the cemetery, accorded proper burials, but not a place among those with whom they worked, and possibly ate and played and prayed. Two sets of relationships distinguished the planters from their servants: kinship and legal rights of accession and inheritance. Archival data indicate that those legal rights were expressed in terms of kinship. Archaeological data suggest that the link was expressed and rationalized symbolically through grave placement. Some individuals retained the right to make consumer choices—to use the wealth of the household—whereas the rights of others, whose contribution to the creation of that wealth was undeniable, were denied. Slaves and servants used household wealth at the direction and discretion of their masters.

There are numerous surviving court cases that demonstrate the conflict over household wealth, allowing us to relate burial patterns to statements of identity and possession. Indentured servants filed lawsuits against their masters for early release from their indentures, maltreatment, poor living conditions, and generally nonfulfillment of the contract. Servants often were brought before the Provincial and County Courts for insubordination, theft, and occasionally murder (e.g., Breen, et al., 1983); theft, however, was among the most common of allegations. Whether or not the thefts were rationalized by the servants or slaves is beside the point: clearly, some believed they could, and should, assert their rights to the household wealth, even if clandestinely.

If we take the cemetery data as a direct and unequivocal declaration of the planters' identity with, claim on, and rationalization of rights to household wealth, does it follow that this was the only object domain in which it was expressed? Could a different, or somewhat tempered, statement have been made through other object domains? This possibility was broached in Chapter 10. Architectural spaces, for instance, may have been used to physically separate some forms of wealth from the general household. The construction of pantries or cellars within the principal chamber or parlor could be construed as a statement of ownership and access: namely, the occupants of the parlor (the male and female heads of household) owned the wealth and it was only through them, as represented by their room, that anyone—slave, servant, neighbor, or family member—could gain access to that wealth. The pantry at Patuxent Point, the cellars and pantry at King's Reach, and the multiroom, multistructure complexes at Clifts Plantation and St. John's provide good evidence for such control. Compton, in contrast, lacks cellars and storage rooms. The two outbuildings in which wealth might have been stored were generally accessible, unless locked. But this need not indicate an equitable distribution of wealth. The three dwellings at

Compton suggest some social differentiation, although along what lines cannot be determined.

In Chapter 10, I also suggested that vessel forms may have been used to temper statements made by the planters regarding their identity and rights to wealth. In many households, planters worked alongside of their servants, slaves, and family members, often doing the same kind of work. In many respects, the planters' fare probably differed little from that of their servants, particularly during the lean spring months. A degree of commonality, of mutual goodwill and common interest, may have been expressed in certain contexts. These might have included sharing meals, entertainment, and religious and secular observances. Consumption, in the specific sense of the word as to expend through use, may have provided this integrative role. Sharing eating utensils and food, smoking together, playing, dancing, and praying together are activities that may have brought master and family and servants together into something that we might recognize as a household.

Unfortunately, analysis of seventeenth-century vessels is in its infancy. Little is known of vessel forms, despite the pioneering work of Beaudry et al. (1983) and Janowitz et al. (1985), and there has been little reporting of vessel lists, and the methods by which they were compiled (Yentsch, 1990b). Our best evidence for household commensalism is the lack of kitchen middens that clearly differ in terms of their contents, particularly in terms of frequencies of fine tablewares and tobacco pipes (e.g., Gibb and King, 1991; King and Miller, 1987). Such middens have been identified only at the sites of Colonial period ordinaries (e.g., King and Miller, 1987), where those differences represent social differentiation outside of the household, rather than material expressions of claims to resources inside of the household. The evidence from Compton and Patuxent Point suggests collective eating and recreation.

CONCLUSION

Consumer behavior in the household—the social form in which wealth is produced, stored, and used—holds promise for analysis and interpretation of domestic site assemblages. The focus is on choices made within the household, by members of the household, as statements about identity and possession. Choices are made in terms of how wealth is to be used, the forms into which it will be transformed, and the claims that individual household members have on that wealth. Distinctions between production and consumption are rejected as arbitrary, imposing analytic barriers where goods and services once flowed. Expressions of prestige and ethnic identity are based on decisions made in the household about how resources are to be used and what images of itself the household will project to the community.

A consumer behavior approach to the analysis of domestic site assemblages does not portend a helter-skelter approach in which contemporary assemblages bear nothing in common other than as products of household decisions. There are constraints—moral and physical—confronted by every household in a particular cultural context. There are widely agreed upon means and ends toward which households both contribute and strive. This can be seen, for instance, in the pattern of plantation siting in the Chesapeake region during the seventeenth-century: the first consideration was access to navigable water; the second, access to productive tobacco soils. The goal was to achieve security for present and future generations through commodity production. Success in selection was constrained by the distribution of preferred sites, the extent of settlement when a particular tract was selected, and the practices of other colonists in selecting their own tracts, whether in keeping within prescribed practices or in breaking the rules through such actions as engrossment, trespass, and illegitimate land sales. Most of the colonists in the region adopted similar strategies that included the selection of similar sites for establishing their plantations.

The variability extracted from analyses of household decisions and practices provides a basis from which to clarify acceptable means and ends, and for understanding the cultural–historical trajectory of a particular area. The development of slavery in the Chesapeake colonies, for example, has been described as a necessary development in the face of declining European immigration. This interpretation, however, ignores the fact that enslavement represents a decision by some planters to maintain certain agricultural, economic, and social practices in the light of rapidly changing conditions. Moreover, not all planters employed slaves, and some groups (e.g., Quakers) eventually rejected slavery outright. The decisions made by households in respect to this one issue affected the cultural development of the region during the eighteenth century, and continues to do so to the present.

The consumer behavior approach—as developed in this book—does not reject such issues as public expression of status and ethnicity. On the contrary, these are important aspects of social behavior that generally were realized through the manipulation of material culture. What I have attempted to do is to make a case for examining these behaviors in the context of household decision making: as extensions of those choices made by household members as to their individual and group identities. There are many avenues of theoretical and methodological research that must be pursued to further develop the approach. In terms of theory, we need to model the processes by which members of a household debate choices and arrive—or do not arrive—at a consensus. Methods must be developed to better identify activity areas on homelot sites. The potential of written documents, particularly literary works, for developing meaningful cultural contexts is far from being realized by archaeologists. Methods must be devised to better identify, sample, and analyze such data. The most critical part of the process, however, is the thorough and timely reporting of archaeological data from seventeenth-century sites. A plea for more data commonly accompanies archaeological writings. I submit that the data are there; they simply have not been made available, and that lack of availability shows in the limited influence that seventeenth-century studies have had in historical archaeology, and in anthropology in general.

NOTES

1. McCracken (1988) and Miller (1987) tend to emphasize acquisition.
2. No doubt sociologists and marketing researchers have made far more progress than anthropologists in this particular area.
3. Data recovery reintroduces artifacts into cultural contexts, but not necessarily those contexts with which the archaeologist is most interested. This point raises intriguing questions: Are the bits of trash that we recover archaeologically new forms of wealth in our society? Do they have use value or exchange value? How can we determine their value? Supply and demand? Costs of recovery? The importance that museums and other collecting institutions place on deeds of gift for donated artifacts indicates that archaeological specimens have value, but our society has not determined the nature of that value.
4. A concern for documentary research and analysis requires some alteration of methods and techniques previously developed by anthropological archaeologists. Rigorous analysis of environmental resources, for example, is of dubious value if those resources were not recognized as such by our subjects. Archival work also demands some concessions in writing style, for example the extensive use of footnotes.
5. These are ideal types. Variation stems from the degree of overlap between the two, and it is by identifying those variations at individual sites that we may gain a better understanding of what the colonists were trying to do.
6. Pogue's (1988) artifact distributions at King's Reach are greatly influenced by materials plowed out of the seven artifact-rich cellars within the principal dwelling.

References

Abercrombie, Nicholas, Stephen Hill, and Bryan S. Turner
1980 *The Dominant Ideology Thesis.* G. Allen and Unwin, London.

Aceves, Joseph B., and H. Gill King
1978 *Cultural Anthropology.* General Learning Press, Scott, Foresman and Co., Morristown, New Jersey.

Alsop, George
1988 A Character of the Province of Mary-Land [1666]. In *Narratives of Early Maryland, 1633–1684,* edited by Clayton Coleman Hall, pp. 340–387. Heritage Books, Bowie, Maryland.

Anderson, Jay Allan
1971 *"A Solid Sufficiency": An Ethnography of Yeoman Foodways in Stuart England.* University Microfilms, Ann Arbor, Michigan.

Anonymous
1963 A Perfect Description of Virginia. In *Tracts and Other Papers, Relating Principally to the Origin, Settlement, and Progress of the Colonies in North America,* edited by Peter Force, pp. 1–18. Peter Smith, Gloucester, Massachusetts.
1972a Bill of Wages and Price Legislation, Submitted to the General Court, Massachusetts Bay Colony, May 17, 1670. In *Remarkable Providences, 1600–1760,* edited by John Demos, p. 250. George Braziller, New York.
1972b Petitions of Richard Preston and His Servants to the Provincial Court. In *Remarkable Providences, 1600–1760,* edited by John Demos, pp. 135–137. George Braziller, New York.

Appadurai, Arjun
1986 Introduction: Commodities and the Politics of Value. In *The Social Life of Things: Commodities in Cultural Perspective,* edited by Arjun Appadurai, pp. 3–63. Cambridge University Press, Cambridge [UK].

Archives of Maryland (Arch. Md.)
1883 *The Archives of Maryland.* 72 volumes, to date. Maryland Historical Society, Baltimore.

Atkinson, David, and Adrian Oswald
1969 London Clay Tobacco Pipes. Reprinted by the Museum of London from the *Journal of the British Archaeological Association* 32.

Aufderheide, Arthur C., Fraser D. Neiman, Lorentz E. Wittmers, and George Rapp
1981 Lead in Bone II: Skeletal-Lead Content as an Indicator of Lifetime Lead Ingestion

and the Social Correlates in an Archaeological Population. *American Journal of Physical Anthropology* 55: 285–291.

Aylmer, G. E.
1980 The Meaning and Definition of 'Property' in Seventeenth-Century England. *Past and Present* 86: 87–97.

Baart, Jan
1987 Dutch Material Civilization: Daily Life between 1650–1776, Evidence from Archeology. In *New World Dutch Studies: Dutch Arts and Culture in Colonial America, 1609–1776*, edited by Roderic H. Blackburn and Nancy A. Kelley, pp. 1–11. Albany Institute of History and Art, Albany, New York.

Bacon, Francis
1955a Of Building. In *Francis Bacon, Selected Writings*, edited by Hugh G. Dick, pp. 114–117. The Modern Library, New York.
1955b Of Riches. In *Francis Bacon, Selected Writings*, edited by Hugh G. Dick, pp. 92–95. The Modern Library, New York.
1955c Of Plantations. In *Francis Bacon, Selected Writings*, edited by Hugh G. Dick, pp. 89–92. The Modern Library, New York.

Baker, Emerson W.
1985 The Clarke & Lake Company: The Historical Archaeology of a Seventeenth–Century Maine Settlement. *Occasional Publications in Maine Archaeology Number 4*. Maine Historic Preservation Commission, Augusta, Maine.

Bankoff, H. Arthur, and Frederick A. Winter
1979 A House-Burning in Serbia. *Archaeology* 32(5):8–14.

Barthes, Roland
1972 *Mythologies*. Hill and Wang, New York.

Barth, Fredrik
1963 *The Role of the Entrepreneur in Social Change in Northern Norway*. Univesitetsforlaget Bergen, Oslo.
1966 Models of Social Organization. *Royal Anthropological Institute of Great Britain and Ireland, Occasional Paper No. 33*, London.
1967 Economic Spheres in Darfur. In *Themes in Economic Anthropology*, edited by Raymond Firth, pp. 149–176. Tavistock, London.

Baugher, Sherene, and Robert W. Venables
1987 Ceramics as Indicators of Status and Class in Eighteenth-Century New York. In *Consumer Choice in Historical Archaeology*, edited by Suzanne M. Spencer-Wood, pp. 31–53. Plenum Press, New York.

Beaudry, Mary C.
1984 Archaeology and the Historical Household. *Man in the Northeast* 28:27–38.
1987 Analytical Scale and Methods for the Archaeological Study of Households. *The Society for Historical Archaeology Newsletter* 20(1):22–25.

Beaudry, Mary C. (editor)
1988 *Documentary Archaeology in the New World*. Cambridge University Press, Cambridge [UK].

Beaudry, Mary C., Janet Long, Henry M. Miller, and Gary Wheeler Stone
  1983 A Vessel Typology for Early Chesapeake Ceramics: The Potomac Typological System. *Historical Archaeology* 17(1):18–43.
Becker, Carl L.
  1932 *The Heavenly City of the Eighteenth–Century Philosophers*. Yale University Press, New Haven.
Becker, M. J.
  1978 An Eighteenth Century Witch Bottle in Delaware County, Pennsylvania. *Pennsylvania Archaeologist* 48(1–2):1–12.
Benson, Donna Lynne
  1978 A Reconsideration of the 'Carolina Pattern.' *The Conference on Historic Sites Archaeology Papers* 12:32–67.
Beresford, Maurice, and John Hurst
  1990 *Wharram Percy: Deserted Medieval Village*. Yale University Press, New Haven.
Bertaux, Daniel
  1981 From the Life-History Approach to the Transformation of Sociological Practice. In *Biography and Society: The Life History Approach in the Social Sciences*, edited by Daniel Bertaux, pp. 29–45. Sage Publications, Beverly Hills, California.
Beverley, Robert
  1947 *The History and Present State of Virginia*. University of North Carolina, Chapel Hill.
Binford, Lewis R.
  1962 Archaeology as Anthropology. *American Antiquity* 28(2):217–225.
  1964 A Consideration of Archaeological Research Design. *American Antiquity* 29(4):425–441.
  1965 Archaeological Systematics and the Study of Culture Process. *American Antiquity* 31(2):203–210.
  1967 Smudge Pits and Hide Smoking: The Role of Analogy in Archaeological Reasoning. *American Antiquity* 32(1):1–12.
  1983 *In Pursuit of the Past: Decoding the Archaeological Record*. Thames and Hudson, London.
Bohannan, Paul
  1955 Some Principles of Exchange and Investment among the Tiv. *American Anthropologist* 57:60–70.
Boone, James L.
  1987 Defining and Measuring Midden Catchment. *American Antiquity* 52(2):336–345.
Bourdieu, Pierre
  1977 *Outline of a Theory of Practice*. Cambridge University Press, Cambridge [UK].
Boxer, Charles Ralph
  1973 *The Dutch Seaborne Empire, 1600–1800*. Penguin Books, New York.
Boyne, William
  1970 *Trade Tokens Issued in the Seventeenth Century in England, Wales, and Ireland, by Corporations, Merchants, Tradesmen, etc.* Burt Franklin, New York.

Breen, T.H., James H. Lewis, and Keith Schlesinger
1983   Motive for Murder: A Servant's Life in Virginia, 1678. *William and Mary Quarterly*, 3rd Series 40(1):106–120.
Brown, Ian W.
1993   The New England Cemetery as a Cultural Landscape. In *History from Things: Essays on Material Culture*, edited by Steven Lubar and W. David Kingery, pp. 140–159. Smithsonian Institution Press, Washington, D.C.
Brown, Marley
1987   Issues of Scale Revisited: A Rejoinder. *The Society for Historical Archaeology Newsletter* 20(1):25–27.
Bruce, Philip Alexander
1964   *Institutional History of Virginia in the Seventeenth Century*, v. 1. Peter Smith, Gloucester, Massachusetts.
Butler, Jon
1992   Thomas Teackle's 333 Books: A Great Library on Virginia's Eastern Shore, 1697. *William and Mary Quarterly*, 3rd Series 49(3):449–491.
Calvert, Cecil [Lord Baltimore]
1988a Instructions to the Colonists, 1633. In *Narratives of Early Maryland, 1633–1684*, edited by Clayton Coleman Hall, pp. 16–23. Heritage Books, Bowie, Maryland. .
1988b Lord Baltimore's Case, 1653. In *Narratives of Early Maryland, 1633–1684*, edited by Clayton Coleman Hall, pp. 167–180. Heritage Books, Bowie, Maryland.
Cameron, Kenneth Neil
1985   *Marx: The Science of Society*. Bergin & Garvey, South Hadley, Massachusetts.
Camp, Helen
1975   *Archaeological Excavations at Pemaquid, Maine (1964–1974)*. Maine State Museum, Augusta, Maine.
Campbell, J. K.
1964   *Honour, Family and Patronage: A Study of Institutions and Moral Values in a Greek Mountain Community*. Oxford University Press, New York.
Carothers, Bettie (compiler)
1977   *1783 Tax List of Maryland, Part I: Cecil, Talbot, Harford, and Calvert Counties*. Privately printed, Lutherville, Maryland.
Carr, Christopher
1987   Removing Discordance from Quantitative Analysis. In *Quantitative Research in Archaeology*, edited by Mark S. Aldenderfer, pp. 185–243. Sage Publications, Newbury Park, California.
Carr, Lois Green, and Lorena S. Walsh
1977   The Planter's Wife: The Experience of White Women in Seventeenth Century Maryland. *William and Mary Quarterly*, 3rd Series 34(4):542–571.
Carr, Lois Green, and Russell R. Menard
1979   Immigration and Opportunity: The Freedman in Early Colonial America. In *The Chesapeake in the Seventeenth Century: Essays on Anglo-American Society and Politics*, edited by Thad W. Tate and David L. Ammerman, pp. 206–242. W.W. Norton & Co., New York.

Carr, Lois Green, Russell R. Menard, and Lorena S. Walsh
1991 *Robert Cole's World: Agriculture & Society in Early Maryland.* Institute of Early American History and Culture and the University of North Carolina Press, Chapel Hill and London.

Carroll, Kenneth
1970 *Quakerism on the Eastern Shore.* The Maryland Historical Society, Baltimore.

Carson, Cary, and Lorena S. Walsh
1981 The Material Life of the American Housewife. Typescript on file at the Jefferson Patterson Park and Museum, St. Leonard, Maryland.

Carson, Cary, Norman F. Barka, William M. Kelso, Garry W. Stone, and Dell Upton
1981 Impermanent Architecture in the Southern American Colonies. *Winterthur Portfolio* 16:135–196.

Chaney, Edward, and Henry M. Miller
1989 Archaeological Reconnaissance and Testing at the Gallows Green Site (18ST1–112), St. Mary's City, Maryland. Historic St. Mary's City Commission, Department of Research. Submitted to St. Mary's College of Maryland, St. Mary's City, Maryland.
1990 An Archaeological Survey of the Fisher's Road Science Building Area (18ST1–23 and 1–265), St. Mary's City, Maryland. Historic St. Mary's City Commission, Department of Research. Submitted to St. Mary's College of Maryland, St. Mary's City, Maryland.

Clark, G. A.
1987 Paradigms and Paradoxes in Contemporary Archaeology. In *Quantitative Research in Archaeology*, edited by Mark S. Aldenderfer, pp. 30–60. Sage Publications, Newbury Park, California.

Clayton, Rev. John,
1972 Letter to the Royal Society of London, August 17, 1688. In *Remarkable Providences, 1600–1760*, edited by John Demos, pp. 318–325. George Braziller, New York.

Cleland, Charles E.
1976 The Focal-Diffuse Model: An Evolutionary Perspective on the Prehistoric Cultural Adaptations of the Eastern United States. *Mid-Continental Journal of Archaeology* 1(1):59–76.

Cole, Charles Woolsey
1964 *Colbert and a Century of French Mercantilism*, 2 vols. Archon Books, Hamden, Connecticut.

Conkey, Margaret W.
1980 The Identification of Prehistoric Hunter-Gatherer Aggregation Sites: The Case of Altamira. *Current Anthropology* 21:609–630.

Cook, Lauren J., and Rebecca Yamin
1994 Shopping as Politics: Toward a Redefinition of Consumption in Historical Archaeology. Paper presented at the annual meeting of the Society for Historical Archaeology, Vancouver, British Columbia, Canada.

Cranmer, Leon E.
1990 Cushnoc: The History and Archaeology of Plymouth Colony Traders on the

Kennebec. *Occasional Publications in Maine Archaeology Number 7*. Maine Historic Preservation Commission, Augusta, Maine.

Craven, Wesley Frank
1970   *The Southern Colonies in the Seventeenth Century, 1607–1689*. Louisiana University Press, Baton Rouge.

Csikszentmihalyi, Mihaly
1993   Why We Need Things. In *History from Things: Essays on Material Culture*, edited by Steven Lubar and W. David Kingery, pp. 20–29. Smithsonian Institution Press, Washington, D.C.

Custer, Jay F.
1992   A Simulation Study of Plow Zone Excavation Sample Design: How Much Is Enough. *North American Archaeologist* 13(3):263–269.

Dalton, George
1971   Introduction. In *Primitive, Archaic and Modern Economies: Essays of Karl Polanyi*, edited by George Dalton, pp. 9–54. Beacon Press, Boston.

Davis, Ralph
1975   *English Merchant Shipping and Anglo-Dutch Rivalry in the Seventeenth Century*. National Maritime Museum and Her Majesty's Stationery Office, London.

Deagan, Kathleen A.
1988   Neither History nor Prehistory: The Questions That Count in Historical Archaeology. In *Questions That Count in Archaeology* (Special Issue), edited by Nicholas Honerkamp. *Historical Archaeology* 22(1):7–12.

DeBoer, Warren R.
1988   Subterranean Storage and the Organization of Surplus: The View from Eastern North America. *Southeastern Archaeology* 7(1):1–20.

Deetz, James
1977   *In Small Things Forgotten*. Anchor Books, New York.
1988   American Historical Archaeology: Methods and Results. *Science* 239:362–367.

Defoe, Daniel
1971   *A Tour through the Whole Island of Great Britain* [1724–1726]. Penguin Books, New York.

Demos, John (editor)
1972   *Remarkable Providences, 1600–1760*. George Braziller, New York.

Dent, Richard J.
1990   Social Change and 18th Century Tidewater Maryland: Reflections in the Archaeological Record. In *New Perspectives on Maryland Historical Archaeology* (Special Issue), edited by Richard J. Dent and Barbara J. Little. *Maryland Archeology* 26(1–2):54–68.

de Roever, Margriet
1987   The Fort Orange "EB" Pipe Bowls: An Investigation of the American Objects in Dutch Seventeenth-Century Documents. In *New World Dutch Studies: Dutch Arts and Culture in Colonial America, 1609–1776*, edited by Roderic H. Blackburn and Nancy A. Kelley, pp. 51–61. Albany Institute of History and Art, Albany, New York.

Donley, Linda Wiley
1982 House Power: Swahili Space and Symbolic Markers. In *Structural and Symbolic Archaeology*, edited by Ian Hodder, pp. 63–73. Cambridge University Press, Cambridge [UK].
Doran, J. E., and F. R. Hodson
1975 *Mathematics and Computers in Archaeology*. Harvard University Press, Cambridge, Massachusetts.
Dougenik, James A., and David E. Sheehan
1979 *SYMAP User's Reference Manual*. Laboratory for Computer Graphics and Spatial Analysis, Harvard University, Cambridge, Massachusetts.
Durand of Dauphiné
1934 *A Huguenot Exile in Virginia, or Voyages of a Frenchman Exiled for His Religion, with a Description of Virginia and Maryland* [1687]. Translated and edited by Gilbert Chinard. The Press of the Pioneers, New York.
Earle, Carville V.
1979 Environment, Disease, and Mortality in Early Virginia. In *The Chesapeake in the Seventeenth Century: Essays on Anglo-American Society and Politics*, edited by Thad W. Tate and David L. Ammerman, pp. 96–125. W.W. Norton & Co., New York.
Edwards, Andrew C.
1987 Archaeology at Port Anne: A Report on Site CL7, an Early 17th Century Colonial Site. Department of Archaeological Research, Colonial Williamsburg Foundation. Submitted to Divaris Real Estate, Virginia Beach, and the City of Williamsburg, Williamsburg, Virginia.
1994 The Archaeological Assessment of Jamestown: Project Overview. Paper presented at the annual meeting of the Society for Historical Archaeology, Vancouver, British Columbia, Canada.
Edwards, Andrew C., and Marley R. Brown III
1993 Seventeenth-Century Chesapeake Settlement Patterns: A Current Perspective from Tidewater Virginia. In *The Archaeology of 17th-Century Virginia*, edited by Theodore R. Reinhart and Dennis J. Pogue, pp. 285–309. Archeological Society of Virginia, Richmond.
Edwards, Andrew C., William E. Pittman, Gregory J. Brown, Mary Ellen N. Hodges, Marley R. Brown, and Eric E. Voigt
1989 Hampton University Archaeological Project: A Report on the Findings. Department of Archaeological Research, Colonial Williamsburg Foundation. Submitted to the Office of the President, Hampton University, Hampton, Virginia.
Falk, Lisa (editor)
1991 *Historical Archaeology in Global Perspective*. Smithsonian Institution Press, Washington, D.C.
Farnsworth, Paul
1992 Comparative Analysis in Plantation Archaeology: The Application of a Functional Classification. Paper presented at the annual meeting of the Society for Historical Archaeology, Kingston, Jamaica.

Faulkner, Alaric, and Gretchen Fearon Faulkner
1987   The French at Pentagoet, 1635–1674: An Archaeological Portrait of the Acadian Frontier. *Special Publications of the New Brunswick Museum and Occasional Publications in Maine Archaeology Number 5.* Maine Historic Preservation Commission, Augusta, Maine.

Fischer, David Hackett
1989   *Albion's Seed: Four British Folkways in America.* Oxford University Press, New York.

Fitzhugh, William
1972   Letter from William Fitzhugh, of Stafford County, Virginia, to Dr. Ralph Smith, of Bristol, England [1686]. In *Remarkable Providences, 1600–1760,* edited by John Demos, pp. 124–126. George Braziller, New York.

Flannery, Kent V.
1972a   The Cultural Evolution of Civilizations. In *Annual Review of Ecology and Systematics 3,* edited by Richard F. Johnston, pp. 399–426. Annual Reviews, Palo Alto, California.
1972b   Culture History versus Culture Process: A Debate in American Archaeology. In *Contemporary Archaeology: A Guide to Theory and Contributions,* edited by Mark P. Leone, pp. 102–107. Southern Illinois University Press, Carbondale.
1973   Archaeology with a Capital 'S.' In *Research and Theory in Current Archaeology,* edited by Charles L. Redman, pp. 47–58. John Wiley, New York.

Force, Peter (editor and compiler)
1963   *Tracts and Other Papers, Relating Principally to the Origin, Settlement, and Progress of the Colonies of North America,* v. 2. Peter Smith, Gloucester, Massachusetts.

Ford, James A.
1962   *A Quantitative Method for Deriving Cultural Chronology.* Pan-American University, Washington, D.C.

Forsman, Michael R. A. and Joseph G. Gallo
1979   The Problem of Archaeological Diversity, Synthesis and Comparison. *The Conference on Historic Sites Archaeology Papers, 1978* 13:238–251.

Fox, George
1988   From the Journal of George Fox [1673]. In *Narratives of Early Maryland, 1633–1684,* edited by Clayton Coleman Hall, pp. 393–406. Heritage Books, Bowie, Maryland.

Frank, Andre Gunder
1966   The Development of Underdevelopment. *Monthly Review* 18:17–31.
1967   Sociology of Development and Underdevelopment of Sociology. *Catalyst* 3:20–73.

Friedlander, Amy
1991   House and Barns: The Wealth of Farmers, 1795–1815. In *Models for the Study of Consumer Behavior* (Special Issue), edited by Terry H. Klein and Charles H. LeeDecker. *Historical Archaeology* 25(2):15–29.

Gainsforth, Thomas
1995   *The Rich Cabinet Furnished with Varieties of Excellent Discriptions, Exquisite*

Charracters, Witty Discourses, and Delightfull Histories (London, 1616). Reprinted in *Elizabethan Households: An Anthology*, edited by Lena Cowen Orlin, p. 127. The Folger Shakespeare Library, Washington, D.C.

Gardner, William M.

1988 Archaeological Investigations at the Proposed Patuxent Point Development (Phase 1) and 18CV279 (Phase 2–3) Near Solomons, Maryland. Thunderbird Associates. Submitted to CRJ Associates, Camp Springs, Maryland.

Gasco' Janine

1992 Documentary and Archaeological Evidence for Household Differentiation in Colonial Soconusco, New Spain. In *Text-Aided Archaeology*, edited by Barbara J. Little, pp. 83–96. CRC Press, Baton Rouge.

Gehring, Charles T.

1987 Material Culture in Seventeenth-Century Dutch Colonial Manuscripts. In *New World Dutch Studies: Dutch Arts and Culture in Colonial America, 1609–1776*, edited by Roderic H. Blackburn and Nancy A. Kelley, pp. 43–49. Albany Institute of History and Art, Albany, New York.

Gibb, James G.

1991 "To Bud Forth, to Spread Further, and Gather Wealth": 17th Century Tobacco Plantations in the Chesapeake Region. Paper presented at the annual meeting of the Society for Historical Archaeology, Richmond, Virginia.

1993a POTS in the Midden: Vesselization and a Re-Analysis of the Stevens Land Plantation Middens. Paper presented at the annual meeting of the Society for Historical Archaeology, Kansas City, Missouri.

1993b English Trade Tokens from a 17th Century Colonial Site in Southern Maryland. *Maryland Archeology* 29(1 & 2):55–60.

1994 Dutch Goods, English Pits, and the Spirit of Mercantilism: Trading with the Enemy? Paper presented at the annual meeting of the Society for Historical Archaeology, Vancouver, British Columbia, Canada.

Gibb, James G., and Wesley J. Balla

1993 Dutch Pots in Maryland Middens: What Light from Yonder Pot Breaks? *Journal of Middle Atlantic Archaeology* 9:67–86.

Gibb, James G., and Julia A. King

1991 Gender, Activity Areas, and Homelots in the 17th Century Chesapeake Region. In *Gender in Historical Archaeology* (Special Issue), edited by Donna J. Seifert. *Historical Archaeology* 25(4):109–131.

Gibb, James G. and Esther Doyle Read

1992 Variability in Plantation Siting in the Chesapeake Bay Region, 1650–1725. Paper presented at the annual meeting of the Society for Historical Archaeology, Kingston, Jamaica.

Gibb, James G., and Abigail W. Turowski

1994 Household Organization in Early Colonial Chesapeake Society as Seen through Patterning within Rural Cemeteries. Paper presented at the annual meeting of the Council for Northeast Historical Archaeology, Williamsburg, Virginia.

Gittings, Clare
1984 *Death, Burial and the Individual in Early Modern England.* Croom Helm, London and Sydney.

Glassie, Henry
1975 *Folk Housing in Middle Virginia.* University of Tennessee Press, Knoxville.

Goodenough, Ward H.
1965 Rethinking 'Status' and 'Role': Toward a General Model of the Cultural Organization of Social Relationships. In *The Relevance of Models for Social Anthropology,* edited by Michael Blanton, pp. 1–20. Tavistock, London.

Gosden, Chris
1992 Production Systems and the Colonization of the Western Pacific. *World Archaeology* 24(1):55–69.

Gramly, Richard Michael
1978 *Fort Laurens, 1788–9: The Archaeological Record.* Privately printed, Stony Brook, New York.

Greene, Jack P. (editor)
1966 *Settlements to Society: 1584–1763.* McGraw-Hill Book Company, New York.

Grettler, David J., and Brian H. Seidel
1993 "Owned, but Not Necessarily Conveyed, " Landowner and Tenant Opportunity in 17th Century Delaware: The Whitehart and Powell Plantations. Paper presented at the 1993 Middle Atlantic Archaeological Conference, Ocean City, Maryland.

Griffith, Matthew
1995 Bethel: Or a Forme for Families, in which all Sorts of both Sexes, are so Squarde, and Framde by the Word, as Thay may best Serve in theire Severall Places, for Usefull Pieces in Gods Building (London, 1633). Reprinted in *Elizabethan Households: An Anthology,* edited by Lena Cowen Orlin, pp. 147–148. The Folger Shakespeare Library, Washington, D.C.

Griffiths, Dorothy M.
1978 Use–Marks on Historic Ceramics: A Preliminary Study. *Historical Archaeology* 12:68–81.

Guelke, Leonard
1976 Frontier Settlement in Early Dutch South Africa. *Annals, Association of American Geographers* 66(1):25–42.

Hall, Clayton Coleman (editor)
1988 *Narratives of Early Maryland, 1633–1684.* Heritage Books, Bowie, Maryland.

Hammond, John
1988 Leah and Rachel, or, the Two Fruitfull Sisters Virginia and Maryland [1656]. In *Narratives of Early Maryland, 1633–1684,* edited by Clayton Coleman Hall, pp. 281–308. Heritage Books, Bowie, Maryland.

Hall, Jerome Lynn
1994 Spanish Coins, German Weights, Dutch Clay Pipes, and an English Ship: The 17th Century Merchant Vessel in Monti Christi Bay, Dominican Republic: 1993 Interim Report. Presented at the annual meeting of the Society for Historical

Archaeology's Conference on Historical and Underwater Archaeology, Vancouver, British Columbia.

Hanna, Susan D., Barry Knight, and Geoff Egan
1992 Marked Window Leads from North America and Europe. Manuscript on file, Jefferson Patterson Park and Museum, St. Leonard, Maryland.

Hanson, Lee H.
1971 Kaolin Pipe Stems—Boring in on a Fallacy. *The Conference on Historic Site Archaeology* 4:2–15.

Harrington, Jean C.
1954 Dating Stem Fragments of Seventeenth and Eighteenth Century Clay Tobacco Pipes. *Quarterly Bulletin, Archeological Society of Virginia* 9(1):9–13.

Harris, R. Cole
1977 The Simplification of Europe Overseas. *Annals, Association of American Geographers* 67(4):469–483.

Harrison, William
1968 *The Description of England* [1587]. Cornell University, Ithaca, New York.

Hartley, Michael O.
1989 Elizabethan Policies and the Charles Town Colony: An Ethnohistorical-Archaeological Analysis. *Volumes in Historical Archaeology VIII.* The South Carolina Institute of Archaeology and Anthropology, The University of South Carolina, Columbia.

Hawley, Jerome [attributed]
1988 A Relation of Maryland. In *Narratives of Early Maryland, 1633–1684* [1635], edited by Clayton Coleman Hall, pp. 70–112. Heritage Books, Bowie, Maryland.

Heite, Edward F.
1992 Letter to the Editor. *The Council for Northeast Historical Archaeology Newsletter* 21:15–16.

Henry, Susan L.
1991 Consumers, Commodities and Choices: A General Model of Consumer Behavior. In *Models for the Study of Consumer Behavior* (Special Issue), edited by Terry H. Klein and Charles H. LeeDecker. *Historical Archaeology* 25(2):3–14.

Herlihy, David
1985 *Medieval Households.* Harvard University Press, Cambridge, Massachusetts.

Hinke, William J. (editor)
1916 Report of the Journey of Francis Louis Michel from Berne, Switzerland, to Virginia, October 2, 1701–December 1, 1702. *The Virginia Magazine of History and Biography* 24(1):1–43.

Hobbes, Thomas
1968 *Leviathan, or the Matter, Forme, and Power of a Common-Wealth Ecclesiasticall and Civill.* Penguin Books, New York.

Hobson, John A.
1919 *The Science of Wealth.* Henry Holt, New York.

Hodder, Ian
1982 Theoretical Archaeology: A Reactionary View. In *Structural and Symbolic Ar-*

chaeology, edited by Ian Hodder, pp. 2–16. Cambridge University Press, Cambridge [UK].

1991   Reading the Past: Current Approaches to Interpretation in Archaeology. Cambridge University Press, Cambridge [UK].

Holifield, E. Brooks

1989   Era of Persuasion: American Thought and Culture, 1521–1680. Twayne Publishers, Boston.

Horn, James

1979   Servant Emigration to the Chesapeake in the Seventeenth Century. In The Chesapeake in the Seventeenth Century: Essays on Anglo-American Society and Politics, edited by Thad W. Tate and David L. Ammerman, pp. 51–75. W.W. Norton & Co., New York.

Hudgins, Carter

1980   "Too Much Muckworms": Colonial Planters and the Course of Conspicuous Consumption in Early Virginia. Paper presented at the annual meeting of the Society for Historical Archaeology, Albuquerque, New Mexico.

Huelsbeck, David R.

1991   Faunal Remains and Consumer Behavior: What Is Being Measured? In Models for the Study of Consumer Behavior (Special Issue), edited by Terry H. Klein and Charles H. LeeDecker. Historical Archaeology 25(2):62–76.

Hurry, Robert J.

1990   An Archaeological Survey of a Portion of St. Leonards Town. Jefferson Patterson Park & Museum Occasional Papers No. 5. Maryland Historical Trust, Crownsville, Maryland.

Hurry, Silas D., and Robert W. Keeler

1991   A Descriptive Analysis of the White Clay Tobacco Pipes from the St. John's Site in St. Mary's City, Maryland. In The Archaeology of the Clay Tobacco Pipe. XII. Chesapeake Bay, edited by Peter Davey and Dennis J. Pogue, pp. 37–71. Liverpool Monographs in Archaeology and Oriental Studies, No. 14. BAR International Series 566.

Hutchinson, Harold

1976   Sir Christopher Wren: A Biography. Stein and Day, New York.

Janowitz, Meta F.

1993   Indian Corn and Dutch Pots: Seventeenth-Century Foodways in New Amsterdam/New York. Historical Archaeology 27(2):6–24.

Janowitz, Meta F., Kate T. Morgan, and Nan A. Rothschild

1985   Cultural Pluralism and Pots in New Amsterdam-New York City. In Domestic Pottery of the Northeastern United States, 1625–1850, edited by Sarah Peabody Turnbaugh, pp. 29–48. Academic Press, Orlando, Florida.

Jansson, Maija, and William B. Bidwell (editors)

1987   Proceedings in Parliament 1625. Yale University Press, New Haven, Connecticut.

Jones, Alice Hanson

1980   Wealth of a Nation to Be: The American Colonies on the Eve of the Revolution. Columbia University Press, New York.

1984 Wealth and the Growth of the Thirteen Colonies: Some Implications. *The Journal of Economic History* 44(2):239–254.

Jones, George T., and Robert D. Leonard

1989 The Concept of Diversity: An Introduction. In *Quantifying Diversity in Archaeology*, edited by Robert D. Leonard and George T. Jones, pp. 1–3. Cambridge University Press, New York.

Jones, Hugh (the Elder)

1987 Letter to Benjamin Woodruff, Dated 23 January 1698/9. *Huntia* 7:39–41.

Jones, Hugh (the Younger)

1724 *The Present State of Virginia. Giving a Particular and Short Account of the Indian, English, and Negroe Inhabitants of That Colony*. J. Clarke, London.

Jones, Olive R. (compiler)

1987 Historical Archaeology Index, Volumes 1–20, 1967–1986. *Historical Archaeology*. Society for Historical Archaeology, California, Pennsylvania.

Keeler, Robert W.

1978 *The Homelot on the Seventeenth-Century Chesapeake Tidewater Frontier*. University Microfilms, Ann Arbor, Michigan.

Keesing, Roger M.

1972 Simple Models of Complexity: The Lure of Kinship. In *Kinship Studies in the Morgan Centennial Year*, edited by Priscilla Reining, pp. 17–31. The Anthropological Society of Washington, Washington, D.C.

Kelly, Kevin P.

1979 "In Dispers'd Country Plantations": Settlement Patterns in Seventeenth-Century Surry County, Virginia. In *The Chesapeake in the Seventeenth Century: Essays on Anglo-American Society and Politics*, edited by Thad W. Tate and David L. Ammerman, pp. 183–205. W.W. Norton & Co., New York.

Kelso, William M.

1984 *Kingsmill Plantation, 1619–1800: Archaeology of Country Life in Colonial Virginia*. Academic Press, New York.

Kenyon, W. A.

1986 The History of James Bay, 1610–1686: A Study in Historical Archaeology. *Royal Ontario Museum Archaeology Monograph 10*.

Kimmel, Richard H.

1993 Notes on the Cultural Origins and Functions of Sub-Floor Pits. *Historical Archaeology* 27(3):102–113.

King, Julia A.

1988 A Comparative Midden Analysis of a Household and Inn in St. Mary's City, Maryland. *Historical Archaeology* 22(2):17–39.

1989 A Proposal for Phase III Excavations at a Late 17th Century Dwelling Site, Calvert County, Maryland. Submitted to the Division of Historical and Cultural Programs, Maryland Department of Housing and Community Development, Crownsville, Maryland.

1990 *An Intrasite Spatial Analysis of the van Sweringen Site, St. Mary's City, Maryland*. University Microfilms, Ann Arbor, Michigan.

1990   The Importance of Plow Zone Data. *The Society for Historical Archaeology News-letter* 23(4):8–9.

1993   An Archaeological Analysis of Rural and Urban Households in the 17th-Century Chesapeake. Paper presented at the annual meeting of the Society for Historical Archaeology Conference on Historical and Underwater Archaeology, Kansas City, Missouri.

King, Julia A., and Henry M. Miller

1987   A View from the Midden: An Analysis of Midden Distribution and Composition at the van Sweringen Site, St. Mary's City, Maryland. *Historical Archaeology* 21(2):37–59.

King, Julia A., and Abigail Turowski

1993   The Patuxent Point Cemetery: Historical and Archaeological Background. Paper presented at the Middle Atlantic Archaeological Conference, Ocean City, Maryland.

Kintigh, Keith W.

1984   Measuring Assemblage Diversity by Comparison with Simulated Assemblages. *American Antiquity* 49(1):44–54.

1989   Sample Size, Significance, and Measures of Diversity. In *Quantifying Diversity in Archaeology*, edited by Robert D. Leonard and George T. Jones, pp. 25–36. Cambridge University Press, New York.

1990   Intrasite Spatial Analysis: A Commentary on Major Methods. In *Mathematics and Information Science in Archaeology: A Flexible Framework*, edited by Albertus Voorrips. *Studies in Modern Archaeology* 3:165–200. Holos, Bonn.

1992   *Tools for Quantitative Archaeology: Programs for Quantitative Analysis in Archaeology*. Privately published, Tucson, Arizona.

Kintigh, Keith W., and Albert J. Ammerman

1982   Heuristic Approaches to Spatial Analysis in Archaeology. *American Antiquity* 47(1):31–63.

Kintigh, Keith W., and Hans Peter Blankholm

1992   KMEANS: Non-Hierarchical Cluster Analysis. In *Tools for Quantitative Archaeology: Programs for Quantitative Analysis in Archaeology*, edited by Keith W. Kintigh, pp. 19–27. Privately published, Tucson, Arizona.

Klein, Terry H.

1991   Nineteenth Century Ceramics and Models of Consumer Behavior. In *Models for the Study of Consumer Behavior* (Special Issue), edited by Terry H. Klein and Charles H. LeeDecker. *Historical Archaeology* 25(2):77–91.

Klein, Terry H., and Charles H. LeeDecker

1991   Models for the Study of Consumer Behavior. In *Models for the Study of Consumer Behavior* (Special Issue), edited by Terry H. Klein and Charles H. LeeDecker. *Historical Archaeology* 25(2):1–3.

Kohl, Philip L.

1981   Materialist Approaches in Prehistory. *Annual Review of Anthropology* 10:89–118.

Kopytoff, Igor

1986   The Cultural Biography of Things: Commoditization as Process. In *The Social*

Life of Things: Commodities in Cultural Perspective, edited by Arjun Appadurai, pp. 64–91. Cambridge University Press, Cambridge [UK].

Kulikoff, Alan

1986 *Tobacco and Slaves: The Development of Southern Culture in the Chesapeake, 1680–1800*. The University of North Carolina Press, Chapel Hill.

Laslett, Peter

1972 *The World We Have Lost*. Cambridge University Press, Cambridge [UK].

LeeDecker, Charles H.

1991 Historical Dimensions of Consumer Research. In *Models for the Study of Consumer Behavior* (Special Issue), edited by Terry H. Klein and Charles H. LeeDecker. *Historical Archaeology* 25(2):30–45.

1993 Life in Wilmington's East Side: The Standard of Living in a Late 19th–Century Industrial Neighborhood. Paper presented at the annual meeting of the Society for Historical Archaeology, Kansas City, Missouri.

LeeDecker, Charles H., Terry H. Klein, Cheryl A. Holt, and Amy Friedlander

1987 Nineteenth-Century Households and Consumer Behavior in Wilmington, Delaware. In *Consumer Choice in Historical Archaeology*, edited by Suzanne M. Spencer-Wood, pp. 233–260. Plenum Press, New York.

Lees, William B., and Teresita Majewski

1993 *Ceramic Choices West of the Mississippi: Considering Factors of Supply and Ethnicity*. Paper presented at the annual meeting of the Society for Historical Archaeology, Kansas City, Missouri.

Lemire, Beverly

1990 The Theft of Clothes and Popular Consumerism in Early Modern England. *Journal of Social History* 24(2):255–276.

Leone, Mark P.

1982 Some Opinions About Recovering Mind. *American Antiquity* 47(4):742–760.

1983 Land and Water, Urban Life, and Boats: Underwater Reconnaissance in the Patuxent River on Chesapeake Bay. In *Shipwreck Anthropology*, edited by Richard Gould, pp. 173–188. University of New Mexico Press, Albuquerque.

1984 Interpreting Ideology in Historical Archaeology: Using the Rules of Perspective in the William Paca Garden in Annapolis, Maryland. In *Ideology, Power and Prehistory*, edited by Daniel Miller and Christopher Tilley, pp. 25–35. Cambridge University Press, Cambridge [UK].

1986 Symbolic, Structural, and Critical Archaeology. In *American Archaeology: Past and Future*, edited by David J. Meltzer, Don D. Fowler, and Jeremy A. Sabloff, pp. 415–438. Smithsonian Institution Press, Washington, D.C.

1988a The Georgian Order as the Order of Merchant Capitalism in Annapolis, Maryland. In *Recovery of Meaning: Historical Archaeology in the Eastern United States*, edited by Mark P. Leone and Parker B. Potter, pp. 235–261. Smithsonian Institution Press, Washington, D.C.

1988b The Relationship between Archaeological Data and the Documentary Record: 18th Century Gardens in Annapolis, Maryland. In *Questions That Count in Archaeology* (Special Issue), edited by Nicholas Honerkamp. *Historical Archaeology* 22(1):29–35.

Leone, Mark P., and Constance A. Crosby
1987 Epilogue: Middle–Range Theory in Historical Archaeology. In *Consumer Choice in Historical Archaeology*, edited by Suzanne M. Spencer-Wood, pp. 397–410. Plenum Press, New York.

Leone, Mark P., and Parker B. Potter
1988 Introduction: Issues in Historical Archaeology. In *Recovery of Meaning: Historical Archaeology in the Eastern United States*, edited by Mark P. Leone and Parker B. Potter, pp. 1–22. Smithsonian Institution Press, Washington, D.C.

Leone, Mark P., and Paul A. Shackel
1990 The Georgian Order in Annapolis, Maryland. In *New Perspectives on Maryland Historical Archaeology* (Special Issue), edited by Richard J. Dent and Barbara J. Little. *Maryland Archaeology* 26:69–84.

Lewis, Kenneth E.
1975 *The Jamestown Frontier: An Archaeological Study of Colonization*. University Microfilms, Ann Arbor, Michigan.

Lewis, Oscar
1970 The Possessions of the Poor. In *Anthropological Essays*, edited by Oscar Lewis, pp. 441–460. Random House, New York.

Lewis, Peirce
1993 Common Landscapes as Historical Documents. In *History from Things: Essays on Material Culture*, edited by Steven Lubar and W. David Kingery, pp. 115–139. Smithsonian Institution Press, Washington, D.C.

Little, Barbara J.
1992a Explicit and Implicit Meanings in Material Culture and Print Culture. *Historical Archaeology* 26(3):85–94.
1992b (editor) *Text-Aided Archaeology*. CRC Press, Baton Rouge.
1993 Consuming Choices: Ceramic Assemblages and Expressions of Ideology. Paper presented at the annual meeting of the Society for Historical Archaeology, Kansas City, Missouri.

Little, Barbara J., and Paul A. Shackel (editors)
1992 Meanings and Uses of Material Culture (Special Issue). *Historical Archaeology* 26(3).

Louis Berger & Associates (LBA)
1989 The Compton Site, circa 1651–1684, Calvert County, Maryland (18CV279). Louis Berger & Associates, East Orange, New Jersey. Submitted to CRJ Associates, Camp Springs, Maryland.

Luckenbach, Al
1995 *Providence 1649: The History and Archaeology of Anne Arundel County Maryland's First European Settlement*. Maryland State Archives and the Maryland Historical Trust, Annapolis, Maryland.

Luckenbach, Al, and James G., Gibb
1995 Dated Window Leads from Colonial Sites in Anne Arundel County, Maryland. *Maryland Archeology* 30(2):23–28.

Lukezic, Craig
1990 Soils and Settlement Location in 18th Century Colonial Tidewater Virginia. *Historical Archaeology* 24(1):1–17.

Macfarlane, Alan
1978 *The Origins of English Individualism.* Basil Blackwell, Oxford [UK].

Main, Gloria L.
1982 *Tobacco Colony: Life in Early Maryland, 1650–1720.* Princeton University Press, Princeton.

Markham, Gervase
1986 *The English Housewife* [1615]. McGill-Queen's University Press, Kingston and Montreal.

Marshall, Nellie M.
1965 *Tombstone Records of Dorchester County, Maryland, 1678–1964.* Dorchester County Historical Society, Cambridge, Maryland.

Martin, Ann Smart
1989 The Role of Pewter as Missing Artifact: Consumer Attitudes toward Tablewares in Late 18th Century Virginia. *Historical Archaeology* 23(2):1–27.

Marx, Karl
1906 *Capital: A Critique of Political Economy. Volume I: The Processes of Capitalist Production.* Charles H. Kerr and Co., Chicago.

Maslow, Abraham
1943 A Theory of Human Motivation. *Psychological Review* 50:370–396.

McBride, W. Stephen, and Kim A. McBride
1987 Socioeconomic Variation in a Late Antebellum Southern Town: The View from Archaeological and Documentary Sources. In *Consumer Choice in Historical Archaeology*, edited by Suzanne M. Spencer-Wood, pp. 143–161. Plenum Press, New York.

McCarthy, John P.
1991 Review of Material Culture and Mass Consumption, by Daniel Miller. *Historical Archaeology* 25(2):115–116.

McCarthy, John P., Jeffrey B. Snyder, and Billy R. Roulette
1991 Arms from the Addison Plantation and the Maryland Militia on the Potomac Frontier. *Historical Archaeology* 25(1):66–79.

McCracken, Grant
1988 *Culture and Consumption: New Approaches to the Symbolic Character of Consumer Goods and Activities.* Indiana University Press, Bloomington.

McGuire, Randall H.
1992 *A Marxist Archaeology.* Academic Press, San Diego, California.

McKendrick, Neil
1982 Josiah Wedgewood and the Commercialization of Potteries. In *The Birth of a Consumer Society: The Commercialization of Eighteenth-Century England*, edited by Neil McKendrick, John Brewer, and J. H. Plumb, pp. 100–145. Indiana University Press, Bloomington.

McKendrick, Neil, John Brewer, and J. H. Plumb (editors)
1982 *The Birth of a Consumer Society: The Commercialization of Eighteenth-Century England.* Indiana University Press, Bloomington.

Meillassoux, Claude
1981 *Maidens, Meal and Money: Capitalism and the Domestic Community.* Cambridge University Press, New York.

Menard, Russell R.
1973 Immigration to the Chesapeake Colonies in the Seventeenth Century: A Review Study. *Maryland Historical Magazine* 68:323–329.
1975 *Economy and Society in Early Colonial Maryland.* University Microfilms, Ann Arbor, Michigan.

Menard, Russell R., Lois Green Carr, and Lorena S. Walsh
1988 A Small Planter's Profits: The Cole Estate and the Growth of the Early Chesapeake Economy. In *Material Life in America, 1600–1860,* edited by Robert Blair St. George, pp. 185–201. Northeastern University Press, Boston.

Menard, Russell R., P. M. G. Harris, and Lois Green Carr
1974 Opportunity and Inequality: The Distribution of Wealth on the Lower Western Shore of Maryland, 1638–1705. *Maryland Historical Magazine* 69(2):169–184.

Miller, Daniel
1987 *Material Culture and Mass Consumption.* Basil Blackwell, New York.

Miller, Daniel, and Christopher Tilley (editors)
1984 *Ideology, Power, and Prehistory.* Cambridge University Press, Cambridge [UK].

Miller, Henry M.
1983 A Search for the 'Citty of Saint Maries': Report on the 1981 Excavations in St. Mary's City, Maryland. *St. Mary's City Archaeology Series No. 1.* St. Mary's City Commission, St. Mary's City, Maryland.
1984 *Colonization and Subsistence Change on the Seventeenth Century Chesapeake Frontier.* Unpublished Ph.D. Dissertation, Department of Anthropology, Michigan State University.
1986 Discovering Maryland's First City: A Summary Report on the 1981–1984 Archaeological Excavations at St. Mary's City. *St. Mary's City Archaeology Series No. 2.* St. Mary's City Commission, St. Mary's City, Maryland.
1988 Baroque Cities in the Wilderness: Archaeology and Urban Development in the Colonial Chesapeake. *Historical Archaeology* 22(2):57–73.

Miller, Henry M., and Julia A. King (editors)
1988 Exploring a "Splendid and Delightsome" Land: Research on the 17th Century Chesapeake (Special Issue). *Historical Archaeology* 25(2):1–3.

Miller, Henry M., Timothy Riordan, Susan Hanna, and Silas Hurry
1993 Project Lead Coffins: A Report on the Initial Findings. Paper presented at the Middle Atlantic Archaeology Conference, Ocean City, Maryland.

Milton, John
1950 Of Reformation. In *The Complete Poetry & Selected Prose of John Milton,* edited by Cleanth Brooks, pp. 509–519. Random House, New York.

More, Sir Thomas
1975 *Utopia: A New Translation, Backgrounds, Criticism.* W.W. Norton & Co., New York.
Morgan, Edmund S.
1975 *American Slavery, American Freedom: The Ordeal of Colonial Virginia.* W.W. Norton & Co., New York.
Mrozowski, Stephen A.
1987 Exploring New England's Evolving Urban Landscape. In *Living in Cities: Current Research in Urban Archaeology*, edited by Edward Staski. *Special Publication Series No. 5:1–9.* Society for Historical Archaeology, California, Pennsylvania.
1988 Historical Archaeology as Anthropology. In *Questions That Count in Archaeology* (Special Issue), edited by Nicholas Honerkamp. *Historical Archaeology* 22(1):18–24.
1993 The Dialectics of Historical Archaeology in a Post-Processual World. *Historical Archaeology* 27(2):106–111.
Mukerji, Chandra
1983 *From Graven Images: Patterns of Modern Materialism.* Columbia University Press, New York.
Muraca, David
1989 The Carter's Grove Museum Site Excavation. Department of Archaeological Research, Colonial Williamsburg Foundation, Williamsburg, Virginia.
Nass, John
1989 Household Archaeology and Functional Analysis as Procedures for Studying Fort Ancient Communities in the Ohio Valley. *Pennsylvania Archaeologist* 59(1):1–13.
Neiman, Fraser D.
1980 Field Archaeology of the Clifts Plantation Site, Westmoreland County, Virginia (44WM33). Unpublished report, Robert E. Lee Memorial Association, Stratford, Virginia.
1989 Letter reviewing the Compton Site, Circa 1651–1684, Calvert County, Maryland (18 CV 279) by Louis Berger & Associates. Dated 06 August 1989. On file at the Jefferson Patterson Park and Museum, St. Leonard, Maryland.
1990 *An Evolutionary Approach to Archaeological Inference: Aspects of Architectural Variation in the 17th-Century Chesapeake.* University Microfilms, Ann Arbor, Michigan.
Nicholls, Mark
1991 *Investigating Gunpowder Plot.* Manchester University Press, New York.
Noel Hume, Ivor
1975 *Historical Archaeology.* Knopf Press, New York.
1992 *Martin's Hundred*, 2nd edition. Victor Gollancz, London.
Norton, Mary Beth
1984 The Evolution of White Women's Experience in Early America. *American Historical Review* 89(3):593–619.
Notestein, Wallace
1954 *The English People on the Eve of Colonization.* Harper Torchbooks, New York.

O'Mara, James
1982 Town Founding in Seventeenth-Century North America: Jamestown in Virginia. *Journal of Historical Geography* 8(1):1–11.
Orser, Charles E.
1987 Plantation Status and Consumer Choice: A Materialist Framework for Historical Archaeology. In *Consumer Choice in Historical Archaeology*, edited by Suzanne M. Spencer-Wood, pp. 121–137. Plenum Press, New York.
1988 Toward a Theory of Power for Historical Archaeology: Plantations and Space. In *Recovery of Meaning: Historical Archaeology in the Eastern United States*, edited by Mark P. Leone and Parker B. Potter, pp. 313–343. Smithsonian Institution Press, Washington, D.C.
1992 Beneath the Material Surface of Things: Commodities, Artifacts, and Slave Plantations. In *Meanings and Uses of Material Culture* (Special Issue), edited by Barbara J. Little and Paul A. Shackel. *Historical Archaeology* 26(3):95–104.
Otto, John S.
1984 *Cannon's Point Plantation, 1794–1860: Living Conditions and Status Patterns in the Old South.* Academic Press, New York.
Outlaw, Alain Charles
1990 *Governor's Land: Archaeology of Early Seventeenth-Century Virginia Settlements.* University Press of Virginia, Charlottesville.
Overbury, Thomas
1964 Sir Thomas Overbury's Observations, His Travels, Upon The State of the Seventeen Provinces, as they Stood, Anno Domini 1609; the Treaty of Peace Being then on Foot. In *An English Garner: Stuart Tracts, 1603–1693*, edited by C. H. Firth, pp. 211–220. Cooper Square Publishers, New York.
Paynter, Robert
1982 *Models of Spatial Inequality: Settlement Patterns in Historical Archaeology.* Academic Press, New York.
Paynter, Robert and Randall H. McGuire
1991 The Archaeology of Inequality: Material Culture, Domination and Resistance. In *The Archaeology of Inequality*, edited by Randall H. McGuire and Robert Paynter, pp. 1–27. Basil Blackwell, Cambridge, Massachusetts.
Pendery, Steven R.
1992 Consumer Behavior in Colonial Charlestown, Massachusetts, 1630–1760. *Historical Archaeology* 26(3):57–72.
Pepys, Samuel
1923 *Passages from the Diary of Samuel Pepys.* The Modern Library, New York.
Pogue, Dennis J.
1984 Town Rearing on the Maryland Chesapeake Frontier: A Reinterpretation. Paper presented at the annual meeting of the Society for Historical Archaeology, Williamsburg, Virginia.
1985 Calverton, Calvert County, Maryland: 1668–1725. *Maryland Historical Magazine* 80:271–276.
1988 Spatial Analysis of the King's Reach Plantation Homelot, ca. 1690–1715. *Historical Archaeology* 22(2):40–56.

1990 King's Reach and 17th Century Plantation Life. *Jefferson Patterson Park & Museum Studies in Archaeology No. 1.* St. Leonard, Maryland.
1992 Letter to the Editor. *The Council for Northeast Historical Archaeology Newsletter* 23:14–16.
1993 Standard of Living in the 17th–Century Chesapeake: Patterns of Variability among Artifact Assemblages. In *The Archaeology of 17th-Century Virginia*, edited by Theodore R. Reinhart and Dennis J. Pogue, pp. 371–400. Archeological Society of Virginia, Richmond.

Polanyi, Karl
1971a Our Obsolete Market Mentality. In *Primitive, Archaic and Modern Economies: Essays of Karl Polanyi*, edited by George Dalton, pp. 59–77. Beacon Press, Boston.
1971b Societies and Economic Systems. In *Primitive, Archaic and Modern Economies: Essays of Karl Polanyi*, edited by George Dalton, pp. 3–19. Beacon Press, Boston.
1971c The Self-Regulating Market and the Fictitious Commodities: Labor, Land and Money. In *Primitive, Archaic and Modern Economies: Essays of Karl Polanyi*, edited by George Dalton, pp. 26–37. Beacon Press, Boston.

Posnansky, Merrick
1992 Archaeology: A World Perspective. Paper presented at the annual meeting of the Society for Historical Archaeology, Kingston, Jamaica.

Prior, Mary
1990 Wives and Wills, 1558–1700. In *English Rural Society, 1500–1800: Essays in Honor of Joan Thirsk*, edited by John Chartres and David Hey, pp. 201–225. Cambridge University Press, Cambridge [UK].

Purser, Margaret
1991 'Several Paradise Ladies Are Visiting Town': Gender Strategies in the Early Industrial West. In *Gender in Historical Archaeology* (Special Issue), edited by Donna J. Seifert. *Historical Archaeology* 25(4):6–16.

Reeve, Andrew
1980 Debate: The Meaning and Definition of 'Property' in Seventeenth–Century England. *Past & Present* 89:139–143.

Reitz, Elizabeth J.
1987 Vertebrate Fauna and Socioeconomic Status. In *Consumer Choice in Historical Archaeology*, edited by Suzanne M. Spencer-Wood, pp. 101–119. Plenum Press, New York.

Reps, John W.
1972 *Tidewater Towns: City Planning in Colonial Virginia and Maryland.* Colonial Williamsburg Foundation, Williamsburg, Virginia.

Rheinhart, Theodore R., and Dennis J. Pogue (editors)
1993 *The Archaeology of 17th-Century Virginia. Special Publication No. 30 of the Archeological Society of Maryland.* Dietz Press, Richmond, Virginia.

Riordan, Timothy B.
1988 The Interpretation of 17th Century Sites through Plow Zone Surface Collections: Examples from St. Mary's City. *Historical Archaeology* 22(2):2–16.

Rousseau, Jean-Jacques
1984 *A Discourse on Inequality.* Penguin Books, New York.

Ryan, Mary
1989 The American Parade: Representations of the Nineteenth-Century Social Order.
      In *The New Cultural History*, edited by Lynn Hunt, pp. 131–153. University of
      California Press, Berkeley.
Rutman, Darrett B., and Anita H. Rutman
1979 'Now-Wives and Sons-in-Law': Parental Death in a Seventeenth-Century Vir-
      ginia County. In *The Chesapeake in the Seventeenth Century: Essays on Anglo-
      American Society and Politics*, edited by Thad W. Tate and David L. Ammerman,
      pp. 153–182. W.W. Norton & Co., New York.
Sanchez-Saavedra, E. M.
1975 *A Description of the Country: Virginia's Cartographers and Their Maps, 1607–
      1881*. Virginia State Library, Richmond.
Schaefer, Richard
1994 Smoke and Mirrors: Dutch 17th-Century Ceramics for Heating and Illumina-
      tion. Paper presented at the annual meeting of the Society for Historical Ar-
      chaeology, Vancouver, British Columbia, Canada.
Schama, Simon
1988 *The Embarrassment of Riches: An Interpretation of Dutch Culture in the Golden
      Age*. University of California Press, Berkeley, California.
Schiffer, Michael B.
1976 *Behavioral Archaeology*. Academic Press, New York.
Schneider, Harold K.
1974 *Economic Man: The Anthropology of Economics*. The Free Press, New York.
Schumpeter, Joseph A.
1961 *The Theory of Economic Development: An Inquiry into Profit, Capital, Credit, In-
      terest, and the Business Cycle*. Oxford University Press, New York.
Schuyler, Robert L.
1988 Archaeological Remains, Documents, and Anthropology: A Call for a New Cul-
      ture History. In *Questions That Count in Archaeology* (Special Issue), edited by
      Nicholas Honerkamp. *Historical Archaeology* 22(1):36–42.
Seifert, Donna J.
1991 Within Sight of the White House: The Archaeology of Working Women. In
      Gender in Historical Archaeology (Special Issue), edited by Donna J. Seifert. *His-
      torical Archaeology* 25(4):82–108.
Shackel, Paul A.
1992a Modern Discipline: Its Historical Context in the Colonial Chesapeake. *Historical
      Archaeology* 26(3):73–84.
1992b Probate Inventories in Historical Archaeology: A Review and Alternatives. In *Text-
      Aided Archaeology*, edited by Barbara J. Little, pp. 205–215. CRC Press, Baton
      Rouge.
Shaffer, Gary D.
1993 An Archaeomagnetic Study of Wattle and Daub Building Collapse. *Journal of
      Field Archaeology* 20(1):59–75.
Shepard, Steven Judd
1987 Status Variation in Antebellum Alexandria: An Archaeological Study of Ce-

ramic Tableware. In *Consumer Choice in Historical Archaeology*, edited by Suzanne M. Spencer-Wood, pp. 163–198. Plenum Press, New York.

Simek, Jan F.
1989 Structure and Diversity in Intrasite Spatial Analysis. In *Quantifying Diversity in Archaeology*, edited by Robert D. Leonard and George T. Jones, pp. 59–68. Cambridge University Press, Cambridge [UK].

Smith, Abbott Emerson
1947 *Colonists in Bondage: White Servitude and Convict Labor in America, 1607–1776*. University of North Carolina Press, Chapel Hill, North Carolina.

Smith, Adam
1937 *An Inquiry into the Nature and Causes of the Wealth of Nations*. Modern Library, New York.

Smolek, Michael A.
1984 "Soyle Light, Well-Watered and on the River": Settlement Patterning of Maryland's Frontier Plantations. Paper presented at the 3rd Hall of Records Conference on Maryland History, St. Mary's City, Maryland.

Snyder, Jeffrey B., and B. R. Roulette
1990 An Analysis of a Seventeenth Century Earthfast Structure from the Addison Plantation: New Light on an Old Building. Paper presented at the annual meeting of the Council for Northeastern Historical Archaeology, Kingston, Ontario.

South, Stanley
1977 *Method and Theory in Historical Archeology*. Academic Press, New York.
1988 Whither Pattern? In *Questions That Count in Archaeology* (Special Issue), edited by Nicholas Honerkamp. *Historical Archaeology* 22(1):24–28.

Spencer-Wood, Suzanne M.
1980 Workshop on Research Problems in Historic Archaeology: A Report. In *Proceedings of the Conference on Northeastern Archaeology*, edited by James A. Moore, pp. 161–165. University of Massachusetts Press, Amherst.
1987a Preface and Introduction. In *Consumer Choice in Historical Archaeology*, edited by Suzanne M. Spencer-Wood, pp. xi–24. Plenum Press, New York.

Spencer-Wood, Suzanne M. (editor)
1987b *Consumer Choice in Historical Archaeology*. Plenum Press, New York.

Starbuck, David R.
1980 Industrial Archaeology: World Systems and Local Engineers. In *Proceedings of the Conference on Northeastern Archaeology*, edited by James A. Moore, pp. 179–187. University of Massachusetts, Amherst.
1984 The Shaker Concept of Household. *Man in the Northeast* 28:73–86.

Steward, Julian H.
1955 *Theory of Culture Change*. University of Illinois Press, Urbana.

Stewart-Abernathy, Leslie C.
1986 Urban Farmsteads: Household Responsibilities in the City. *Historical Archaeology* 20(2):5–15.

St. George, Robert Blair
1983 Maintenance Relations and the Erotics of Property. Paper presented at the annual meeting of the American Historical Association, San Francisco, California.

Stiverson, Gregory A.
1977   *Poverty in a Land of Plenty: Tenancy in Eighteenth-Century Maryland.* The Johns Hopkins University Press, Baltimore.

Stiverson, Gregory A., and Patrick H. Butler (editors)
1977   Virginia in 1732: The Travel Journal of William Hugh Grove. *The Virginia Magazine of History and Biography* 85(1):18–44.

Stone, Garry Wheeler
1982   *Society, Housing and Architecture in Early Maryland.* University Microfilms, Ann Arbor, Michigan.

Swift, Jonathan
1958   *Gulliver's Travels and Other Writings.* Random House, New York.

Tate, Thad W., and David L. Ammerman (editors)
1979   *The Chesapeake in the Seventeenth Century: Essays on Anglo-American Society and Politics.* W.W. Norton & Co., New York.

Thomas, Keith
1971   *Religion and the Decline of Magic.* Charles Scribner's Sons, New York.

Thomas, Ronald A., and Martha J. Schiek
1988   A Late 17th-Century House Site in Gloucester City, New Jersey. *Bulletin of the Archaeological Society of New Jersey* 43:3–11.

Toulouse, Julian H.
1970   High on the Hawg: Or How the Western Miner Lived, as Told by Bottles He Left Behind. *Historical Archaeology* 4:59–69.

Ubelaker, Douglas H., Erica J. Bubniak, and Abigail Turowski
1993   Skeletal Biology of the Patuxent Point Human Remains. Department of Anthropology, National Museum of American History, Smithsonian Institution, Washington, D.C. Submitted to the Maryland Historical Trust, Crownsville, Maryland

United States Bureau of the Census
1970   *Historical Statistics of the United States, 2 vols.* U.S. Government Printing Office, Washington, D.C.

United States Department of the Interior, Soil Conservation Service
1971   *Soil Survey: Calvert County, Maryland.* United States Government Printing Office, Washington, D.C.
1978   *Soil Survey: St. Mary's County, Maryland.* United States Government Printing Office, Washington, D.C.
1979   *Soil Survey: Anne Arundel County, Maryland.* United States Government Printing Office, Washington, D.C.

Veblen, Thorstein
1934   *Theory of the Leisure Class.* Modern Library, New York.

Virkus, Frederick Adams (compiler)
1972   *Immigrant Ancestors: A List of 2, 500 Immigrants to America Before 1750.* Genealogical Publishing Co., Baltimore.

Walker, Iain C.
1977   *Clay Tobacco Pipes, with Particular Reference to the Bristol Industry* (4 vols). Parks Canada, Ottawa.

Wallerstein, Immanuel
1974 *The Modern World-System: Capitalist Agriculture and the Origins of the European World-Economy in the Sixteenth Century.* Academic Press, New York.
Walsh, Lorena S.
1977 Servitude and Opportunity in Charles County, Maryland, 1658–1705. In *Law, Society, and Politics in Early Maryland,* edited by Aubrey C. Land, Lois Green Carr, and Edward C. Papenfuse, pp. 111–133. Johns Hopkins University Press, Baltimore.
1979a A Culture of 'Rude Sufficiency': Life Styles on Maryland's Lower Western Shore Between 1658 and 1720. Paper presented at the annual meeting of the Society for Historical Archaeology, Nashville, Tennessee.
1979b 'Till Death Us Do Part': Marriage and Family in Seventeenth-Century Maryland. In *The Chesapeake in the Seventeenth Century: Essays on Anglo-American Society and Politics,* edited by Thad W. Tate and David L. Ammerman, pp. 126–152. W.W. Norton & Co., New York.
1983 Urban Amenities and Rural Sufficiency: Living Standards and Consumer Behavior in the Colonial Chesapeake, 1643–1777. *Journal of Economic History* 43(1):109–117.
Walsh, Lorena S., and Russell R. Menard
1974 Death in the Chesapeake: Two Life Tables for Men in Early Colonial Maryland. *Maryland Historical Magazine* 69:211–227.
Warfel, Stephen G.
1982 A Critical Analysis and Test of Stanley South's Artifact Patterns. *The Conference on Historic Sites Archaeology Papers, 1979* 14:137–190.
Weinand, Daniel C., and Elizabeth J. Reitz
1993 Report on the Faunal Remains from Patuxent Point (18Cv271), Near Solomons, Calvert County, Maryland. Submitted to the Maryland Historical Trust, Crownsville, Maryland.
Weissner, Polly
1983 Style and Social Information in Kalahari San Projectile Points. *American Antiquity* 48(2):253–276.
White, Fr. Andrew
1988 A Briefe Relation of the Voyage unto Maryland [1634]. In *Narratives of Early Maryland, 1633–1684,* edited by Clayton Coleman Hall, pp. 29–44. Heritage Books, Bowie, Maryland.
White, Leslie A.
1945 Diffusion versus Evolution: An Anti-Evolutionist Fallacy. *American Anthropologist* 47(3):339–356.
1947 Evolutionism in Cultural Anthropology: A Rejoinder. *American Anthropologist* 49(3):400–413.
Wilcoxen, Charlotte
1987 *Dutch Trade and Ceramics in America in the Seventeenth Century.* Albany Institute of History and Art, Albany, New York.
Wilk, Richard R.
1990 The Built Environment and Consumer Decisions. In *Domestic Architecture and*

the Use of Space: An Interdisciplinary Cross-Cultural Approach, edited by Susan Kent, pp. 34–42. Cambridge University Press, Cambridge [UK].

1991   *Household Ecology: Economic Change and Domestic Life among the Kekchi Maya in Belize*. The University of Arizona Press, Tucson.

Wilk, Richard R., and William L. Rathje

1982   Household Archaeology. *American Behavioral Scientist* 25(6):617–639.

Winter, Marcus C.

1976   The Archeological Household Cluster in the Valley of Oaxaca. In *The Early Mesoamerican Village*, edited by Kent V. Flannery, pp. 25–31. Academic Press, New York.

Wobst, H. Martin

1977   Stylistic Behavior and Information Exchange. In *Papers for the Director: Research Essays in Honor of James B. Griffin*, edited by Charles E. Cleland, pp. 317–342. Museum of Anthropology, University of Michigan, Ann Arbor.

Worsley, Peter

1984   *The Three Worlds: Culture and World Development*. The University of Chicago Press, Chicago.

Wyckoff, V. J.

1937   The Sizes of Plantations in Seventeenth-Century Maryland. *Maryland Historical Magazine* 32(4):331–339.

1938   Land Prices in Seventeenth-Century Maryland. *American Economic Review* 28(1):82–88.

Yentsch, Anne

1990a   An Interpretive Study of the Use of Land and Space on Lot 83, Annapolis, Md. In *New Perspectives on Maryland Historical Archaeology* (Special Issue), edited by Richard J. Dent and Barbara J. Little. *Maryland Archeology* 26:21–53.

1990b   Minimum Vessel Lists as Evidence of Change in Folk and Courtly Traditions of Food Use. *Historical Archaeology* 24(3):24–53.

1991a   Engendering Visible and Invisible Ceramic Artifacts, Especially Dairy Vessels. *Historical Archaeology* 25(4):132–155.

1991b   The Symbolic Division of Pottery: Sex-Related Attributes of English and Anglo-American Household Pots. In *The Archaeology of Inequality*, edited by Randall H. McGuire and Robert Paynter, pp. 192–230. Basil Blackwell, Oxford [UK].

Zierden, Martha A., and Jeanne A. Calhoun

1986   Urban Adaptation in Charleston, South Carolina, 1730–1820. *Historical Archaeology* 20(1):29–43.

Index

INTERDISCIPLINARY CONTRIBUTIONS TO ARCHAEOLOGY
Chronological Listing of Volumes

THE PLEISTOCENE OLD WORLD
Regional Perspectives
Edited by Olga Soffer

HOLOCENE HUMAN ECOLOGY IN NORTHEASTERN NORTH AMERICA
Edited by George P. Nicholas

ECOLOGY AND HUMAN ORGANIZATION ON THE GREAT PLAINS
Douglas B. Bamforth

THE INTERPRETATION OF ARCHAEOLOGICAL SPATIAL PATTERNING
Edited by Ellen M. Kroll and T. Douglas Price

HUNTER–GATHERERS
Archaeological and Evolutionary Theory
Robert L. Bettinger

RESOURCES, POWER, AND INTERREGIONAL INTERACTION
Edited by Edward M. Schortman and Patricia A. Urban

POTTERY FUNCTION
A Use-Alteration Perspective
James M. Skibo

SPACE, TIME, AND ARCHAEOLOGICAL LANDSCAPES
Edited by Jacqueline Rossignol and LuAnn Wandsnider

ETHNOHISTORY AND ARCHAEOLOGY
Approaches to Postcontact Change in the Americas
Edited by J. Daniel Rogers and Samuel M. Wilson

THE AMERICAN SOUTHWEST AND MESOAMERICA
Systems of Prehistoric Exchange
Edited by Jonathon E. Ericson and Timothy G. Baugh

FROM KOSTENKI TO CLOVIS
Upper Paleolithic–Paleo-Indian Adaptations
Edited by Olga Soffer and N. D. Praslov

EARLY HUNTER–GATHERERS OF THE CALIFORNIA COAST
Jon M. Erlandson

HOUSES AND HOUSEHOLDS
A Comparative Study
Richard E. Blanton

THE ARCHAEOLOGY OF GENDER
Separating the Spheres in Urban America
Diana diZerega Wall

ORIGINS OF ANATOMICALLY MODERN HUMANS
Edited by Matthew H. Nitecki and Doris V. Nitecki

PREHISTORIC EXCHANGE SYSTEMS IN NORTH AMERICA
Edited by Timothy G. Baugh and Jonathon E. Ericson

STYLE, SOCIETY, AND PERSON
Archaeological and Ethnological Perspectives
Edited by Christopher Carr and Jill E. Neitzel

REGIONAL APPROACHES TO MORTUARY ANALYSIS
Edited by Lane Anderson Beck

DIVERSITY AND COMPLEXITY IN PREHISTORIC MARITIME SOCIETIES
A Gulf of Maine Perspective
Bruce J. Bourque

CHESAPEAKE PREHISTORY
Old Traditions, New Directions
Richard J. Dent. Jr.

PREHISTORIC CULTURAL ECOLOGY AND EVOLUTION
Insights from Southern Jordan
Donald O. Henry

STONE TOOLS
Theoretical Insights into Human Prehistory
Edited by George H. Odell

THE ARCHAEOLOGY OF WEALTH
Consumer Behavior in English America
James G. Gibb

STATISTICS FOR ARCHAEOLOGISTS
A Commonsense Approach
Robert D. Drennan

DARWINIAN ARCHAEOLOGIES
Edited by Herbert Donald Graham Maschner

CASE STUDIES IN ENVIRONMENTAL ARCHAEOLOGY
Edited by Elizabeth J. Reitz, Lee A. Newsom, and Sylvia J. Scudder

HUMANS AT THE END OF THE ICE AGE
The Archaeology of the Pleistocene–Holocene Transition
Edited by Lawrence Guy Straus, Berit Valentin Eriksen, Jon M. Erlandson, and
David R. Yesner